Also by Tim Hollister

*Not So Fast: Parenting Your Teen
Through the Dangers of Driving*
(Chicago Review Press)

His
Father
Still

a parenting memoir

Tim Hollister

Author's Note

This is a true story depicting real events and real people.
I have used fictitious names when necessary to protect
privacy or confidentiality.

For information, address RSH, LLC c/o David Black Agency, 335 Adams Street, 27th Floor, Brooklyn, NY 11201.

www.fromreidsdad.org

Print ISBN: 978-0-7867-5632-2
eBook ISBN: 978-0-7867-5632-2

Cover design by Maria Ramsay
Distributed by Argo Navis Author Services

Distributed by
Argo Navis Author Services
www.argonavisdigital.com

To Ellen,
for giving me permission and time to write this.

To Martha, for persevering.

To Gracie, for wagging her tail through the darkest days.

To Reid, my son still.

Contents

Introduction:
What a Parent Does

As our kids grow into teens, we let out a tether, allowing our sons and daughters to experience life and its risks firsthand. We try to strike the right balance, allowing them to face danger because it's part of growing up, but pulling them back before they see for themselves what happens when they touch a live wire, lean too far over a cliff, or put the accelerator too far down. Fear and frustration unavoidably haunt this process, because granting freedom means seeing less of what is happening at the tether's other end. We hope that the tension in the extended line is our kids' remaining connected to us, but we are less and less sure. Presence and control give way to being satisfied with our teens' returning to us, wiser for their experiences but physically unharmed. We thank our stars for the strides they have taken toward adulthood, and the gods for their having sidestepped the worst-case scenario.

Sometimes, however, the tether breaks, and at a time when the life that had been pulling it taut is largely hidden by this maddening phenomenon of raising teens by letting them go and giving them space. With teens, car crashes are the most frequent cause of these breaks, though there are many others.

Yet when a catastrophe occurs, we don't, can't, and won't just walk away, because of course, parents are never untethered. Slack in the line, especially when it involves a teen, forces a retracing of how we let out that tether and ultimately creates a need, in lieu of what was, for a sustainable connection. In other words, the parent-child connection never really breaks, and in the aftermath of a cataclysmic change, we yearn for a renewed attachment.

This book is the story of a tether that broke and how I set about evaluating my letting go vs. reeling in, learning who had been at its other end, and devising a hereafter. That is, in the months after my seventeen-year-old son's passing in a one-car crash, I considered, reconsidered, and agonized over this balance of exposing vs. protecting, and how I had handled it—or not. As I tended to the many unrelenting and surprising demands that were thrust upon me as a father who had lost a son, I revisited the choices, decisions, and assumptions I had made as a father. Yes, of course there was grief and despair, but also a review, all while I was attending to an unthinkable set of new responsibilities. My reflection was spurred not by guilt or a need to absolve myself over his driving on one night; my focus was the life I had given him, including the lengths to which the tether had extended, and what he had taken from his degrees of freedom. My inquiry was less burdened by the feeling that I had made an obvious mistake than confused by the sense that I hadn't. Our father-son relationship, now entirely rearranged by his loss, needed to settle, and I started by replaying the metaphorical tape and taking notes.

I began by talking to dozens of people, including relatives, friends, co-workers, neighbors, and therapists. While many engaged me in conversation I desperately needed, the most frequent response was that books and patient reflection would best help me.

So I began to read. The shelves of my study were soon filled with *A Broken Heart Still Beats* and *Teen Angel* and *Andy's Mountain* and *Beyond Tears* and *The Worst Loss* and *Why Men Grieve* and *The Bereaved Parent* and *Hello From Heaven!* and *The Death of a Child* and *Lament for a Son* and *The Grieving Garden* and *The Grief Recovery Handbook,* and many more. Most of the books offered advice from psychologists, therapists, and ministers about stages of grief. Several were reflections by parents talking about common questions, including how to create a "new normal," how to deal with remarks such as "Thank God you have another child," and when to give away possessions. Some were memoirs by parents who explained how faith, literature, conversation, music, art, or a new hobby had lit their path through grief.

Each one in some way reminded me that I am hardly the first parent to lose a child, and that thousands have endured similar and in some cases much worse tragedies. Each taught me that grief is a process, that hard anguish dissolves over time into softer sorrow, and that there are steps that parents can take to speed up these progressions.

Yes, these books—"the Grief Books," I now call them—were helpful, but as I read them, I was left still searching. Ultimately, I did what many people do when they can't find the book they need—I started to write. When I began, I had no plan other than to put down what seemed to be unaddressed in the Grief Books. My scribbles became a journal, but I found myself focusing not on suffocating despair morphing into breathable sadness, but recounting and reevaluating my successes and failures as Reid's father, and whether my experiences paralleled the challenges that occupy parents, especially of teenagers, every day. That I was rethinking my life as a father *after* my son had died began to illuminate aspects of parenting that I had not and in many cases could not have discerned clearly when Reid was alive.

As sentences became paragraphs, pages, and then chapters, it dawned on me that the books that had been recommended to me, purporting to advise on emotional management for bereaved parents, addressed the bereavement but not the parenting. Put another way, embedded in the important things I was doing and still had to do as a father after my son passed away were valuable perspectives for parents whose kids are very much alive and promising to remain so: After Reid's passing, I learned much more about parents, choices, freedoms, tethers, and the depth and quality of his character. At ages fifteen, sixteen, and seventeen, Reid had lived more and more beyond my gaze, but after he was gone, well, we were reintroduced. My eventual reward—though I struggle for a better word—was a clarity about him that was gratefully received, even though it arrived late.

Eventually, it occurred to me that parents would benefit from a story of attending to a teenager's legacy after a tumultuous life, a sudden death, a barrage of questions and doubts, a reassessment of what had happened and what might have been done differently, and eventually a wistful and new appreciation of my son's life and a way for us to go forward as father and son. I considered that parents might be emboldened to say no and to make better decisions, or at least approach their choices with an added perspective and be more appreciative of what they have, by considering what happened to Reid Hollister and me, his father, Tim.

I was encouraged by the thought that many parents would identify with the particulars of this story: fathers and mothers of teenagers, of boys, of students struggling with a lack of confidence and self-worth, of ADD or ADHD kids. Of teens who excel not in academics, sports, or the arts, but in humor, kindness, and empathy. Parents struggling with school choices or school discipline gone wrong. Those deciding whether to make car keys available. I wondered if my assembling the pieces after the fact might spur parents to consider how to keep a tighter rein and maintain a clearer view.

The utility of this book may be visceral, in the sense that it invites mothers, fathers, and guardians to draw inferences from my experience, as opposed to providing direct parent-to-parent or expert-to-parent advice. I say this because, in truth, I started on this detailed reconsideration of Reid's life and my parenting not to counsel others but to meet my own stark emotional need, one that emerged as I wrote: How do I address my son, talk to him, now that he is not physically here? Does a child who is gone have a face? A purpose? A voice? Is he an absence or a presence? A fact or an emotion? Is he within me, next to me, above me, somewhere else, all of the above, or nowhere to be found?

I worked backward from our new reality, which needed to be comprehensible and tangible but, most important, comfortable—his texture, weight, and position in relation to my body and spirit had to be just so, if Reid and I were to be in this mode for decades, until we would "meet again at God's right hand." I had to figure out how to carry him. This need propelled me to rediscover who he was. That is, this cautionary tale for parents arose not only from a conversation in my head *about* my son, but from discussions I had *with* him as I worked to position him within our new relationship. Even though he was physically gone, once I got to know him better we plotted our future, starting by agreeing on where we had been when he left.

1

Passing Into Memory

Friday, December 1, 2006, dawned clear and cool in the Northeast, but Chicago was bracing for an unprecedented late-fall snowstorm. I was headed there, for a dinner and an all-day work meeting on Saturday.

That is, assuming I could become comfortable about leaving Reid.

Most recently, Reid had undergone his final growth spurt, so he was now tall, nearly six feet, and thin, because his weight had not yet caught up with his enlarged frame. His head of thick, dark brown hair framed a perfectly proportioned and still boyish face whose most memorable features were his sparkling aqua-blue eyes and a smile that betrayed mischief ahead. Yet his pieces did not quite yet work together; "gangly" might have described him. Nor had his maturity kept pace with his size; he was, in a phrase, happy-go-lucky, one whose presence in a group most often launched curiosity about what hilarious

antic was next. The challenges ahead, in his senior year of high
school and beyond, did not yet concern him.

But at that moment, Reid's uneven growth and irregular
focus were our secondary concerns. So much had happened in
the past two weeks. In that time, he had been accused of serious
misconduct by his school, a claim he had adamantly denied.
As the disciplinary process had proceeded, rumor and skewed
perception had crowded out the facts and contorted what had
actually happened. There had been an expulsion hearing, a
committee's decision, a nearly violent confrontation in our
kitchen, and a subsequent meeting with a guidance counselor at
a new high school to try to patch together courses so Reid could
graduate in June. Emotions were running high. Yet a counseling
session with Dr. Jarvis, who had overseen his treatment for
attention deficit disorder and had become a trusted family advisor,
seemed to have settled Reid during the previous two days.

By mid-morning Friday, it was evident that I was not going
to Chicago; it had already started to snow there. Around 10:30
a.m., an email came from our group's chair: "Meeting moved
to Washington, D.C. Get there if you can." I did not realize that
this was my first lucky break of the day. With things seemingly
stable with Reid, I rearranged my trip so that I would fly to
Baltimore, take a bus and a train to Washington, spend one night
there, attend my meeting, and fly back late Saturday afternoon.

While I was at work, I texted Reid; he had recently
taught me how—Dad entering the twenty-first century. I
reconfirmed our signed behavior contract and his plans for the
coming weekend. On Friday morning, Reid would meet with
the guidance counselor at his new public high school, take
placement tests in math and Spanish, and then see Dr. Jarvis

for more counseling at 1:00 p.m. He would then be allowed
to visit his girlfriend, Lauren, in the afternoon, and then he
would be home Friday night. That evening my wife, Ellen,
would be either home or nearby, at the monthly meeting of her
women's group. Our daughter, Martha, two years younger than
Reid, would be watching movies in the basement. On Saturday
morning, Reid would show up at the Department of Motor
Vehicles for driver retraining, a mandatory class that had been
triggered by his having received a ticket a few weeks earlier, for
going 42 miles per hour in a 25-mph zone. And I would be back
from Washington for dinner on Saturday.

I decided that the situation was calm enough that I could go
to Washington.

As I arrived at the airport, the bad weather was wreaking
havoc across the country, and my flight was delayed three times,
for four hours in total. As a result, I missed the last commuter
train that I could have taken from the Baltimore airport to
downtown Washington, so I rented a car. This proved to be
another then-unrecognized stroke of luck.

At dinner in northern Virginia, I turned off my cellphone,
out of courtesy. As a result, it wasn't until 10:40 p.m., as I
waited at a traffic light while en route to the Wyndham Hotel,
that I found a text message from Reid, sent at 9:25 p.m.: "Gone
to Mike's house to see him and family."

I was concerned but not overly. Mike's house was not part
of the plan, and 9:25 p.m. was late to be going out, and why was
he texting me instead of asking his mother? On the other hand,
he had checked in as he was supposed to, and Mike's house was
a safe haven, a place we would have let him go just about any
time.

I called Reid's cellphone. No answer; I got his voicemail. He was supposed to answer if I called when he was on the road or out of the house. Maybe he was on the phone.

I tried again at 10:50. Same thing.

I arrived at the Wyndham just after 11:00 p.m., left the car with the valet parking attendant, checked in, went to my room, dropped my bag on the bed, and reached again for my cellphone. The instant I touched it, it rang.

Ellen.

"Reid has been in an accident," she said. Her tone was even.

"What happened? Where?"

"On 84 in Plainville." Interstate 84 is the main highway through central Connecticut. "We're trying to find out what happened. I'll call you back." Still, she did not sound alarmed.

Plainville? That was the opposite direction from Mike's house.

Within five minutes, Ellen called back. Her tone was still matter-of-fact. "He was in his car with Jessica and Rachel." Jessica and Rachel lived in our neighborhood. They were classmates and friends of Martha. I was still baffled by why Reid had been in Plainville with these two in his car.

Ellen said, "They're taking Reid to the hospital," and that she was now with our nephew Mark Pierce, a nurse practitioner. "We're going to the hospital. I'll call you back."

Three minutes later, Ellen called back to say that they had begun driving to New Britain General, which is in the next town from Plainville, but had now learned that Reid was being transferred to Hartford Hospital.

For a few moments, in absolute silence after that call, I slumped in the chair, unopened suitcase on the bed, weary and wondering if I would need to wake myself up.

In the next call, Ellen was clearly upset. "We're at Hartford
Hospital. They just wheeled him in. He looked good. He has burns
on his hand and feet. He had tubes in him." She handed her phone
to Dr. Kuntz. Rich Kuntz and his wife, Joanne, also a doctor, were
the people on whom our neighborhood imposed when one of our
children spiked a high fever or suffered a bad bruise.

"Rich, is this serious?" I asked. "Do I need to get home?"
It was both comforting and terrifying to be talking to a doctor,
because I knew that the answer I was about to get would be
professional analysis.

"You'd better come," he said. Then he added, "Now."

I asked to speak to Ellen again. She explained what she
now knew: Somehow, Reid had taken Jessica and Rachel for
a ride, she was not sure why. They had ended up in Plainville
and gotten lost. Then, the crash. The two girls were already
at Hartford Hospital and were "OK." Reid had been taken by
ambulance to New Britain, and then someone had decided that
he should be transferred to the emergency room at Hartford. I
knew that Hartford Hospital handles the region's most serious
injuries; it has a Life Star helicopter.

Ellen mentioned that a state trooper at the hospital had been
bugging her about Reid and why he was in a car with those two
girls. She had walked away from him.

I wondered where the eastern edge of the Midwestern
snowstorm was and whether I could outrace it. I momentarily
considered that I was lucky to be in Washington, where it was
still clear and relatively warm, and not snowbound in Chicago.
Once I did the math, though, it was clear I had missed any
chance of making any late flight to New England.

I called Ellen. "I'm going to drive—no other way. I will get
there as soon as I can."

I thought my declaration sounded like the script of a bad movie.

I picked up my suitcase and smoothed the few rumples on the bed. At the registration desk, I presumed the clerk could see the tension in my face. "I just checked in. I have a life-and-death emergency at home. I didn't use the room at all, not even the bathroom. I would be pleased not to be charged, but I have to leave now." I handed her the room key without waiting for a response.

I hurried outside to the valet and began the same pitch. The young man remembered me from thirty minutes earlier, knew exactly where my car was, and sprinted toward the garage, and in less than one minute screeched to a halt in front of me. I handed him a ten-dollar bill, the smallest I had.

His accent was Caribbean. "No. You go." He refused the money.

Having lived in Washington for three summers during college, I knew well the route I would have to take, and how congested it usually was. But it was nearly midnight, and the streets I needed to use were clear; I was on the expressway north in ten minutes. For the next five and a half hours, my default speed was seventy.

Murphy's Law of Cellphones states that when you most need your phone, the battery runs low and you cannot charge it. As I got into the car, this law kicked in. Just before midnight, I told my sister-in-law, Linda, who answered Ellen's phone, that to conserve the battery I would call each hour at the top of the hour but would turn the phone off in between. Of course, part of the unspoken reason was that, as I was driving through the night, continual updates from the operating room would not be what I needed. Unless there was unequivocally good news.

As I was about to shut off the phone for the next hour, my inner child stirred. I wanted to talk to my mom and my dad. My mother was a night owl; I knew she would be awake. I reached her at home in eastern Connecticut. I told her that Reid had been "in a serious car accident."

Maybe I just needed to practice those words.

She drew her breath and then asked for more details. I immediately felt foolish for calling. Why in heaven's name had I alarmed my eighty-three-year-old mother at midnight, when all I knew was that Reid was in an operating room and I was driving hundreds of miles by myself in the middle of the night after an exhausting week?

I said I would call back if and when I knew more. When I hung up, I was sure that I had done the wrong thing.

As I turned off the phone for its midnight rest, I went into full compartmentalization—a mental discipline that lawyers are taught to invoke when needed. A voice in my head started saying that Reid might be dead. There were plainly indications in that direction, but I stuffed that voice into a box, nailed the lid shut, taped it, and for good measure sealed the cracks with putty so nothing would leak out. I forced myself not to think about it, if for no other reason than that I still had several hours to drive.

I was certainly not, however, able to wall off fear of dreadful possibilities, a tap-tap-tap from the inside of that sealed compartment, and so for the next three hours I played a mind game of speculation and diversion, sentences passing through my mind, punctuated by the geographic progress I was making along the highways. As I sped toward Hartford, the staccato dread went like this:

Passing the Baltimore-Washington airport. Midnight. Good morning, Baltimore. Lucky thing I didn't try to make that last plane. Tank is nearly full. Five to ten miles per hour over the speed limit. Go.

What if he's seriously injured like that girl in our church? She was in the hospital for months.

Delaware River Bridge, 1:00 a.m. I turned the phone on for a few minutes but decided not to call. If they needed to call, they would. I knew they would call with good news, but would not call a dreary man with hours to drive to tell him that his son had died. No calls, no messages.

Ellen had seen him being wheeled into surgery. He "looked good." "Burns on his hand and feet."

Just before 2:00 a.m., I called Ellen's number. My brother-in-law Ferg answered. He said Ellen was in the bathroom and "not doing well." I didn't ask for details. I projected my arrival as after 5:00 a.m. I put the phone down with no intention of calling anyone anymore, even on the hour.

New Jersey Turnpike rest stop, 2:00 a.m. Gas, bathroom, black coffee. Ten minutes uselessly charging the cellphone while I tried to drink the coffee before it was cool enough.

At some point, I realized that I was wide awake, as though I had just slept ten hours on satin sheets in a king-size bed. Part of my mind was racing, part was compartmentalizing, and part was driving. Adrenaline? Caffeine?

Newark Airport, 3:30 a.m. Empty.

Hackensack, Paramus.

Why was he in Plainville? He was supposed to be in Wethersfield! Can he go to school? Will he graduate?

The Meadowlands.

Why did Ferg say, "She's not doing well"?

George Washington Bridge. Two cars and me. "Burns on his hand and feet?"

Just after 4:00 a.m., I reached the Merritt Parkway— Connecticut. "You'd better come," Dr. Kuntz had said. "Now."

I can drive this road in my sleep. Don't.

He is not getting a new car, dammit.

Rocky Hill. Lord, please get me through this.

He will be all right.

Hartford, Connecticut, the Seymour Street parking garage at Hartford Hospital, 5:15 a.m., December 2, 2006.

I'm not sure why, but I looked at the odometer and the clock. Perhaps I was proud of myself, or in disbelief that I had not been stopped for speeding. Three hundred and forty miles in three hundred and thirty-five minutes, with one ten-minute stop.

I pulled in, took a deep breath, and unsealed the mental compartment I had constructed. It was time to find out what had happened and start to deal with it.

From the garage entrance, it is a half-block, slightly downhill, to the semicircular entrance plaza of the hospital. The overhead lights were bright. I wasn't running, but I wasn't walking either.

Through the double sliding-glass entrance doors, thirty yards ahead, I saw Gary Miller, the senior minister of our church. For some reason, I took this as a hopeful sign. Decades ago, Gary used his barrel chest and his strong arms to bring down running backs. He is, even now, a powerfully built man. As I approached, Gary was rocking side-to-side. He was, however, expressionless.

As the second slider opened, I raised my hands to Gary's shoulders and looked him in the eye and asked, "Is he OK?"

Gary paused, and returned my gaze, and said, "No, Tim." He paused again, measuring me. "He never made it out of surgery."

I recall first, instantly, my body tightening. My chest and legs were like a wet towel with each end attached to a propeller. At that moment, the propellers began to spin in opposite directions. The towel—my physical body and my consciousness—was immediately pulled tight. As the tension magnified, the force was centrifugal, separating my physical self from its compass, its bearings, and its direction. Hope, joy, coordination, certainty—everything—evaporated.

I was in emotional free fall. No structure, no boundaries, no anchors, no floors; certainly no windows or light. Suddenly, there was no grammar, no punctuation, no diction, no sentence structure; just formless incoherence. Even though I was now being supported by Gary's arms, I felt as though I had jumped backward off a building.

And while my body was twisting, and my soul was descending into an abyss, there was a sensation that is best described by an unavoidable cliché: Everything that had ever been nailed down was coming undone.

As I collapsed further into Gary's arms, I began crying, screaming, "This is all my fault! This is *my* fault. I never should have left. Gary, I never! . . . should! . . . have! . . . left!" Wail upon wail, gasping for breath. I don't recall if Gary said anything. I continued, weeping and mumbling, figuratively trying to dig a hook into something hard and stable that would arrest the sensation of falling.

After a few minutes, I remembered that Gary and I were still in the lobby, draped over a leather couch in a sitting area, but my family was upstairs. I said, "I need to see Ellen." With Gary's arm across my back and his hand under my shoulder, we went to the elevator, up, out, into a corridor.

The waiting room was enclosed in slightly tinted glass. Leather couches, institutional brown and pale yellow. And too small for the group: Ellen; her sister Linda and her husband, Ferg; my niece Emily and her boyfriend, Pat; our close friend Mary Way; our associate minister, Peter Grandy. My niece Sara and her husband, Mark. And Martha, my sandy-haired, freckle-faced, inquisitive marshmallow, rousted from her bed by her cousins, without warning or explanation, to go to the hospital. Just outside the door, Ellen and I collapsed into each other's arms, simultaneously letting out a cry that emanated from the bottom of our souls.

Months later, Mary described the moment, which I do not remember: "I was by myself in the hallway. I heard someone screaming in the elevator and I thought it was a patient in distress. I looked up and saw you walking with Gary. I wanted to hide because I was ashamed to witness something so personal. But at the same time, seeing you with Gary made me feel that God was with you."

The others began to emerge from behind the glass. As Martha approached me, this poor, shattered fourteen-year-old somehow managed to say something at once courageous, thoughtful, and mature beyond her years. "I love you, Daddy," she said tenderly. Ellen, Martha, and I melted into one.

More than a year later, I asked my relatives to explain what had happened before my arrival at the hospital. My niece's husband, Mark, the nurse practitioner, well acquainted with doctors delivering news, obliged:

> The surgeon comes in. The look on his face is like every surgeon you see in the movies who is about to deliver grim news. My muscles tighten. My heart races. I do not want anyone to know that I am instantly alarmed, even before he starts talking. Maybe my senses are wrong. He tells us that Reid was in critical condition upon arrival. He says something about brain activity. He wants to know if we want them to keep his heart beating and keep trying. Ellen says yes, keep trying. I am aware that the information means something different to me than to everyone else in the room.
>
> I chase the surgeon down the hall. I ask for more information. He tells me more of the same, but his words, tone, and expression tell me everything. I go back to the room. They look at me and ask me. "What did that mean?" All I can do is shake my head "no."
>
> The surgeon returns. I suspect it was less than 20 minutes. He walks in with an even more somber expression. He says what they always say in the movies. I am thinking, as the words come out, screaming in my head, NO! NO! NO! "By the time I got back to the OR, Reid was gone." NO! NO! NO! Ellen collapses, screaming, crying, Linda crying, wailing, everyone on the ground hugging.
>
> This is the part I cannot get out of my head. The crying. The screaming.

~

The corridor was poorly lit, tiled in gray and green, dull, unadorned. I was seeing a part of the hospital that few ever get to see and certainly no one wants to. At some point, it dawned on me that this was the morgue, and its lack of light and the absence of anything welcoming was by design, an acknowledgment of its limited, specific, and gruesome function.

I walked in slowly, with Gary Miller and Peter Grandy continuing to support my steps. I saw first a billowing white that was bigger than a body. It was not just a sheet resting on a human form through which legs or feet, chest or arms, were visible, but a kind of canopy draped across the body, covering everything but Reid's head with a thick sheet, maybe several, tucked in at his neck, shielding his body from my sight.

I studied his head and noticed first a stitched-up cut on his right temple. Then the weight of his closed eyes. The stillness of no breathing. My son, long afflicted with attention deficit disorder, suddenly free of his problems with sequencing and prioritizing, without any need to focus. And then, his chin.

Probably for the rest of my life I will think about Reid's chin at that moment.

I have many wishes and some anger at myself in retrospect, principally because I did not ask one of the hospital staff who had prepared him for my visit what I could or should touch, or not. His chin precipitated this question; it was pushed up slightly and at an odd angle. Simply, it was closer to his nose than it should have been. And his lower jaw seemed, well, soft. Mushy.

I can't say that as I observed this I recoiled in horror—I was already well past that point—but I distinctly recall being afraid to touch him—that is, the little that was available to me at all—for fear that I would . . . what, hurt him? Feel with my own fingers the extent of the blow from the accident?

So, I confess, at my last moments with my son—and it turned out to be the last time I saw him—I got scared, and I did not touch him or kiss him or run my fingers through his hair. All because of his chin.

Gary and Peter lowered me into a chair. The room was only six or seven feet wide, so even as I sat with my back to the opposite wall from where Reid lay, I was still close enough that I could speak just above a whisper so he could...hear me.

I addressed him as "Buddybear," a name I'd coined when he was a baby and never stopped using—he hadn't seemed to mind. Struggling even to speak, much less find words, I began talking about a letter I had written to him in July 2005, on his sixteenth birthday, a letter in which I had listed "The Very Best Days I Have Spent With My Son, Reid." I tried to summon good times we had had together, and that letter, as best as I could recall it, seemed like the best place to start.

Because he could not—or would not—respond as I reviewed our special days together, in my head I answered for him. I was talking aloud—Gary and Peter heard me—but Reid's voice was answering inside my head. There, in that room, off the main corridor of the morgue, just after 6:00 a.m. on a Saturday morning in early December, I did not touch my son, but we had a chat. I used his nickname, he called me "Dad," and we remembered our best times together.

~

To describe the hours that followed as containing any rational thought, deliberation, intelligence, logic, or order, or as the start of anything resembling healing, would be a lie. To write now about those hours is to impose a semblance of structure on what was still an emotional free fall with no floor or bottom.

Back in the waiting room, I learned the basics of the evening. After dinner, Reid had fallen asleep on the couch, Martha was watching television, and Ellen had decided that things were quiet and she could visit with her Christian sharing group. Reid would check in and ask permission if he wanted to go somewhere. Eventually, Jessica and Rachel arrived and woke Reid, and they decided to go for a ride.

Reid had only gotten half of his responsibilities right; he had "checked in" with me, but not with Ellen. He had not gotten permission before he left the house. Mike was not aware of Reid being en route to his house.

The quick spin with the girls had been that rite of passage among teenagers, a joyride. They had headed toward Plainville, where they had gotten lost. Trying to get back onto I-84 East to head back to West Hartford, they had mistakenly gotten onto I-84 West, which took them on a long stretch before the next exit.

In Southington or Cheshire, Reid had gotten off the highway and reversed direction, onto I-84 East, heading toward Plainville. That section is straight for two miles, but at the end of the straightaway is a sharp corner to the right, and then Exit 34, where the ramp inclines at an odd angle from the highway. At sixty-five-plus miles per hour, that big turn to the right and the odd angle arise in four to five seconds. As soon as I learned the vicinity of the accident, I understood. That was not a stretch of highway that Reid knew, and on a dark night that right curve probably surprised him.

The last bit of information I received at the hospital was that Jessica and Rachel had been due home by their curfew of 10:30 p.m., and the crash, about ten minutes from our neighborhood, had happened just about then. So perhaps Reid had been rushing to get the girls home on time.

It was now after 6:00 a.m. Most had been at the hospital for five or six hours. We verified that Jessica, mental state unknown, was physically recovering and would be released soon, and that Rachel had received some stitches in her lip and had other bruises, and would remain in the hospital for another day. They did not yet know that Reid had died. There was nothing more to do at Hartford Hospital.

Ferg drove Ellen, Martha, and me home in my rental car. I mostly recall a continuing inability to think.

We rode home in silence. Perhaps a few whimpers. Ellen and Martha were cried out, I guess. As we pulled into the driveway, our house had a different feel. This was not the place I had left twenty-three hours ago.

We opened our kitchen door and there was Gracie, needing to go outside, pleading for her breakfast, wanting to play with a towel, wagging her tail.

I went to my study. I emptied my pockets—my travel itinerary, the Hertz rental agreement, stuff.

I stared at the phone. I forced a list into my head. I needed to call Mom and Dad; my law partner, Joe Williams; and Duane Desiderio, who would be expecting me at that meeting in Washington in about an hour.

My mom picked up the phone immediately, as though she had been sitting there all night waiting for it to ring.

"Is he all right?" she blurted out.

"Is Dad on the phone with you?" I asked. I was not sure if she understood the implication.

She held the phone away and said, "Ken, go in the kitchen." My father picked up, barely awake. "Yeah, hi."

"No, Mom. He died."

"He . . . what?" An extended, uncomprehending shriek.

My parents lived an hour away, and they said they would get in the car right away, though after some back and forth they said they would take some time to compose themselves, to get ready to stay several days, and would come in the late morning.

By mid-morning, my first semblance of organized thought was forced consideration of what to do about my work. I was scheduled to argue a complicated appeal on Wednesday. There was a lot going on at the office. I was about to offload a great deal of responsibility and time, just before the holidays, on my co-workers, starting with my partner and friend, Joe.

Joe's wife, Tracy, answered. I knew this call would be devastating because their son Ethan was one of Reid's charges at Sunday school, and one of Reid's favorites.

Joe had already left the house, she said. She was no doubt expecting some call about an upcoming public hearing or a brief that had to be filed.

"Reid died in a car accident last night," I said, now training my voice for the second time. She too drew her breath. "Oh my God. . . ."

Next was Duane. We had worked together extensively on a case during the past two years. I didn't need to give my last name. Nor did I need to explain who Reid was; Duane is also the father of a boy, so we had compared notes.

He was his usual cheerful self. "Hey, Tim! What's up?"

"I'm back in Connecticut." I used my voice-in-training to explain why. As with my parents and Tracy, our voices trailed off; there was not much else to say. Duane began to repeat, "Tim, I am so sorry."

Elsewhere in the house, our relatives and our indefatigable friend Mary Way had started making other essential calls, to the families of Reid's best friends. By 8:00 a.m. or so, I concluded that I had made the calls I needed to. Ellen was in the den with Martha; they were crying on the shoulders and in the arms of several people, a tangle of grief. On the kitchen counter was Reid's class schedule for his new school for Monday. I put it in a drawer. I decided to go upstairs to our master bedroom.

I lay down on the bed and closed my eyes. In that moment, some other person inside me sat up and buried his head in his hands. My on-the-bed body became so frightfully conscious of this second presence that I could not rest. There was no discussion or communication between the body sitting and the body lying, just one presence too exhausted to sleep and another too devastated to lie down. Because resting requires at least the belief that the bed is not going anywhere, my effort was going to be futile.

After maybe half an hour, I could hear people starting to come into the house, I could smell coffee and something baking. Months later, my niece Sara described the scene: "By mid-morning, we had made some calls to our close friends. People were starting to show up. Food, flowers, tears, repeat. Cleaning, laundry, making coffee—were things I kept busy with. Cars were lining the street." Night had ended, but only in the sense that if one looked out the window, it was daylight.

Reid's death was statewide news. Katie Melone, a *Hartford Courant* reporter, called late-morning. I was glad it was her; I had talked to her on occasion in the past when she had covered some cases in which I had been involved, and I knew from those interactions that she was one of the paper's most capable people. She was gentle and empathetic in her questioning, deftly balancing her professional obligation to inquire with minimizing the intrusion.

The story she produced, published the next day, was news without sensationalism. There was a photo of the charred wreckage of the car but, again, I understood that Katie and her colleagues were only doing their jobs. No indictment or conviction. Under a headline of "17-Year-Old Dies in Wreck," the article said:

PLAINVILLE – A 17-year-old West Hartford boy died early Saturday of injuries sustained when the car he was driving struck a guard rail on I-84 on Friday night. Two passengers, also West Hartford teens, were injured.

All three were taken to Hartford Hospital. The driver, Reid S. Hollister, 17, died. The passengers were in stable condition Saturday night, a hospital spokesperson said.

Police said Hollister lost control of the Volvo he was driving at 9:28 p.m. He struck a metal guardrail where the Exit 34 off-ramp splits from the highway, and the car caught fire.

Hollister is the son of Ellen and Timothy Hollister, a partner at Shipman & Goodwin known for his expertise in land-use law.

The only inaccuracy in the article was the time of the accident, which was 10:28 p.m.

Saturday night, Greater Hartford's television stations carried the story. In my new role of caretaker of my son's name, I forced myself to watch. I am familiar enough with news coverage and its potential for misinformation and distortions that I wanted to know immediately if anything was said that would inaccurately shape the public perception of the accident. My stomach was churning and my hand on the remote was trembling, but the stories, each told by the in-studio anchor with the photo of Reid's car in the background, spoke only of "a teenage driver who lost control of his car on Interstate 84" and "the police identifying the deceased driver" as "Reid Hollister, 17, of West Hartford."

The news coverage was the bare essentials, nothing more. I was thankful.

Breaking the news to my parents, Tracy, and Duane; talking to the reporter; and using the remote to turn on the news were acts of willpower, a summoning from the chaos of enough emotional energy to form a sentence or press a button. Otherwise, I was a feather in the wind, buffeted, unable to control anything I was doing or where I was going. The arms and shoulders of others propped me up and received my tears, at least until the well ran dry and I needed to stop for refilling.

I was about to learn, however, that I had jobs to do, ones that would not wait for me to regain my balance. Parent jobs.

2

❧

Instantaneous and Irreversible

Starting on Saturday, December 2, no more than twelve
hours after Reid's passing, Ellen and I were suddenly confronted
with a list of decisions on matters that neither of us had ever
considered in our lives, due to the good fortune of never
having lost a parent or sibling. We certainly had never given a
moment's thought to what choices we would make if we had to
bury one of our children. Each decision had to be made more or
less instantaneously, and each was essentially irreversible. And
with every choice, whether made by his sister, Martha; by his
or our friends; or by anyone else we felt we had to consult, we
faced a question for which the best spokesman was unavailable:
What would Reid have wanted?

Overlaid on these decisions was one issue we had to face
quickly. Reid had died four days after being expelled from his

private school, accused of being "a drug dealer." Reid, who
had never been in disciplinary trouble before, had vehemently
denied that he had ever sold drugs to anyone. In the days before
his disciplinary hearing, we had established that Reid, with
other students, had tried marijuana several times and had given a
single marijuana cigarette to one student, one time, off campus,
for no money. Reid conceded his part in the matter, apologized
profusely, and was genuinely contrite. We also knew that his
school was not "zero tolerance," and in the past had meted out
less than expulsion to serious offenders. Reid pleaded with us
that the drug-selling claim was not true, and was devastated
by the school's faceless accusation and bewildered at how to
respond to it. Meanwhile, the school's claim somehow did
not remain confidential, and the drug-dealer rumor overtook
the campus and our community. Reid, in our view, was then
expelled because the punishment had to be consistent with the
rumor and the perception it had created, never mind the facts.

In the months ahead, we would learn much more about the
expulsion, but the dilemma of the moment was our certainty that
these events were being discussed widely and further distorted,
and thus were shaping how Reid would be remembered.
Stopping, reversing, and correcting these distortions were
vital, immediate tasks. We had to rescue his character from the
speculation that his having been kicked out of school and dying
in a crash, so soon thereafter, were undoubtedly generating. Any
teenager's life cut short is a canvas with few lines and colors,
but now we needed to complete the portrait—and repair the
image—immediately.

Meanwhile, with regard to his life, friends, and memory,
we had to be very careful not to miss something, not to discover

days, weeks, or months later that we had forgotten an important obligation or task. We had to bear in mind and pay appropriate attention to the norms and traditions of our society and our faith, yet we also had to be true to ourselves, to make sure that we did not make decisions simply to please others. No one would live with these choices in the future as we would.

Yet at that moment, as we began to make these consequential decisions, neither of us was mentally fit to decide what socks to wear, much less to define our son's memory. We were grief-stricken, sleep-deprived, overwhelmed even by where to start, host to an escalating stream of visitors and arriving relatives, inundated by condolence messages, and angry at the school.

My challenge began with life's basics: In the hours and then days immediately following Reid's death, my life's conventions and routines disappeared, and I was forced to relearn life's simplest tasks—to think through every step. This began after my unsuccessful attempt to sleep on Saturday morning; as I rolled off the bed, I thought to myself, "I am now getting out of bed, *which Reid will never do again.*"

This continued with everything I did:

"I am now washing my face, *which Reid no longer needs to do because he is dead.*"

"I am now getting dressed, *which Reid will soon do, with the assistance of an undertaker, for the very last time.*"

"I am breathing, *which Reid is not.*"

"I can see the sun, *which Reid cannot.*"

Every single thing I did, every action, every gesture, was now a comparative analysis, freighted with injustice and disbelief.

"I am now eating, *which Reid did for the last time on Friday evening.*"

I looked out the window at a car driving down our street. *"That is the activity that killed my son."*

Grief had reduced me to learning everything anew. Each action was now a maddening juxtaposition of the facts that I was still thinking and functioning, but Reid was not. I was deliberating about every motion and thought. My simplest action was saddled with disbelief.

Meanwhile, devastated though Ellen and I were, our to-do list was growing, and sometime in the late morning on Saturday, we realized that our community and our friends were now awaiting directions from us. We needed to submit the obituary to our region's newspaper, the *Hartford Courant*, by 5:00 p.m.

Midday on Saturday, the Rev. Sarah Verasco, who had been an associate minister at our church for several years before leaving a few months before Reid's accident, stopped in. She was the first of several angels who swooped down to prop us up and help us think through our choices. Sarah joined Ellen and me in my study.

We talked first about memorial donations, probably because this emerged as the easiest decision. Our church, just three months earlier, had opened a new day-care facility, the School for Young Children on Asylum Hill, known as SYCAH, to serve the Asylum Hill neighborhood of Hartford, one of the city's most economically distressed. The school needed tuition assistance and an endowment. Reid was at his best taking care of young kids. The school, on weekdays, inhabited the space on the church's lower level, where Reid had gathered his Sunday-school class—and perhaps found his future. So, in lieu of flowers, we would ask for donations to SYCAH.

That we would hold calling hours at a local funeral home was also assured, because it is a Protestant tradition and our community was undoubtedly expecting it. Although I suppose Ellen and I could have decided on a private burial and no other event, and perhaps our communities and friends would have understood, privacy seemed cowardly. Ellen and I, and Martha, now needed to open ourselves to our various communities, to allow Reid's passing to be shaped by those who had inhabited and enriched his life.

For this same reason, we needed to facilitate some form of communal grieving. We needed a memorial service. It became clear that this would be held at our church, where Ellen and I had met and were married, both Reid and Martha had been baptized and confirmed, and Ellen had worked for the past twenty-one years.

When? For practical and spiritual reasons, the universal recommendation of our relatives and ministers was as soon as possible. I felt a chill as I considered that we needed to expedite for no other reason than that Reid's body was just lying at the hospital, and this was not right. He needed to be laid to rest. And, I thought, the sooner we received hugs from multitudes, perhaps the sooner we could make some of the pain more bearable by sharing it among the supportive friends and neighbors we are privileged to have.

We considered the weather; thankfully, the forecast for the coming days was clear and cold but with no rain, snow, or ice.

West Hartford and Hartford offered us several choices of funeral homes for the calling hours. When our neighbor Steve Quish volunteered that Randy Molloy, of the Molloy Funeral Home, was a long-standing friend who would take good care of us, this too fell into place.

On Saturday afternoon, after roughing out these basic
directions with Sarah's help, Ellen and I excused ourselves from
the house to meet with Rev. Miller and Rev. Grandy to plan
the events. And we did: Calling hours at Molloy on Tuesday,
burial Wednesday morning, and a public memorial service on
Wednesday evening.

I turned my attention to my core obligation: writing a
description of Reid's life for his obituary.

As I confronted this surreal task at midday on Saturday,
our house was filling with relatives and friends who were there
to comfort us, and certainly I needed to lay my head on each
person's shoulder, but this writing would not wait. I knew it was
up to me to try a first pass. This was not a time, and there was no
time, for a committee. And who but Reid's parents could know
and decide what should be said?

My initial thoughts were panicky. I was stymied by my
fear of being unable to say much, to fill the space, to show
the *Courant*'s readers that Reid's life *mattered*. And then
emerged the critical issue: whether this obituary was going
to state the truth about a boy for whom educational struggles
were a defining characteristic, and for whom expulsion from
school was a penultimate event. Reid had no college, no
career, no leadership positions with charitable organizations,
and no children. He was handsome, gregarious, and gifted
with children, but from my vantage point, during the past four
years—almost a quarter of his life—his ADD, his educational
meltdown, our confrontations, his expulsion, and his fear of
the future had predominated. And, of course, all of this while
Ellen and I had seen and talked with him, and understood who
he was, less and less. Reid's final years had been, unfortunately,

intermittent dark clouds; no description of his life could accurately state that it had been only sunshine. So would his obituary be accurate or misleading, a portrait or a whitewash? As newly appointed and unwilling guardian of his memory, what was my duty?

I began to realize that creating an obituary for any teenager is a more delicate task than it is for someone who dies after years of employment and community and charitable activities and the raising of a family. Writing an obituary for *this* teenager would be a battle between need and format, between the need to explain and space limitations, between fact and rumor.

I started with the basics: *"Reid was born in Norwalk, Connecticut, on July 22, 1989, and adopted by Ellen (Deutsch) and Tim Hollister on October 19, 1989."*

In mid-October of 1989, I was walking through the parking lot adjacent to the office building in which I worked when who should come around the corner but Ellen. It was highly unusual for her to be in downtown Hartford. I thought that something bad had happened. But Ellen was smiling nervously and blurted out, "We have a baby!"

As we hugged in the parking lot, Ellen was bubbling with plans. I, on the other hand, in my lawyerly manner, was deliberating, formulating questions, such as "What do we know about the birth parents?" and "Don't we want a newborn?" It had taken us so long to reach this point that it seemed to me that a bit of due diligence wouldn't hurt.

We had been married on Pearl Harbor Day, December 7, in 1985, and after a couple of years of carefree young-coupledom, we began to think about children. Two stressful years followed. When we finally concluded that biological conception was unlikely, we discovered that neither of us had any hesitation in considering adoption. We researched and prayed. We prepared a detailed profile for a reputable adoption agency, complete with as appealing a photo as we could muster and a plaintive letter to an as-yet-unknown pregnant girl or young woman. Our letter described the home and the life we would provide, including our suburban street overflowing with kids, our church-based life, and my parents' summer cabin by a lake. And then, one day, we got the call.

The baby had been born on July 22 and was now eleven weeks old. When I mentioned my preference for a newborn, our social worker said, "Sir, this baby is sleeping through the night." Oh.

As it turned out, this baby had never been part of any earlier discussions with the adoption agency. His birth mother had changed her mind twice.

The next day we drove ninety minutes to Norwalk, the ride mostly enshrouded by the same if-we-don't-talk-about-it-we-won't-jinx-it silence that had characterized the previous nine months. We had studiously avoided any mention of decorating, toys, and baby clothes. Now that we were so close, we were too fearful to say anything that might dash our hope.

At the agency, the social worker referred to the birth parents as a "movie-star couple"—he was handsome and she was beautiful. They were not married, and apparently they doubted their future together. By the end of the conversation we were ready to be parents. On the way home, along Interstate 84, we called all of our relatives on a new contraption called a cellphone.

We learned that the baby's birth mother had named him Kyle, but because he was so young, we felt no hesitation about renaming him. Our process was as silly as most: We wanted a short, simple name that could not be nicknamed and was slightly unusual—and I knew a guy named Reid who I thought was very nice.

As I sat in my study scribbling obituary notes, commotion in our kitchen broke my concentration.

What to say next?

We would have to mention Reid's stunning eyes, the trait for which he was best known. His birth mother's eyes. *"Reid was widely known for his piercing aqua-blue eyes,"* I wrote.

From the moment we returned from the foster mother's home in Danbury to our own, filled with relatives and friends camped out, the words "Look at those eyes!" became a never-ending refrain. His eyes combined the best of aqua and blue. They were the color of the water next to a sparkling beach on a tropical island, transparent in the sense that those snowflake-like formations that surround the pupil were sharply defined and symmetrical. They were, in a word, stunning.

Now, because Reid was adopted, his eyes were the regular cause of awkward interactions with people we did not know. Ellen would be in Stop & Shop with Reid perched in the shopping cart's foldable seat, and the checkout clerk or someone in line would say, "Look at those eyes!" and then would inspect Ellen's eyes, looking for the baby's genetic roots. If I was not present, this puzzled person would then remark, "Oh, he has his father's eyes." On one occasion, when Ellen and I were both present but did not get around to explaining that Reid was adopted, someone said, "Oh, the mailman!"

On my pad of paper, I jumped years ahead.

"Reid's true gift was caring for and nurturing children."
After attending Sunday school and summer camp for years,
Reid began to see that his ability to empathize with others and
to identify the fun in every situation could be put to use in a role
as a teacher and counselor. He volunteered for Sunday-morning
duty at church with the three-, four-, and five-year olds and
then as a trainee counselor at a summer sports camp. In both
places the directors identified him early on as one who had an
uncommon ability to connect with young children, to gain their
trust, to help them overcome their fears, and to help them learn
through laughter.

*"Reid lent his tenor voice to West Hartford's Inter-El Choir
and Spartan 7."* Singing—he had a beautiful tenor voice. In
fifth grade, he won a spot in the town-wide elementary school
chorus. Then, at the beginning of Reid's freshman year in high
school, his voice and personality led to one of those moments
in which talent rises to an opportunity and sets a young person
on the road to a confidence-building success. David, a senior,
formed a boys' a cappella group called "Spartan 7." The group
was mentored by the school's choral director, a teacher revered
by both students and parents for his demands that the kids sing
professional-level material and his precise, inspiring instruction
about exactly how to do it.

Spartan 7 needed a tenor. In a "bring-in-the-understudy!"
moment, David told the director that "Reid Hollister can do it."
And he did. When we saw Spartan 7's first performance at the
end of Reid's freshman year, we were awestruck by the sight
of our boy seamlessly contributing to a blend of voices that
enraptured a packed auditorium.

"Offbeat sense of humor." Reid perfected an Elvis Presley imitation, throwing his head back and his pelvis forward, running his hand through his hair, summoning that familiar low and husky tone, "Thankya vera muuuuccchh . . . ." His repertoire also included characters from television and the movies; Jim Carrey's funniest scenes frequently echoed throughout our house.

"Amazing ability to whistle." At any time he would burst into song or whistle perfectly any melody that popped into his head, from the opening of Beethoven's Ninth to Lou Bega's "Mambo No. 5."

"Fierce loyalty to his friends." For two years Reid had been inseparable from his classmates Tom Gersky and Mike Borea, each of them friendly and respectful to Ellen and me and, we could tell, looking out for Reid in the same way he did for them. This threesome spent many of their out-of-school hours in our house, watching television and movies, subsisting on chicken wings and pizza, taking showers every now and then, making a horrendous mess of our downstairs recreation room. Ellen and I were completely comfortable with all of this because the boys were in our house when their whereabouts could have been unknown. It also did not hurt that Tom and Mike were capable students whose habits we thought might seep into Reid's routines. These two boys became to us like second and third sons.

"The Hollister family owes a great debt of gratitude to countless others who loved him as their own." Next door to us was the Quish family, with Steve a year older than Reid and Tom a year younger. The Quish basement sported a big-screen

television that was far superior to ours, and Reid began to spend hours on end in the Quish house, playing video games mostly. He made it clear to us many times that the grass was greener on the other side of the backyard fence. Ellen and I tolerated this because the Quishes are a wonderful, loving family and Reid seemed genuinely happy when he was there.

With Reid's most noteworthy and positive traits now on paper, it was time for me to try to confront what was boiling within me. Would the obituary put a happy but false face on his troubled life, or would it state the less comfortable truths?

Reid's first-grade teacher, Mrs. Sebolt, was a veteran who had interacted with hundreds of youngsters. Commenting on Reid's social development, she wrote that "he is the first to sense and respond to the needs of other children, and in this sense he is truly unusual." Another teacher described him as "an extroverted youngster with many friends" while another wrote that "Reid's sense of humor and wit are priceless."

But as early as second grade, we also began to hear the drumbeat of what would be Reid's albatross, attention deficit disorder. Through a series of "age-appropriate diagnostic skills evaluations," his teachers and the school staff skillfully pinpointed Reid as a boy of "high average" intelligence, but with problems focusing and tackling open-ended assignments. One evaluator elicited Reid's view of himself: "Writing takes too long" and "my fingers get sweaty and start to hurt" and "I get an idea in my head but when I try to write it, it goes blank and I forget it." Said the counselor, "Reid shows frustration with his minimal accomplishments."

As Reid reached fourth and fifth grades, his capabilities continued to emerge, but so did his obstacles. His teachers continually commented on his ability to learn but frequently added that "his impulsivity interferes with his focus." They observed intelligence but also lagging fine-motor skills, and resulting interference with transferring his thoughts to paper and handling tasks that required sustained effort.

At the school's recommendation, we had Reid evaluated by a psychologist. After exercises and tests, he reported "strong verbal reasoning and perceptual organization" and "inferential problem-solving skills" but "low-average use of a pencil." He stated, "In terms of practical real-world problem-solving and thinking, Reid has significant positive capabilities," but was "in the clinical range on the impulsive scale," "clinically significant for hyperactivity," and at-risk for attention deficit. More colloquially, Reid was an ADD kid, with some symptoms of ADHD. The psychologist described him as intellectually able, but with difficulty in holding his thoughts long enough to speak them or write them down.

Then there were Reid's sleeping problems, specifically, difficulty falling asleep and nightmares. He began to subsist on less sleep—six or seven hours per night—than most adults get. Yet the fact that Reid was not an adult was underscored by the many nights when, after a nightmare, he made a place for himself on the floor next to our bed.

As Reid entered fifth grade in 1997, Ellen and I again sought out professionals to help us evaluate Reid's potential and challenges and decide where he would attend sixth grade. We were fortunate to be able to afford private-school tuition; we had choices that many families do not.

Reid was not a candidate for special education, but he clearly needed help to keep him on task and to implement the day-to-day strategies that the psychologist had recommended. We feared he might get lost in the larger public school.

We pursued two private-school options, a mainstream school with a creditable reputation for academics and athletics, and a smaller school known for providing alternatives to a conventional schedule and a competitive environment. Both offered academic excellence and small classes, but the larger school seemed to offer more of the sports and other activities that we thought Reid would need to have the most opportunities to shine. We decided on bigger and mainstream.

During his first year there, Reid got the full dose of the expectations and workload at a demanding private school. He passed his courses, barely, but was constantly bewildered by comparisons to his peers. Often, struggling with homework, he dissolved into tears, pleading, "Dad, I can't do this!"

We brought him to another psychologist, Dr. Carver, who specialized in ADD and knew his school well. We asked her to help him try to make sense of his attention deficit and sequencing challenges. She again diagnosed his combination of substantial intelligence, deficient fine-motor skills, and resulting frustration and low self-esteem.

At that time, August 2001, when Reid was twelve, I marveled at Dr. Carver's ability to get inside my child's head and make clinical sense of what was happening there. Her predictions of what was to come were spot-on. Her report opened with a charming description of Reid as "a handsome dark-haired adolescent with notably expressive eyes." She identified his penchant for losing things and his inability to handle a verbal assignment of three tasks without forgetting one or getting the intended order wrong. Her assessments suggested an "overanxious disorder" related to "peer humiliation and rejection." In other words, "he worries about people laughing at him or doing something stupid" and "becomes nervous in public" and thus "lacks self-esteem." She concluded that "Reid has the IQ and the ability to succeed, but needs a full program of tools and support." She recommended a series of coping strategies.

Though Reid was only twelve at the time, Dr. Carver threw into her report one piece of advice for the future: Reid would need to be careful when he learned to drive.

When Ellen and I met with Dr. Carver to review her conclusions, she cautioned us that "telling him to try harder won't work." In other words, there were limits on Reid's ability that more homework or tutoring was unlikely to overcome, and the best we could do was provide reasonable support and encouragement.

Her last recommendation was that his dose of attention deficit medication should be increased. She referred us to an M.D., Dr. Jarvis, to oversee a prescription of Ritalin. Naturally, Reid resisted the idea of yet another doctor. His protests included "I'm fine!" and "You guys think I'm some mental case, don't you?" and "I'm not taking any pills."

Nevertheless, when he meet Dr. Jarvis, they got along well. The good doctor reeled him in by displaying an intimate knowledge of video games. Still, the very idea of drug therapy was discomforting to Ellen and me; for parents, administering pills requires a nuanced differentiation between "good drugs" that assist the mind and "bad drugs" that harm it. In the best

circumstances, giving medication to a physically healthy
kid creates the impression that life's mental challenges can
be addressed by popping pills. On the other hand, drugs for
attention deficit have been on the market for a generation and
seem to have a track record as a benign form of intervention.
And in moments of candor, Reid conceded that with the
medication he could sense an improvement in his attention span.
Yet Ellen and I felt compelled to try to soften what the doctors
recommended by referring to Reid's ADD medication as his
"vitamins."

As age twelve gave way to his teenage years and high
school loomed, Reid's academic struggles began to dominate
our family life. We put in place the steps that Dr. Carver had
directed. We regularly called and emailed his school to explain
what we were seeing at home. It may be that we wore out our
welcome there, but with each step and communication, we
tried to strike the right balance between intervening and leaving
things in the hands of his teachers and advisors.

So often during this period, I was not sure what to do. I
listened to the school's polite reassurances that all would be fine,
that kids mature at different times, boys more slowly than girls.
Kids need to learn that they will sometimes fail, and so we need
to let them, they told us on occasion. I understood the subtext:
Leave us alone; we will educate your child. Nonetheless, mostly
at Reid's insistence, I hunkered down with him night after night
over homework.

As Reid worked his way through sixth and seventh grade,
Ellen and I worried about how his learning challenges would
play out as he got older, as he sought to put more distance

between himself and his parents, as teenagers do. Our fear was that he would rebel and start blaming the closest available humans—us—for his frustrations.

3

And Unrelenting

Sure enough, as he started his eighth-grade year, Reid began to announce far too early in the evenings that he had done "enough" homework. When we upped the stakes by referring to his future, or how lucky he was to be in a private school, or what discipline we would impose, he would bellow, "It's my life!" When we made it clear that more time and effort was needed, he would say, "I hate you." On a few occasions, Reid even threatened us with phrases such as "Don't push me too far." We always took these moments seriously, including bringing Reid to Dr. Jarvis to make sure that he was not really at risk. At each visit Dr. Jarvis reassured us, and we began to take them somewhat in stride.

Meanwhile, Reid began to flounder even more in school. His class notes were a shambles, his handwriting mostly unreadable. Every bad grade had an excuse: a forty-six on a quiz? "No one else got over fifty." Homework assignment unknown? "The teacher never explained it." Can I help you get organized? "I don't need help. I hate my life. Get out of my room."

Yet while this nightly theater drove Ellen and me to question everything we were doing as parents, some of the feedback from school provided hope that these challenges were temporary, that better days were ahead. This was simultaneously comforting and baffling. Emblematic was this comment from Reid's advisor at the end of eighth grade:

> When we met for our parent/teacher conference this spring, there were three issues of concern: The first was Reid's confidence, the next his ability, and the last his effort. In reading over Reid's final comments for the year and in talking to his teachers, it is clear that Reid is headed in the "right" direction on all three counts. For starters, Reid does seem to be taking himself and his studies more seriously, feeling more confident in his own ability, and opting out of playing the class clown. While he still likes to crack a joke or two in class, they are actually quite clever and appropriate and never self-denigrating. He has also stopped publicly announcing his quiz scores and his expectations for failure just before he takes a quiz.

But these comments came accompanied by a report card of C's, some of which were plainly generous. Thus emerged the contrasting pattern that we would see for the next four years: a bad attitude and complete disorganization at home, and at school barely passing grades and descriptions of minimal effort, but leavened with praise for his ability, potential, and personality.

Reid's academic travails led us to reexamine whether he should transfer somewhere else for high school. In response to our direct questions, Reid's teachers were equivocal. In our darker moments, we wondered whether the school, in its encouraging messages, was simply trying to retain a paying customer. Reid's advisor led with faint praise: "None of us is convinced that Reid should not attend the Upper School." She pointed out that Reid was now socially integrated and popular within his eighth-grade peer group and that "the social stuff is important too."

Academically, Reid squeezed by again at the end of the year. He desperately wanted to stay with his friends, and so Ellen and I took another leap of faith. Off he went to the Upper School.

Before Reid's freshman year began, we sat down with the two teachers in charge of the ninth graders and his advisor, a well-meaning young man but brand new to teaching. We recounted Reid's middle school ups and downs, the support system we had put in place at home, and the steps we needed his teachers and the school to take. Nonetheless, Reid's high school years began with a score of five out of one hundred on a chemistry test and comments like this one from his math teacher: "I do not believe that Reid suffers from deficiency in skills but I do not believe he works particularly hard in applying them." Said another, "I patiently await Reid's awakening."

Ellen and I began to sound the alarm. In October, Ellen wrote to his advisor:

> My biggest concern is that even though you say he seems to want to do well, I am seeing no effort at home. When I question Reid about homework he says that he is all done. He seems clueless on how to study and that he needs to study. I'm getting frustrated because weeks seem to be flying by and it is not getting any better. Someone has to say to him that he is going to flunk out

if he doesn't start to buckle down. We can't wait any longer.

We were told last year that this school was the right place for him. I was talked into it. I once again need to be talked into it.

In November, after another month of hearing from the school that "Reid can do it if he wants to" and what a joy he was to have in class, I sent a further plea:

We get the sense that Reid simply does not understand what it means or what it takes at this level of school to work hard and to achieve mastery rather than just the passing familiarity that gets you a D on a quiz. It may be that his teachers are *assuming* that he knows all of the basic study habits, when he really does not. We see a string of failing grades—what does he think this means? He seems mostly unconcerned.

There were some steps from the school that seemed to help temporarily, but ultimately Reid got the same poor results. His science teacher, for example, explained that the course's textbook "has served as a reference and we have had assignments in it on all the main topics." He neglected, however, to tell us what we should do when Reid declined even to open the book.

By the end of Reid's freshman year, the situation was becoming clear—and it was a trap. We had enrolled Reid in a competitive private school in which he was continually, if not failing, then teetering. His self-esteem was taking a constant beating, in large part because he was not exposed in his peer group there to the 70 percent or so of students whose entrance-exam scores were lower than his, as well as those who did not have his economic advantages. He was the "dumbest" not because he was dumb, but because he was in the company of academic achievers.

Our parent-child conflicts, Reid's barely passing grades, his lack of concern about them, and his hostility to our efforts to help led us back to Dr. Carver during the summer after his freshman year. She spent a day and a half with him, and as before captured precisely his capabilities and obstacles. She took him through an exercise called the Million Adolescent Personality Inventory and identified Reid as being in the category of teens who attempt to maintain an image of cool strength, arrogance, and fearlessness. "Such a youngster," the scoring code said, "may display a rash willingness to risk harm and is notably fearless in the face of threats and punitive actions." Dr. Carver prepared a revised, age-appropriate list of recommendations.

As Reid's sophomore year began, the pattern repeated itself: signs of promise but ultimately near-failures—that is, just enough academic success to confound our annual decision about whether to keep Reid at this private college-prep school. The best course once again appeared to be to await the success that his teachers said was probably, hopefully, on the horizon.

His teachers continued to extol his personality and promise: "Reid adds liveliness to the classroom with his humor, which makes it enjoyable for all of us," said one. Midway through that first semester, his English teacher remarked, "Reid seemed to have an epiphany midway through the term, reading the books and preparing for class," but this comment accompanied a charitable grade of C.

In an email to Reid's advisor, we described one evening that summarized much from those sophomore months:

> We had a rather bizarre conversation with Reid last night. He was focused on the fact that he raised two C-minuses to C's, while we were focused on the two grades that went down (math and history) and the pointed comments from all five teachers about lack of effort, or at least lack of consistent effort. Ellen and I felt that we had no choice but to cut back further on the at-home electronics (video games now totally gone, computer access for homework only), and to make it clear that if he wants to have the privilege of driving this summer when he turns sixteen, we are going to need a report card that shows effort (as always, not any particular grade, but effort). Needless to say, he is now furious at both of us. This morning he threatened to quit Spartan 7 just to show us who's the boss.

A short time later, Reid did indeed quit Spartan 7.

~

Anna Quindlen once described how the job of family obituarist defaulted to her after she demonstrated her talent for the task. She ended up writing obituaries for her mother and several other relatives and close friends. In an article, she described the peculiar challenge: "I could only be accurate. The limitations of the form eliminate the more subjective truths: a good heart, a generous soul." She concluded, "How little the facts suffice."

As I sat in my study mid-afternoon on Saturday, I stared at my obituary notes. The clock was ticking; the afternoon light was fading. The *Courant*'s deadline was approaching.

I tried a few phrases that contained the word "education," but scratched each one out before I had finished. I began to realize that his academic struggles, though a defining characteristic of his life, would have no mention in his obituary. It became obvious that his educational struggles could not be reduced even to a paragraph. I could not muster one appropriate sentence. "In school, Reid tried his best" or something similar seemed to mock him, implying that he tried and failed, damning with faint praise. And since I was going to omit his educational struggles, even alluding to, much less trying to explain, the more particular and pointed problems of the weeks just prior to his death were now out of the question. I was beginning to comprehend the reason for the axiom that one does not speak ill of the dead. No, I came to realize, an obituary is not an evenhanded explanation of a life or a truthful summary of the deceased's time on earth. It is certainly not a vehicle for correcting an injustice—though that need was still burning inside. An obituary is a ledger of relatives, an announcement of times and places, and a highly filtered list of virtues and high points. No asterisks, no explanations.

Ultimately, I gave up on the full truth. Reid's obituary would adhere to the traditional, and it would mention only those traits for which he would be fondly recalled. I remember thinking that Reid's memorial service and eulogy might provide another opportunity to correct the record, so to speak, but with the *Courant*'s deadline looming and all of the other decisions demanding more immediate attention, I concluded that the truth of Reid's life would be shelved. Whether this was temporary remained to be seen.

As the afternoon progressed, I enlisted relatives to help with making sure nothing and no one had been omitted or misdescribed. I noted that until 5:00 p.m., I could still correct my mistakes, *which Reid could not.*

I typed the notes I had into the format of the other obituaries, and then I discussed my draft with Ellen and my niece Sara, with Ellen's sister, and with Ellen's mother, Nadia. This was the published piece:

> **HOLLISTER, Reid Samuel.** Reid Samuel Hollister, 17, of West Hartford, died in the early morning of Saturday (December 2, 2006), from injuries sustained in an automobile accident. Reid was born in Norwalk on July 22, 1989, and was adopted by Ellen (Deutsch) and Tim Hollister on October 19, 1989. Reid will be missed by many, many throughout West Hartford and the region. Reid's true gift was caring for and nurturing children, which he demonstrated for several years both at Asylum Hill Congregational Church and at Camp Overlook. Reid had a beautiful tenor voice, which he lent to West Hartford's Inter-El Choir and "Spartan 7," an a cappella group. He played soccer, basketball, and lacrosse. Reid was widely known for his piercing aqua-blue eyes, handsome face, happy-go-lucky attitude, an amazing ability to whistle, lightning-fast text-messaging skills, an offbeat sense of humor, fierce loyalty to his friends, and his abiding love of his family. Reid leaves his parents, Ellen and Tim; his beloved sister, Martha; his affectionate golden retriever, Gracie. . . .

And then the details of the calling hours, burial, memorial service, donations, and online condolences. Finally:

> The Hollister family owes a great debt of gratitude to countless others who loved him as their own.

We scanned and emailed what would have been Reid's high school graduation photo. Navy blazer, pinstriped shirt, pink-and-blue striped tie perfectly knotted but askew, pushed half an inch to the right of center. Reid at his most dapper, looking squarely into the camera, his short soccer-season haircut framing his sparkling eyes and his perfect smile. One would say that this photo nearly jumped off the page in the December 3 and 4 editions of the *Courant*, in which Reid's obituary started at the top of the page, and in which his age presented itself as perhaps the most tragic fact in that section of the newspaper.

In Reid's obituary, the limitations of the form and his age when he died eliminated what usually fills a death notice and reduced us to happy but appallingly incomplete truths. We ended up with the facts recited telling so, so little of the story. In my first obligation on my first day as the father of a child who had passed away, I had come up short. That most basic parental instinct, to protect a defenseless child, had kicked in, and my response had been to recall the good, catalogue the bad, but omit the truth.

Deadline, indeed.

~

Throughout that Saturday, as we devoted our first attention to the obituary and the memorial service, people arrived and the implications of this new role of custodian of the posthumous started to unfold, without pause and often with no rationale as to why one question followed another.

As my mother, bent at the waist with anguish, got out of the car, I began to wonder: Should Reid's vital organs be harvested and donated? When a neighbor asked what she could do to help, into my head crept: What type of casket should we choose?

Teenagers at our doorstep, Reid's and Martha's friends, their faces most revealing the realization that life is never assured, gave rise to: What should Reid wear in his casket? Aunts and uncles, cousins, classmates, parents, co-workers, friends, people we had not seen or talked to in quite some time, seemed to prompt us to formulate essential, immediate questions: What personal effects should accompany Reid in his casket? What photos of Reid's life should we display? Should the casket be open or closed? Should we bury Reid or cremate him? If we buried him, where? If a burial, who should be pallbearers? What should be said to eulogize Reid, and who should say it? What role, if any, should Martha, who was mostly huddling in the basement watching movies with friends, play in all this? Should we try to contact his birth mother and birth father?

Mid-afternoon on Saturday, while others considered the obituary draft, Ellen and I excused ourselves and drove across town to the Molloy Funeral Home. Randy Molloy was well prepared to receive and guide us. He looked the part: solidly built, a clean-shaven head, dressed in black. Every sentence he uttered, every question he asked, and every explanation he gave were paced so as to convey both sympathy and patience; he would spend as much time with us as necessary.

Ellen and I followed Randy into an inner room, the casket display. Without discussion or comparison, I knew that we did not want for Reid the fanciest or finest, but the fittest. We had to figure out what type of casket would be best suited to our boy, matching a type of wood, style of carving, handles, and finishes to the body they would comfort.

Among the issues, decisions, and choices that Ellen and I, as parents, had never before contemplated, surely this one was the strangest—even formulating the question made me wonder what in God's name we were doing: Would we be most comfortable burying Reid in mahogany, cherry, oak, or pine? Brass fittings? Wooden handles? Intricate or plain or somewhere in between? The interior bed—plush, smooth, satin?

Ultimately, we made the decision as if we were decorating our home or buying clothes for Reid. He wasn't fancy or pretentious, so we focused on oak. Similarly, Reid did not need to rest on satin—seventeen-year-olds do not covet luxury, but comfort. Reid would want a basement sofa, not a chaise longue.

Next on this bizarre agenda was what mementos of Reid's life would go into the casket to keep him company. Randy had informed us that we could assemble the items for display at the calling hours and his staff would then place them inside before the burial. Thus, as to this one task, we had some time, Monday and Tuesday, to think.

I don't recall a great deal of deliberation about these items; more accurately, after we spread the word to family and Reid's closest friends of what we needed to do, things just materialized. It was as if we were helping Reid pack for one of those life-planning retreats at which the participants introduce themselves with a show-and-tell of items that best illustrate who and where they are at that time in their lives. Martha offered the bottle of cologne that she had already bought Reid for Christmas, a pencil sketch of Reid she had drawn on Saturday night, and several photos of herself and Gracie. With Martha's help, Ellen and I selected, in addition to more photos, a T-shirt from the West Hartford Wolverines, Reid's triumphant U-11 travel soccer team, and three items from which he was rarely separated: PlayStation games, gum, and Blistex.

Reid's clothes drawers contained several baseballs. We took one and passed it around the kitchen and the den for relatives to sign. In an extraordinary gesture, Mike Borea contributed his actual black belt in karate. Our neighbor Scott Schpero put in some of Reid's favorite DVDs. Tom Gersky donated his ticket stub from a Red Sox game and a condom. (Well, why not? Reid was a head-turning young man who had a harem and, I assumed, some experience in this regard.)

And then there was the question of open or closed casket. Randy Molloy made sure that we understood the potential value of an open casket. He implied that he had seen families later regret their decision to keep the casket closed. He mentioned more than once that some people gain a measure of solitude from seeing the body at peace.

Another powerful consideration was that Ellen had last seen Reid as he was being wheeled into the emergency room at Hartford Hospital. She had not gone with Gary Miller, Peter Grandy, and me to the morgue after I arrived at the hospital. Ellen had told me by her cellphone, right after she saw Reid enter the hospital, that "he looked good"—his cheeks were rosy—but we had since learned that by that time he had been in cardiac arrest for almost an hour. Perhaps Ellen needed to see him.

I, on the other hand, was concerned about that gash on his right temple, his injuries, and his surgery at the hospital. Randy assured us that his staff could mend the wound, but I was not persuaded. And when I considered the idea of our handsome, blue-eyed gentleman with the electric smile, now to be embalmed, eyes and mouth closed, right temple repaired at best, looking shrink-wrapped, I decided that I did not want our family and friends to see him like that. An open casket for an eighty-year-old is one thing; showing Reid's body in a way that would hide or cover up the physical features that had endeared him to so many was, in my mind, out of the question. I insisted on a closed casket, Ellen did not disagree, and Randy felt that we had suitably discussed this option.

The decision about cremation or burial was surprisingly easy. Ellen was so certain that she gave me the impression she had thought about this previously. Envisioning ashes being scattered, degraded, and dissolved by wind and rain, Ellen said firmly, "I need a place to go." Although I toyed briefly with a vision of sprinkling ashes in one or more meaningful places—Fenway Park or the pond in eastern Connecticut or at the base of a new tree in our backyard—I quickly realized that even if we buried or interred cremated remains, Ellen's fear was justified. We would bury Reid's body in a cemetery.

(Weeks later, a friend whose twenty-five-year-old daughter had died several years earlier told us, "If we had scattered the ashes, my soul would have scattered as well." Ellen had the same intuition.)

As we were finishing our tasks at the Molloy office, Randy advised that he needed clothes for Reid. Since Reid's casket would be closed, this decision would be consequential only for Ellen, Martha, and me. As Ellen and I drove home, we agreed that this was one decision in which his sister should participate, so we momentarily deferred.

Then Randy led us to the Fairview Cemetery to select a plot. At the time of Reid's death, I had lived in West Hartford for twenty-four years and had therefore driven past Fairview hundreds of times, but had never paid it a moment of attention or been inside the fence; now, it was to become a center of my universe. On its east side is Fernridge Park, where I had spent countless days with Reid and Martha on the swings, swimming, and playing tennis, soccer, softball, and baseball.

Randy explained that the cemetery had few remaining plots and the available section was to the immediate right of the entry gate. The area had some agreeable features: It is easily found, due to its proximity to the cemetery's entrance. The main gate is at the north end of Pleasant Street, a name we liked. Across the street is a church. There was even a feature for a father and son bonded by their devotion to the Mets and Red Sox, and hatred of the Yankees: Section 15 is within sight and earshot of Fernridge Park's baseball diamond.

Randy explained the geometry of our choices: against the fence and closest to the street, where Reid could have a full-size, upright headstone; the middle, where the rules allowed only headstones less than two feet high and with a slanted face; and closest to the driveway, where each grave must be marked only with a flat stone.

This decision was another that effectively made itself as soon as we examined the options. Our boy deserved more than a flat headstone that would be repeatedly stepped on and covered with dirt and grass clippings. A full-size headstone was an inducement, but the stone and the grave would be next to the cemetery's chain-link perimeter fence and close to the street. We opted for the middle, especially when we saw that the plot was shaded by a large, lovely pine tree.

At home, as soon as we broached with Martha what Reid should wear, she revealed that she had already thought about it. "Pink polo, khakis, red boxers," she said. Brilliant, I thought.

The pink polo had become Reid's trademark of sorts. He looked fabulous in it; it set off his eyes. Girls loved it. We knew he would have liked the pink. The khakis were part of the default uniform at his school, where blue jeans are not allowed. And the plaid red boxers recalled the time at Crabby Bill's restaurant in St. Petersburg, Florida, when Reid, age thirteen, had won a prize by being the first patron to prove to the owner, acting as master of ceremonies, that he was wearing red underwear.

With expert help from our friend Karen Tomasko, a graphic designer, we approached another painful task—preparing a mounted display of seventeen years of photographs for the calling hours. Actually, we quickly determined that one large board would not be sufficient, so the project quickly morphed into two boards, one for his early childhood and one for his teenage years. Martha and her cousins took the lead in pulling photos. The early pictures displayed the passages of Reid's life: a face full of chocolate; sitting on a pumpkin; holding Martha in his lap the day we brought her home from the adoption agency; saving the world in his Superman costume; showing off his Power Ranger lunchbox; dressed up in a turtleneck and navy blazer in front of a Christmas tree; donning a bright-orange life preserver during our boat trip on Lake Powell; wearing his New York Mets cap on Opening Day, 1994.

The "older" board, once assembled, was harder for me to look at, and always will be. To look at those pictures is to calculate how long he had left to live when each was taken. Two years, one year, six months. Three weeks. Five days. My contribution to that board was my favorite photo of him. On our trip to Zion National Park, when Reid was fifteen, he and I took a hike up "the Narrows," a river framed by a high-walled

canyon. The walk is one of the most dramatic in the United
States because of the depth of the canyon, the irregular flow and
depth of the water as one crisscrosses it, the wildlife (we had
to move quickly to avoid a deer), and the dramatic contrasts
between light and shadows, due to the sun being above the
canyon for only minutes at a time and at constantly changing
angles. In my photo, Reid is perched on a rock in the middle
of the flowing river, with dark shadows in the foreground and
background, but right where Reid is standing, a bright beam of
sunlight reflects off the water and the rock.

On the rest of that board, our last family portrait, taken in
July 2006; Reid toasting with a glass of champagne; and finally,
Reid with his arm around Martha, five days before he died, the
last photo taken of him.

Seventeen years, four months, and nine days compressed
into fifty-one photos onto a pair of two-by-three-foot foam
boards.

Late Saturday afternoon, Reid's friends began to arrive
at our home in large groups. Their anguish was qualitatively
different from that of the adults, those more familiar with death
and loss. While the adults arrived to comfort Ellen and me in
our shock and disbelief, the teens arrived baring their disbelief
that life can end so suddenly and so early, and their need for
the most basic guidance about what to do, think, and say. Their
tears seemed tentative, cries to simply understand what had just
happened. They were plainly struggling not only with Reid's
death but with what death is.

Mr. West, a former principal of Reid's school and father of
one of his classmates, arrived. I hesitated, not knowing if he was
an unofficial emissary. We had sent word through several people

that the school's administrators responsible for his expulsion were not welcome at our house, the calling hours, or the service. This was painful but prudent. Probably understanding the situation and our anger, Mr. West did not try to speak for the school. The focus of the moment was elsewhere, and I thanked him for his visit.

Our decision-making picked up momentum on Sunday and Monday, but Ellen and I deferred one decision—whether to try to contact Reid's birth mother, Laura. We knew where she lived, sort of. We also knew that the adoption agency in Norwalk could contact her if necessary, though we had no idea how quickly. Laura was aware of Reid's adopted name, but there was no way to know whether she had heard the reports of the crash or had seen the story that had appeared in the *Courant*.

Deciding whether to reach out to Laura involved several unknowns. How would she feel about all of this? How had seventeen years affected her feelings about her biological son? Would she think of Reid as her own child or more of a distant relative? Would she blame us for what had happened? The memorial service did not seem like the time for a reunion, much less introductions. While Ellen and I always have felt a debt of gratitude to Laura and always will, and although in that moment we both respected her grief—if she was yet aware—as profound yet unique, we were simply unsure what to do.

So we delegated. We informed the adoption-agency staff of Reid's death and asked the staff to inform his birth parents, and left the how and when to them.

As we made our decisions, catalogued Reid's virtues, assembled photographs, and selected music, poetry, and Bible verses to help burnish his memory, the reality that we had omitted from his obituary the tumult of the final year of his life gnawed at me. My thoughts and feelings were nothing more or less than a parent's most basic gut reaction: We defend our children. Had I been with Reid just after his crash, I would have whispered in his ear, "Don't worry, Bud, I will protect you," and he would have known what I meant. I had to find a place and a way, fair and appropriate, to illuminate the truth about his struggles, and I had to do it fast.

4

❦

Truths They Will
Recognize

As the list of matters to decide got shorter amid the noise
and chaos of our house, I struggled with Reid's eulogy. Now
that I had pulled from the obituary the slightest hint that his life
had been anything but wonderful, the eulogy loomed as Truth's
Last Chance.

I have long been intrigued with eulogies as a literary form
and as the occasion for some of the greatest speeches of our
time. The Rt. Hon. The Earl Spencer's homage to his sister,
Princess Diana, in 1997, has always been my favorite. At a
moment of monumental pressure, with one billion people
watching or listening, the earl achieved the brilliant feat of
speaking one-on-one to each of those billion. He presented
himself as "representative of a family in grief, in a country
in mourning, before a world in shock." Then, incredibly—I

remember watching it live, astounded—he took direct aim at the smothering, profit-driven paparazzi who had hounded Diana and her entourage and induced her driver to the excessive speed that led to her, and his, death. Asking why Diana's good deeds and nobility were "sneered at" by the media, he offered that "genuine goodness is threatening to those at the opposite end of the moral spectrum." The earl finished by thanking God for "small mercies," for taking Diana "at her most beautiful and radiant."

Our country's foremost expert on eulogies is a gentleman from New York City named Cyrus Copeland. In 2004, he published an article, a bit of instruction for eulogists, entitled "Death, Be Not Ponderous." His article outlined five essentials of a good eulogy: a strong beginning, personal details, truth, specificity, and a memorable closing. Illustrating his first instruction, Copeland quoted from the opening of Diane Sawyer's tribute to Lucille Ball:

> I've been told that there is a debate that is one of the longest-running minor theological arguments in Christianity. A debate that has engaged everyone from dusty, old scholars in the Middle Ages to Baudelaire. The issue is this: Is there laughter in heaven?

Author Tom Chiarella has explained that a eulogy is "a simple and elegant search for small truths," which "do not have to be truths that everyone will agree on, just ones they will recognize."

I began thinking about Reid's eulogy sometime on Saturday afternoon, and by Sunday morning, I started to panic. I had three or four days to prepare a speech for more than a thousand people, and my work needed to be suitable, accurate, and memorable. Writer's block is almost never a problem for me, but on that day it was. Words, thoughts, outlines, themes, anecdotes—nothing was coming except fear of not being up to the task and embarrassing myself and tarnishing Reid's memory.

Almost out of desperation, at 9:30 Sunday morning I made a fast decision and did something that an hour earlier would have been unthinkable: I went to church. I often do my best thinking in the pews; the solitude has a way of uncluttering my mind and helping me focus. Seeking both this unburdening and perhaps also divine intervention in my hour of literary need, I excused myself from the house.

Normally, I enter our church's sanctuary through its side door and then its reception hall, so that when I enter I am at the right front side, facing and visible to most of the congregation. Had I done that that morning, I would have started a riot of whispers. By then, I'm sure that most of Asylum Hill's fifteen hundred or so members had heard the news.

So I waited in my car until the service was just about to start, and then I slipped into the back of the church. My good friend Sally Pickett was the usher stationed there. She was shocked to see me, but I quickly put my finger in front of my lips to signal that I did not want to draw any attention to my presence. I moved into the far right seat of the last pew, in a shadow, lowered my head to remain out of sight, and took out my pen.

Rev. Miller always begins with announcements before the religious part of the service, and he began, with the congregation totally silent, by announcing Reid's death. His own continuing shock was evident. He asked church members not to stampede our house or bombard us with flowers or calls, and explained the calling hours and the memorial service, albeit that the details were still taking shape.

Thoughts began. I pondered how Reid's relationship with Martha, two years younger, provided a striking and at times amusing comparison for Ellen and me. Reid and Martha were buddies and confidants. He was her protector, and she adored him. Martha, however, had emerged as an excellent, self-motivated student, one who quickly mastered the subjects that befuddled Reid. She did her homework religiously and perfectly, without prompting or oversight, and her grades reflected her effort and ability. Reid was frequently confounded by his sister's academic success.

Ellen and I confronted typical teen-rearing issues: We tried to foster responsible use of money through allowance, a list of household chores, and a savings account for that not-too-distant day when Reid would surely want a car. Meanwhile, at that time, video games were beginning to dominate the leisure hours of boys of Reid's age. We tried everywhere we could to draw and enforce lines on the number of hours spent on electronics. We did our best to outlaw profanity and otherwise to set limits on his messages, but with computers now widely available in the homes of Reid's friends, it was plain that our limits were easily evaded.

Other challenges of that time: Reid keeping us informed of his whereabouts, wearing his retainer after he got rid of his braces, doing laundry, taking regular showers, brushing his teeth properly. His horizon was the next twenty-four hours, the next pizza or video game. Reid even discovered another way to rankle us, adopting the "gangster" style of wearing his pants low on his hips so that the top of his underwear was visible.

Ellen and I imposed discipline when the situation warranted, though we often disagreed on when to confiscate the computer or the video-game controllers, ground him, or suspend his allowance. Undoubtedly, Ellen and I were less effective as a parent team than we might have been because our styles were different; Ellen reacted quickly to a fresh remark or a failed chore or a lie, while I was more prone to deliberate and devise a measured consequence. This of course led Reid to view me as the softer parent and Ellen to regard me as undercutting her firmer discipline. I can only say that while I acknowledged that part of discipline is consistency, Reid seemed so frustrated with his attention deficit that I concluded that punishment should be delivered with a measure of sympathy.

Though it was not apparent at the time, the fall of 2004 was a turning point in Reid's life. For a time at the start of that school year, he applied himself as never before. Not that he did his best, but he realized that there were strategies that if used regularly would help unlock his academic potential. He even studied with Martha on occasion, hoping that some of her excellence would rub off. But in that competitive academic environment, Reid's best was mediocre. His hardest work got him C-pluses and B-minuses, but not A's. That he was learning how to work and think, that he was accumulating knowledge, did not matter to him; when one is fifteen, life is measured by comparisons to daily classmates, not national percentiles. So in Reid's mind he had tried, he had failed, and he would never be respected for his intelligence. Ellen and I, and his teachers, knew that this was true at this particular school but not in the world, but for him, school was the world.

Where Reid could stand out, however, where he could be admired, was in being everyone's best friend. He could excel as the funny guy, as the class clown. He could be the one with the biggest social network, the one with the prettiest girls draped over each arm. He began to realize that his comfort zone was in doing what he did best and better than most people, which was make others smile and cheer them up, especially when no one else noticed that they were sad about something. In those months, Reid abandoned the goal of academic success to devote more time to being a buddy, a cheerleader, a boyfriend, and a soft shoulder.

We saw him withdraw, but we did not then see where he went or where he was headed. Perhaps the educational struggles and the disrespect were so predominant that it was difficult to perceive that Reid had an extraordinary and burgeoning network of friends who really loved him. One might say that as Reid grew toward being a young adult, our window on who he was got smaller, and because of our diminishing view, we saw more clouds than sunshine. Reid was positioning himself for status in the company of his peers, not in the classroom but in hallways, cars, electronic communication, and face-to-face conversations with his friends.

What then could I say in the eulogy to balance his challenges with high points? That July 21, 2005 Very Best Days letter—the one I had talked about as Reid lay in the morgue! It was a treasure trove of memories, a pot of gold to be mined for its most precious pieces. Our hike up a river, the Narrows, at Zion National Park—I thought of it as a metaphor for life's journey. Also, Reid was now an angel—what to do with that image? What about the obituary? No rule said that I could not borrow from it.

Yet the eulogy was more challenging than the obituary, because I did not need to adhere to a strict format. Other than not trying the patience of the audience at the memorial service, I had no time limit. My boundaries were propriety and good taste; my requirements were eloquence and clarity. The debate—now the centerpiece of my role as guardian of Reid's memory—was whether to be candid about his struggles and his expulsion. So much about his travails was so unknown or unclear to our friends and our community that, if I did not explain them, the facts would disappear forever, speculation would continue, rumor would go unrebutted, and those with partial or inaccurate information would have a lasting and mistaken impression of Reid's life. I felt an excruciating need to explain, but I had to be sure that my words would be regarded as justified by the higher calling of truth, not dismissed as an unfortunate consequence of our anger.

In contrast to how we had adhered, or perhaps become resigned, to our community's expectations in our other decisions, telling the truth about Reid's downward spiral and railing against the injustice of his final days would most likely surprise and even shock many of the listeners. Whether they knew the facts or not, most who would attend Reid's memorial service would expect an exclusive focus on the positive, and that any misgivings or unfinished sadness would be left for some other day and forum.

~

As Rev. Miller led the church service from announcements to worship, I revisited the roller coaster that was Reid's final two years, starting with the end of his sophomore year.

College loomed, but our conversations with his teachers started to include the thought that "college is not right for everyone." This was immensely frustrating because, after all, the school's stated mission was to prepare students for that very eventuality.

Reid's life and preparation for his future needed a jolt. On the theory that improving his confidence and self-discipline might help in a variety of ways, we introduced the idea of a three-week Appalachian Mountain Club program of canoeing, rock climbing, kayaking, backcountry camping, and rescue and first-aid training, all in the vicinity of Mount Washington, New Hampshire. Needless to say, Reid dismissed as absurd the notion that a physical challenge might help him in school and life, and the idea of being deprived of the comforts to which he was so very accustomed sealed his opposition. But Ellen and I were desperate to try something; we began making a list of the things that would not come Reid's way if he refused to go, with his driving learner's permit being our trump card. Eventually, he relented.

So, in mid-July, I drove him six hours to northern New Hampshire and met up with his two group leaders and twelve fellow campers.

I kept my worries to myself. Reid was the youngest in the group, one of only two with no camping experience. In addition, I was consigning my son to spending his sixteenth birthday in the woods with strangers, and without family. The small birthday party we had at home two days before I took him north, several days before his actual birthday, was palpably inadequate, as was the batch of cards from family that I surreptitiously handed to the head counselor to give to Reid on the actual day, July 22.

The night before he shipped out, in my upper bunk in the camping ground's lodge, I hastily composed a birthday letter. I wrote it with only a night-light while Reid snored in the lower bunk. I stuffed this letter into the bottom of his backpack:

Reid—

I *really* miss you, and I can't believe that you are turning *16* !

Here's my list of the VERY BEST DAYS I HAVE SPENT WITH MY SON, REID H:

1. The day we brought you home (October 21, 1989)
2. The day we filmed "Just a Reidbear"*
3. The day I left the door open and you went down the stairs in your walker (so glad you survived)
4. Your Voluntown [our summer cabin] birthdays
5. The day you scored the game-winning and tournament-clinching goals for the Wolverines
6. The day you got accepted to your school
7. Golf school; your 45-footer for your first birdie
8. Rock-climbing school
9. Our walk up the river in Zion National Park
10. When your wrote "Reid-flections" in 8th grade
11. Your Spartan 7 performances
12. Watching you drive the Big Boat in Voluntown
13. Our trip to the Spy Museum and U.S. House of Representatives
14. Games at Fenway and Shea
15. Our trip to Finland, especially your all-nighter with Mummu [Finnish for grandmother]

---

* A video interview with Reid when he was three. When asked, "Are you a Republican or a Democrat?" he said, "I'm just a Reidbear."

16. "Here ya go"—at the Farm in Simsbury [his first words, 1990]
17. Bucket baths in the sauna [at the lake in eastern Connecticut]
18. The time you flew to Pittsburgh by yourself
19. The time you smashed your finger in the window (you survived)
20. You following the guards at Windsor Castle

Probably many more I'm forgetting. SO WHAT'S ON YOUR LIST?!

> Happy Birthday
>
> Love, Dad
>
> XXOO

While Reid was on the trail, I checked in twice with the AMC director who had been part of the first-aid training of Reid's group, and he assured me that Reid was content, participating, and always entertaining.

When I picked him up three weeks later, he gave me a weary but reluctant hug, like a boxer falling on his trainer after the last round of a fight. Both counselors made a point of telling me what an upbeat presence he had been. As we left the lodge parking lot, Reid took off his socks for what he said was the first time in three weeks. I could not roll the windows down quickly enough as I started to gag.

Then to my amazement, he started in on me: "Why did you send me away?" he said angrily.

"I didn't send you away. I wanted you to have a great experience." I didn't know what else to say, and suspected that a lecture on character building and self-discipline would not be well received.

"You wasted your money and my time."

"How is that?" I asked.

"I *hated* it," he said, turning toward me as he emphasized his second word.

I tried to collect myself, but he knew he had struck a nerve. I began looking up at the mountains as we headed south. "Well, I'm sorry you feel that way. Maybe someday you'll feel different."

I tried another tactic, both to change the subject and to learn whether his complaint was real. I started asking about what he had done on the trail. To my further amazement—and slight relief—he began to describe "stuff" that was "cool" and "crazy" and "neat." A mock safety drill in the middle of the night. Flipping his kayak in white water. Being appointed the group trail guide, a rotating responsibility that one camper assumed each day, which for Reid meant being a newly minted sixteen-year-old in charge of a decidedly older group. Bathing in freezing streams (proof that he had taken his socks off) and then warming his hands by the fire. Portaging a canoe for two miles—in the wrong direction. An intense mid-trip discussion during which the campers started sniping at each other and the counselors demanded that they talk out and resolve their grievances before the group took another step.

These were the energetic, animated words of a more mature young man than the one I had dropped off in mid-July. I almost concluded that the "you sent me away" was his way of ensuring that I would not entertain any thought that the trip had been a fitting measure for what he needed at that time in his life. But I kept that thought to myself.

~

As this memory rushed through me, the congregation rose for the service's first hymn. I kept my seat; I was gathering momentum.

But if those five hours driving back from New Hampshire to Hartford gave me any hope of an epiphany or even an appreciation for the experience, that expectation dissipated in September. It was as if the summer had never happened; the familiar patterns returned. Reid refused to audition for Spartan 7, even though the director assured him that he would be accepted if he would just show up. "I'm not going on stage in front of the other guys," he informed us. He was increasingly disrespectful, profane, and belligerent when we enforced school-day limits on television and computer use.

We started his junior year with the same pleas to his advisor for attention and support as in previous years:

> We have decidedly backed off from our entreaties/ begging/lectures about the need to spend some time in the evening on homework, and we have imposed additional restrictions on electronics in the evening hours to encourage that, but nothing has changed— the backpack hardly ever leaves the place where it is deposited when he gets home. Meanwhile we continue to observe a string of failing grades. We will continue our "understanding"—that we will put the support measures in place and otherwise back off, with the understanding that you are and the teachers are on top of the situation and aggressively working with Reid to try to turn him around. Also, please remember that it will help us greatly to hear periodically your perspective on how things are going. Reid says "fine" and not much else.

But the patterns of his first two years, now well established, persisted. Reid and I remained at loggerheads throughout the winter and into the spring of 2006.

It was not totally surprising, then, that in April, near the end of his junior year, in one of our routine inspections of his car, Ellen and I found, hidden in a gym bag beneath T-shirts that could have walked into the house on their own, a cheap bottle of rum. We had suspected that Reid had tried alcohol when we had gone on vacation the prior month and he had spent some time in the company of teens we did not know. When we confronted him with the bottle, Reid forcefully claimed that he was not drinking himself but was carrying it around as a favor to a friend. I considered this explanation for a nanosecond. It was true that in my regular, up-close interrogations when he had arrived at home, I had never seen him even remotely impaired or smelled anything on his breath; I had been in his face, literally, every time he had come home in his then four months of driving with a full license. Also, it was potentially in character for my son, desperate to be cool, to be a bagman for some older kid.

But plausible story or not, our discipline was immediate. We not only confiscated the keys, we hid the car behind a neighbor's garage in a different section of our town. I lectured Reid again and again about the meaning of the words "criminal offense," including the facts that carrying alcohol in his car and providing it to any other underage person could land him in jail and result in his license being suspended for a year or more. To emphasize my point, I went to my office, photocopied the relevant state statutes, highlighted the key words in yellow, and

taped the page above the desk in his room. Meanwhile, Ellen
and I ratcheted up our oversight. We began screening Reid's
friends at our door. We transferred our own alcohol supply to a
basement hiding place, and from then on we never left the house
for any extended time when our kids were home and visitors
might show up. Without voicing it expressly, Ellen and I knew
that our discovery of that bottle was not just a loss of innocence
or a teenage rite of passage, but a new front in our parenting
campaign.

Reid chafed under that first confiscation of his car. At times
it seemed as though his refusal to study and his indifference to
school in general were his way of showing us, if not who was
in charge, that he could stand up to whatever we imposed. More
often than not, he retreated to his room, turned up his music—
rap was becoming a frequent choice—and sulked.

We found more alcohol bottles, in the garage and in the
basement. He yelled that this stuff was not his, that it had
been smuggled in by his friends without his knowledge. We
confiscated the car again, we took the laptop away, we grounded
him, we lectured, we made more demands that he toe the
behavioral line, or else.

~

As Rev. Miller read the morning's first scripture, I listened
to see if there might be a message in it for me from God, some
road map for my painful recollections. Nothing jumped out.

As Ellen and I began to grapple with this new wave of anger
and alcohol, we took Reid several times to Dr. Jarvis. Though
we of course don't know what he said to Reid during sessions

while we waited outside, Dr. Jarvis always seemed able to settle
Reid down, to help him better appreciate the consequences of
his actions, and to provide the three of us with at least a short-
term plan of, if not compromise or resolution, accommodation.
Dr. Jarvis was not judgmental, and worked to gain Reid's trust
by inducing him not to capitulate and obey, but to meet Ellen
and me approximately halfway. Thus, while we hoped he would
give Reid a stern lecture about heeding his parents, what we
often got was the sense that Reid's belligerence was not going to
dissipate easily or soon, and that we were better advised to live
with as much as we could stand.

Still, confrontation was coming. One of our combative
conversations was destined to boil over.

On May 10, near the end of his junior year, we found
another liquor bottle in the garage in the early evening.
We called Reid on his cellphone and ordered him home
immediately. I made the huge mistake of telling him why.
He refused to come home. What followed were frantic hours
in which he toyed with us in cellphone calls and seemed to
enjoy it; sometimes he would answer and sometimes not. In
succeeding calls, he gave us contradictory information about
where he was.

Around 8:00 a.m. the next morning, he arrived at school
and went to class. I felt I had no choice but to confiscate his car,
so my brother-in-law drove me to the school parking lot, where
I "stole" the Volvo. One of Reid's classmates saw me. Reid
called me on his cellphone and issued a ridiculous threat—that
if he did not get the car back right away he was going to "hurt
someone." I knew that that was absurd, that he was simply
furious, maybe also exhausted. However, Ellen and I felt that

we had no choice but to alert the school to this threat, and with great embarrassment we did so.

We hid the car again. Later in the day, I met with Reid in the company of the school psychologist. After acknowledging that he had demonstrated his moxie, I momentarily broke down. I pleaded with him: "Reid, this has to stop!" I was then furious with myself for this lapse in his presence.

We made another appointment to see Dr. Jarvis. I acknowledged to Reid again that he had made his point, that he had demonstrated that he was old enough to stake a greater claim to independence and to give Ellen and me enough heartache to cause us to listen even more closely to his complaints about his life.

Dr. Jarvis, as always, was quick to understand. Acting partly as a mediator and at times nearly as a third parent, he intervened and skillfully suggested a process and terms for temporary disarmament. He proposed a contract, terms of compromise that, while not resolving the core tensions, would allow us to live together while we tried to restore trust, revisit expectations, and redefine freedom. On May 17, Reid, Ellen and I signed this:

CONTRACT

1. Absolute rules: any violations → no car
   a. No alcohol in car—yours or anyone else's.
   b. No alcohol before or while driving.
   c. No illegal passengers.
   d. No speeding tickets.
   e. No threats of harm, injury, violence.
   f. No driving after midnight.

2. If Reid or any friend calls for a ride, it will be provided, no consequences, no questions.

3. Reid must
    a. Make good decisions about alcohol – it is
        illegal, unhealthy, and dangerous. But we
        cannot monitor your behavior 24/7.
    b. Be respectful.
    c. Be helpful at home, without multiple requests.
    d. Keep Mom or Dad informed of your
        whereabouts.

4. Mom and Dad need to
    a. Continue to back off on homework and TV.
    b. However, this does not mean unlimited TV or
        freedom. This requires Reid to understand his
        obligations at school, including turning things
        in on time. Reid must agree that if he does
        not study and use effort, he is hurting his own
        future and college prospects.

5. Reid, Mom, and Dad will agree on a regular
    weekly budget for gas and food, to be paid in cash
    on Sundays. This money will *not* be paid for any
    weeks from June 12 to August 11 where Reid
    does not have a job of some type. Job can be paid
    or volunteer, and can be part-time, but it must be
    regular work.

6. Mom and Dad will help in finding a job.

Somewhat to our amazement, the contract seemed to placate
Reid. Perhaps he had indeed made his point. Also, summer
was coming; Reid would not have to face for a while the
academics that were giving him so much trouble, and the college
applications that, based on poor SAT and achievement-test results,
were as unappealing as ever. He would spend a few weeks in one
of the roles where he most shined, that of camp counselor.

~

The worship service reached the morning's second hymn, and then the Lord's Prayer.

In June, Reid's travails were overtaken by family matters, an illness and then a tragedy. Ellen had surgery and then developed a serious, painful infection. Reid at her bedside in the hospital was my son at his most empathetic and charming. Then, just a few days later, a distant relative whom we had met only a few times, a fifteen-year-old girl, Brittany, died of leukemia. Ellen was still too sick to attend the calling hours in Oneonta, New York, so Reid stayed home with her while Martha and I drove to pay our respects.

The scene at the funeral home was overpowering. Teenagers weeping around the room. From the parents and stepparents, anguished remembrances of their child's spirit and courage. As I knelt down at Brittany's casket to pray, I said to myself what every parent says: There but for the grace of God go I.

At the start of the summer, Reid got a job and his first taste of real physical labor, demolishing the inside of a former clothing store, disassembling display cases and clothing racks. No one was going to turn on air conditioning for a vacant store, so the work was hard and the conditions miserable. Reid began to take a six-pack of Gatorade to work each day.

On Reid's first day, he met his co-workers. They did not speak English. Reid was concerned that they did not have money for a decent lunch, and asked if he could buy for them— with my money. I told him they were getting paid, just as he was.

I am sure that Reid had several reactions to this experience
that he didn't tell me, but one became evident from how he
arrived home each day, his face covered with dust and his shirt
soaked through with sweat: One benefit of education is that it
may get you out of doing manual labor, inside, on hot, humid
summer days.

With the store's inside demolished and the mess cleaned up,
Reid went off to his camp-counselor job. As always, he reveled
in it; the kids adored him. Eventually, the camp staff would give
him the Best Counselor award. Though by this time I was well
aware of his ability with children, I was proud of him, I praised
him, and I told him that I hoped that what got him his award
would continue in the months ahead.

As the service continued apace, an usher offered me the
collection plate. I waved him off.

During the third week of August, Reid and I embarked
on one of the great parent-child rituals, a college scouting
trip. Being realistic, his advisor had given Reid a list of small
colleges with comparatively less-competitive admission. She
was candid that her list included schools that were not usually
part of her recommendations for students at Reid's school. Yet
for us, on the horizon were five days, just the two of us, an
ambitious itinerary, a beautiful weather forecast, and a focus on
the future.

We drove east from Hartford on a Sunday night and in
the next five days visited the list we had worked out with his
advisor: Salve Regina, Roger Williams, and Bryant in Rhode
Island; Curry College, just south of Boston; Franklin Pierce
and Keene State in southwestern New Hampshire; and finally
Champlain College in Burlington, Vermont. We decided that

Reid on his own could visit the University of Hartford and nearby Central Connecticut State, and he was quite familiar with the University of Connecticut, with his mother and several relatives being graduates and his girlfriend about to enroll there as a freshman.

Salve Regina was an interesting choice. Its undergraduate population is about 70 percent female. Reid's advisor explained that their acceptance rate for men was, therefore, relatively high. I tried to envision my head-turning son among a predominantly female student body.

As we took our tours and I listened to his reactions—I had taken an oath to keep my mouth shut—at lunch or dinner afterward, I was alternately amused and alarmed. As was often the case with Reid and me, I did not know whether he was kidding to elicit a reaction or whether he was actually clueless about what mattered. Curry College's school color was purple—unacceptable. Champlain, four hours away, was too far. So was Curry (two hours). The young lady who was our tour guide at Bryant was "hot." (I agreed with that.) The other girl on the tour at Franklin Pierce was weird. (Ditto.)

Yet there were more constructive and forward-looking conversations:

"Why are you less interested in becoming a teacher when you're obviously so good with kids?" I asked.

"Teachers don't make money," he said.

"Money isn't everything," I replied. "If you're gonna get out of bed every day to do your job, you have to enjoy what you're doing. Making money at a job you don't like isn't any fun."

He did not seem to understand this concept. How could making enough money to buy a fast car not be fun?

We talked about business. "Reid," I said, "you're a born salesman. You get along great with people, you're a nice-looking guy, you're funny and energetic."

I talked about majoring in marketing. "You mean like the guys at Best Buy that sell the iPods and stuff?" he inquired.

I explained that sales—"marketing" being the academic term—involved many different people, places, locations, and functions. I noted that he liked to roam from place to place, communicating by cellphone and computer, and that one of his strengths, due to his looks and personality, was the ability to make a good first impression. "I can just see you schmoozing some receptionist to get in to see the boss."

My efforts to encourage him were counterbalanced several times by his own fears and the daunting, competitive realities of admission to college. At each place we visited, both his "reach" schools and his "safe" ones, the admissions people talked about admitting only students who "are committed to learning" or some similar quality. Then there was the tyranny of grade-point averages and SAT and achievement-test scores. In general, the larger the institution, the more numbers-driven the admission process, and Reid began to realize that this was going to work against him. The bigger schools we saw, such as Keene State, had the newer, fancier athletic and dining facilities and the larger student populations that Reid seemed to find attractive, but these same schools were less likely to give him a personal interview at which he could try to charm the admissions officer into overlooking his borderline scores and grades. On the other end of the size spectrum, Curry College offered a program for ADD kids that seemed perfect for Reid, but of course he was resistant to any program or school that was tinged with a stigma or what others might perceive as one.

By the end of our excursion, as much as I enjoyed those five days one-on-one with my son, when we arrived home it was evident that he was more worried, more scared about what was to become of him, more apprehensive about comparisons to his peers, than before. Three years of belligerent resistance to schoolwork was coming home to roost. Our trip had demystified college but had laid bare how hard it was going to be to get into a place that Reid, among his peer group, was going to find acceptable.

We returned to West Hartford just a few days before school was to begin. In fact, soccer—he had vowed to try out for the varsity team for the first time—had already started. With first-semester grades looming as Reid's last chance to show the colleges the potential that so far had eluded him, I emailed his advisor in late August:

> As you will recall from our discussion in June, the biggest priority now is to get Reid off to a good and disciplined start, with a focus on getting him to understand what, on a daily basis, he needs to do in study halls and at home to keep up and to do well. We discussed your communicating this to his teachers and his advisor at the start of school, and letting them know that they should give Reid *as much specific and daily direction as possible;* unfortunately if they try to treat him like a senior who has already learned to work independently, then we will be right back into the problems of the past two years.

This email coincided with my own conscious decision about how I was going to handle what I assumed would be Reid's last full year living in our house: I decided to back off. Perhaps because I had just spent an unprecedented five fairly enjoyable days with him, but also because I was just too mentally worn out to face another year of continual disputes, I made a decision that I would insist on safety and personal hygiene, I would hope for but not demand respect and politeness, I would no longer lecture, and if he started failing again, I would let him. He knew what was expected of him and what was at stake. Over the course of several conversations in late August and early September I made clear to Reid the approach I intended to take, to make sure he understood what I was doing and why. Once again not wanting to give me the satisfaction of having made a sound parenting decision, Reid's response, in so many words, was "It's about time."

~

The congregation sang the third hymn.

The equanimity of that summer ended on a lovely late afternoon in early September. Our neighbor Karen Reale called me and said that Reid had been taken by ambulance to the UConn Medical Center. He was having trouble breathing. Ellen was with him. By the time I arrived, he was stable. Mike, Tom, and Lauren were beside his bed. The diagnosis was a severe anxiety attack. The emergency-room doctor had given Reid a powerful anti-anxiety drug and had instructed him, if he had the same trouble again, to control his breathing by blowing into and breathing out of a brown paper bag until his pulse was again under control.

Ellen and I had no idea what to make of this, and we took Reid the next day to Dr. Jarvis. Once again, Dr. Jarvis was able to put the situation in terms that we could understand. He explained that the body's and the mind's ability to regulate tension and anxiety are like a bathtub; each of us has a limit, and when the tub overfills, what can result is not a drip but a flood. Reid had reached his overflow point. Dr. Jarvis prescribed rest and anxiety medication—in other words, the opposite of varsity soccer, Spartan 7, college applications, and studying harder.

While obviously bewildered and concerned about Reid's health—an inability to breathe was nothing to take lightly—I recall this evaluation as confirmation that above all, Reid was terrified about what was ahead in his life. He was more than afraid to fail his academic courses and to be rejected by colleges; he was floundering in the face of the most basic question a teenager asks: What am I going to do with my life?

Two nights later, when I was with him at home, Reid had a second anxiety attack. His body tensed. He was having trouble breathing, so much so that he was not able to inflate or deflate the brown bag that I thrust in his face. The muscle relaxant seemed to have no effect. His face started to turn blue, and he started crying in the most pitiful voice I had ever heard. He looked at me and said, "I'm sorry, Dad."

The paramedics put him on oxygen and strapped him to a gurney. Meanwhile, outside, a surreal scene developed of police cars with full flashers, and concerned and curious neighbors converging. At the hospital, the doctors succeeded in stabilizing him, calming him down, but most important, talking to him with more than a hint of impatience about his second visit. A young resident—closer in age to Reid than to me—did a good job of explaining to Reid that there was nothing physically wrong and that when he felt his anxiety level spike, he needed to *breathe*, regularly and slowly. As before, the prescription was rest and medication.

While this second episode appeared to convince Reid that he could handle these anxiety attacks physically, it laid waste to his—our—plan for the fall. Reid stopped practicing with the varsity soccer team, which he had made during tryouts. "I can't play if I can't breathe," he said.

Ellen and I were reduced to walking the finest of lines: making sure first to attend to our son's obviously fragile state, but also figuring out what was left to nudge him toward studying and college. Time was running out. A few times Reid infuriated us by threatening to "have another attack" if we did not back off from our questions about whether he was keeping up with his assignments or making progress with his applications. We were dealing not just with the familiar "you can't just say, 'Try harder'" limitation; we were, or felt we were, face-to-face with choices about parenting where the wrong choice would result in flashing emergency vehicle lights and our son headed back to the hospital.

As September gave way to October, Reid made a start on his college applications. After one false start (a topic and draft that his advisor apparently rejected outright—we never saw it), Reid wrote his personal essay for the so-called Common Application. After cleaning it up for its intended readers over several drafts and revisions, Reid put his best face forward in these words:

> I can't explain it, but I have a natural ability to connect with people, especially kids. I don't think I want my whole career to involve children, but from working with them I have learned the skills of talking, listening, understanding, empathizing with

and convincing others. I hope to apply these skills in a career in business.

To help kids understand me and feel comfortable around me, I "talk them down," which means I calm them, break their problem down into smaller pieces and help them relax. I make them feel like I have been through whatever situation they are dealing with. If they are scared I will show them how to do what they are scared of or I will give them a reward for solving their problem. And lastly I try to make them feel important.

What I have learned about myself from working with children is that children can be stubborn, but if you work with them, ultimately an overall agreement can be achieved. I have also learned to make my point clear and that it must be followed. A child's mind can be easily persuaded, as long as they think that they are winning the argument. If a child or anyone likes you, they will do more for you, rather than being a problem.

Applying what I have learned from working with children to a career in sales or marketing in a business seems to be natural. I would use several strategies to succeed. First, if people like you, they will work with you. Secondly, having people feel as though they are on the same track as you makes them feel more comfortable in a situation. Lastly is that you have their best interest at heart, and they need to feel confident of that commitment. Adults have fears just as children do, but the only difference is that they suppress them. To get someone to work with you, you need to convince them to overcome their fears. I have learned a lot from my years with small children. Who would have guessed they would have taught me so much!

In late October, I drove with him to his interview at the University of Hartford. While he was inside, I walked around, checked my email, mused on this nerve-racking process, calmed myself with thoughts that things would work out somehow. Reid emerged from the Admissions Office upbeat.

"How did it go?" I inquired.

"Great," he said. He smiled mischievously, with an air of self-congratulation. "I told her I enrolled myself in an outdoor survival-skills course in order to improve my self-confidence and leadership skills." He started laughing.

If, in my seventeen years of parenting Reid Samuel Hollister, there was a moment when the urge to laugh and a need to cry were at simultaneous, contradictory peaks, that was it.

~

Rev. Grandy read from the New Testament. I was now scribbling quickly.

The anxiety attacks, it turned out, were the start of the final downward spiral in Reid's life. Ellen and I did not appreciate the cumulative effect of a series of small, incremental changes. His classmates, even his best friends, Mike and Tom, were leaving him behind. They were emotionally on an even keel, optimistic, racking up respectable SAT scores and grade-point averages, compiling lists of achievements, applying to competitive schools.

As the weather got colder, Reid became more withdrawn. We gave him more space, but he used it to retreat into his room, bantering with friends by cellphone, text messages, and instant messages. He started to change in other ways, including hanging out with some students whose influence on him concerned us greatly. Reid was trying hard to be cool, to remain accepted, to hide his anxiety, to show that he had not a care in the world, to be sure that if a good college didn't want him, well, there were lots of pretty girls who delighted in his hilarious and energetic company.

There were other changes. Reid installed a bass speaker in the trunk of his car, the better to play loud rap music. He bought a white hooded sweat suit, made himself a necklace of string and soda-can pull tops, and bought a cheap watch with a wide silver band. In other words, he started to dress like a suburban white kid's stereotype of a pimp.

We started finding "dharma" cigarettes in his car—cheap, foreign-made, illegal because they bypass the federal government's safety labeling and have high levels of tar. Then, in mid-October, Reid got a speeding ticket—for going forty-two in a twenty-five zone on a West Hartford street. A letter arrived from the Department of Motor Vehicles requiring his attendance at a four-hour driver-retraining course. If he did not attend, his license would be revoked. Regardless of his attendance, our insurance was going to go up. He called the DMV and signed up. He obtained an appointment for the morning of Saturday, December 2.

Yes, he scheduled his retraining class for the day he would die.

We immediately outlawed the dharma cigarettes, and thus began a several-week cat-and-mouse game. He would hide them; we would find them and throw them out and impose some additional punishment. He lost his car and his computer intermittently during those weeks. We reminded him that someone who was recovering from anxiety attacks and breathing difficulties was doing exactly the wrong thing by flirting with cigarettes. He said they calmed him down.

If I had to describe how Ellen and I approached Reid at that tense time in one word, it would be "vigilant." We were on him like a wet blanket. But still, in early November, we discovered he had graduated to marijuana.

He had arrived home while Ellen was in the house and he was with a friend, but he was a bit disoriented, giggly, and very hungry. It did not take Ellen long to figure things out; in the morning she went through his clothes while he was sleeping. I went to the drugstore and bought a home-use drug test, which rendered a positive result for marijuana.

And so we confiscated his car again. We visited Dr. Jarvis, both to make sure that he was aware of this development and to force Reid to divulge what he had been doing. We hoped again that Reid might come to understand that most elusive of concepts for teenagers, the big picture. We grounded him for several days and let him know that drug tests were now going to be part of our family routine.

All of this, of course, set back studying and college applications at a critical time. I emptied my latest pound of dismay in an email to his college advisor:

> Everyone is frustrated with him. I keep telling him that he is giving us little evidence that he is ready for college living, much less academics, and that he is setting himself up for some very hard years ahead if he doesn't snap out of this funk. If you have any idea about who can help us deliver this message, forcefully but in a supportive way, we are all ears.

~

As the church service progressed, I paid even less attention. I had found my focus. Had Reid's life ended three weeks earlier, the day after I had sent this email to his college advisor, writing his eulogy would have been difficult only in the sense of having to put grief out of mind long enough to form coherent sentences. But I now needed to put this divinely aided concentration to maximum use, because I needed to find the words to explain the events of Reid's final fourteen days.

5

A Rough Road Ahead

On November 17, 2006, I flew from Hartford to San Jose, California, for a four-day, two-part trip. This was my long-planned fiftieth birthday present to myself, albeit slightly earlier than the actual day, January 3.

The trip was the delightful confluence of events and dreams. During 1978–79, I had worked in St. Louis in a public affairs leadership-training program known as the Coro Fellows Year. A prominent alumnus of Coro had decided to open his house— mansion, actually—in Watsonville, California, for a weekend retreat for graduates of the Fellows program. Two days of intense but friendly discussion of public policy and leadership, along with great food and excellent local wines.

When I received the announcement in July, I immediately noted that Watsonville is about ten miles from the Monterey Peninsula. I proposed to my wife a birthday plan: the weekend at the Coro conference, and Monday morning, fulfilling my lifelong dream as a golfer, playing one of the world's most famous, storied, and expensive golf courses, Pebble Beach. A once-in-a-lifetime trip.

Before I left, I received Ellen's blessing. Reid was grounded; she could handle him. I was free to go. Perhaps the nonrefundable payment for my tee time sealed it.

I arrived in San Jose, drove to Watsonville, checked into my hotel—and then my cellphone rang. It was 4:15 p.m. Pacific Standard Time on Friday, November 17. I now regard that moment as the Continental Divide of my life.

It was Ellen. She had received a call at home asking her to come to school for an urgent meeting. The message was that Reid had been suspended because the school "had evidence" that he had been selling marijuana to underclassmen. The situation was described as a "clear case of expulsion" if presented to the Citizenship Committee, and we were advised to immediately withdraw him.

Now Ellen was frantic, talking quickly in order to get the words out between sobs and chokes. I quickly realized that I had no choice but to return home immediately. I had just flown across the entire United States of America and plopped my suitcase on the bed of my hotel room, and now it was time to turn around and head home.

I called my golf buddy Scott Rogerson. He had been so excited for me as a fellow golfer. I told him that I was coming home, and why, and then to my embarrassment I started to cry.

Scott is one of those friends one counts on for advice. He simply said: "When you get home, hug your son."

I called US Airways. It being the weekend before Thanksgiving, all I could get was San Jose to Las Vegas to

Phoenix to Philadelphia to Hartford, five stops and three plane changes over eleven hours.

I arrived home just after 11:00 Saturday night. It was a cold, perfectly clear night. I found Ellen and Reid on the patio behind the house, looking up at a lunar eclipse that was in progress; I noted the irony. As Scott had so wisely advised, I walked up to Reid, put my hand on his shoulder, turned him toward me, reached up to hug him, and said, "I love you, Buddy." I suppose he had been bracing for a tirade or a tongue-lashing, because he did not react with anything more than a shrug. He had probably spent the past twenty-four hours preparing for combat and was now surprised that I had checked my weapon at the door. Or maybe he thought my words were merely a postponement.

On Saturday night and Sunday morning, we talked at length with Reid. As to the allegation that he was selling drugs on campus, we made it clear that we needed a complete and immediate explanation of everything that had occurred. By the time we were done, we felt that we had obtained the truth in detail. In a letter he wrote several days later to the Citizenship Committee, Reid recounted in his own words what had happened:

> I first tried marijuana two months ago. I was with a
> couple of people from school and everyone was doing
> it so it seemed pretty harmless for me to try it as well. I
> then tried it about three more times, with the same group
> of friends. The smoking was in cars or wooded areas.
> Then in late October I decided to buy a small amount
> for myself. I really had no idea what I was doing but I
> heard about this guy and bought some marijuana. Once
> I had gotten it I met up with my friends and we smoked
> some of what I had bought in my friend's car. I had a

small amount left, which I hid at home, in the stone wall in our backyard.

On November 10, which was Friday night, I bought marijuana for a second time from the same man. I smoked a little, in the company of my friends. We then went back to my house and ate a lot of food. My mom smelled the marijuana when we came in and was more suspicious when we were so hungry. I fell asleep and my mom picked up my clothes, emptying my pockets and finding the marijuana in my jacket pocket. My parents decided to give me a drug test shortly after they flushed it down the toilet to make sure that they had a full understanding of what had been done.

A few days later, after the school day was over and as I was leaving the parking lot, a student asked me if I could get him some marijuana. I knew he was an underclassman but I didn't know his grade level exactly because I didn't know him at all. He did not ask if he could buy it. He asked me if I could get some. I believe that the only reason he asked me was because a large number of upperclassmen at our school are involved in marijuana at one time or another. This student definitely did not come to me because of any previous action of mine in supplying marijuana to him or anyone else, because this had never happened. After the student asked me, I told him I would have to go home to get it. I was willing to give it to him because I was nervous about hiding it at home and wanted to get rid of it. We agreed to meet at a gas station down the street. I went home and picked up what I had, which was about half of what I had bought. This was all that I had. I met him at the gas station. I did not drive him to the gas station. He got in my car, and I then handed it to him in a little bag. He did not offer me any money for it and I did not take any. The reasons I did not take money were because he never asked me if he could pay for it and I didn't want to have the marijuana on me anymore. The student got out of my car at the gas station and I went home.

On Saturday and Sunday, we reached out to several people who knew about disciplinary matters in private and public schools. Each offered the same advice: Be sure that Reid understands the severity of the situation and is willing to accept punishment. Volunteer a strict program of discipline and monitoring, and offer personal oversight and frequent updates. In light of Reid's learning disability and counseling, get a letter from the treating physician explaining the emotional and educational consequences of expulsion. Give the Citizenship Committee letters from those who can demonstrate that Reid is a good person who made a mistake and is not a threat to the school or its students. Based on this advice, we asked Dr. Jarvis to write a letter.

While we were discussing the situation with Reid during the weekend, rumors began flying. On Saturday evening, we began receiving phone calls at home from other students asking us whether it was true that Reid "had been expelled for dealing drugs." We wondered how the accusation had become public information.

In light of Reid's explanation, Ellen and I were now highly disturbed by having been presented with a "clear case" of expulsion. No one at the school had spoken with Reid or allowed him to defend himself. Through our conversations with Reid on Saturday and Sunday, we got a clear picture of a seventeen-year-old who, while experimenting with marijuana in the company of several classmates, had given a small amount to one underclassman on one occasion, off-campus. A serious violation of school rules, but a basis to expel a mid-year senior with an otherwise clean record? The school was not so-called "zero tolerance." Its policy was not that any single incident, especially off-campus, would result in automatic expulsion; had that been the standard, a dozen or more kids could have been expelled. Other parents had told us about previous incidents on campus where students involved with marijuana had been suspended or faced other discipline but had not been expelled, and of other instances, one involving a star athlete, where the school had just looked the other way.

Ellen and I met with a school representative on Sunday. I began by saying that if there was evidence that Reid had been selling drugs or creating a danger to the school, we would withdraw him immediately. But we explained what we had learned and the steps that, with Reid's cooperation, we were prepared to take. As discipline, we offered probation; mandatory weekly drug testing; a substance-abuse counseling program; counseling with Dr. Jarvis; indefinite suspension of off-campus privileges; driving restricted to school and back; community service; and agreement that one more incident would result in expulsion. We guaranteed our personal involvement.

We then pointedly asked why this was a clear case of expulsion. We accepted that the school would not name names as sources. Rather, we pressed for whether the information was reliable. To our disbelief, we were told that the sources were "students who had heard things" about Reid.

This was third-hand information that we could not evaluate and Reid could not challenge. We protested that if vague statements from anonymous sources were presented to the Citizenship Committee as fact, Reid would have no way to dispute them.

Our fears that rumor was morphing became more acute on Monday afternoon, when a teacher who was a member of the Citizenship Committee confided to a student, a friend of Reid's, that his expulsion was "a done deal." The student came to our house later that day to report this conversation.

We met with the principal, who was in his first year at the school, on that same afternoon. We outlined what we had learned, and our proposal. We stated our concern that a rush to judgment had overtaken the campus. We noted the other disciplinary cases that had not resulted in kids being expelled. The principal reinforced our fear, telling us that Reid had a "reputation."

Ellen and I became furious. Why had we not been informed of this "reputation" when we had asked repeatedly for feedback? After years of asking, "Is Reid in the right school?" and begging for candor and being told repeatedly, "Yes, and we will work with him," now the answers suddenly seemed to be "No," and "We won't."

During the next four days we worked hard, in the face of perplexing resistance, to obtain a clear statement of exactly what the claim was against Reid and its basis, to provide support letters to the Citizenship Committee, and to make sure that the committee's process was fair. But the die had been cast. Late Tuesday afternoon, we received an email saying that Reid was now being charged with possession of marijuana "on school grounds." This was a different story. I responded, "This seems to be something new about which we know nothing. When did this occur? Where?" The school replied that since Reid and the underclassman had driven from campus to the gas station and back, what had happened was "on campus."

We discussed with Reid whether he had driven the underclassman from school to the gas station. Reid was adamant that this had never occurred. He swore that his written statement was true. There was desperation in his voice. If he was lying, he was doing it well, because I believed him. He had provided too many precise details on the time, the sequence, and his route to be making it up. We concluded that the school had not considered that we lived four minutes from the school and it was entirely plausible that Reid had driven home first.

We continued to press Reid. He was emphatic. He said he understood what was at stake and we had a complete account.

~

Rev. Miller continued with his sermon. By now, I was completely tuned out, making notes upon notes. I recounted the next day of that frantic week, Thanksgiving.

It was a strange one. The grandparents were befuddled. Younger relatives were plainly curious but kept a respectful distance. At dinner, I asked each of the twenty at the table to offer what they were thankful for. We went counterclockwise, which meant that Reid, sitting two to my left, was next to last. He said, "I'm glad I have a family that stands behind me."

On Saturday, Reid met with his "faculty advocate," the teacher who would accompany him to his Citizenship Committee hearing and, we were told, speak on his behalf. Just after they finished this meeting, Dr. Jarvis emailed a letter to the committee. It explained why expulsion would be emotionally and educationally devastating to Reid.

On Sunday, we received a call at home explaining the Citizenship Committee procedure. We were told that everything would be oral and nothing in writing would be submitted to the Committee.

Those who, like me, are involved professionally with administrative hearings develop a sense of when, to use the vernacular, the hearing's result is "wired"—that is, predetermined. The indicators include information from faceless or undisclosed sources, claims that are repositioned as the hearing approaches, and refusals to put things in writing. We could see it coming.

If the school were a zero-tolerance school and all were being treated the same, so be it, but now the rumor that Reid was a drug dealer had overtaken the school and was distorting the process. Also, it certainly seemed that Reid Hollister, with his low grades and SAT scores, was going to be a blot on the school's college admission record. He was not a star athlete, so no sports team or coach would suffer if he were expelled. The school had failed in its efforts—such as they were—to turn Reid around, so it would be expedient to cut him loose.

At one point during that weekend before the hearing, Reid set me off. I can't recall if it was a request to do a chore to which he responded slowly or some other minor disrespect to my position as his father, but I remember exactly what I said: "You know, Reid, you have ruined my birthday and my Thanksgiving, and if I work really hard at the office from now until Christmas, maybe I can salvage that. I'm doing this because I love you, but a little gratitude would be nice." I knew I had struck a nerve, because he winced. One of his strengths as a person was being attuned to the feelings of others, and he knew his actions had stung badly.

The Citizenship Committee hearing was on November 27. Right after the hearing, Reid told us that his fate was clear as soon as he walked into the room, and his faculty advocate agreed. The committee members were uninterested in Reid's character, his learning disability, or any impact on our family. The committee chair referred to a letter we had sent to the committee and the support letters from Dr. Jarvis, our minister, the head of the Sunday school where Reid taught, and other parents as "outside interference."

The school's rules did not permit parents to attend a hearing involving their son or daughter. As is sometimes the case with private schools, there was no due process—no right for Reid to know fully the accusation, the evidence, or whether the line between fact and surmise would be recognized.

Because we did not know what was going to be said about him, we cautioned Reid to stick to his written statement, to not even try an impromptu response. We were sure that if Reid tried to listen and respond point-by-point, he would fumble and this would reflect poorly. So we told him simply to make a forceful presentation of his own written statement.

Reid followed this direction. The only thing he told us afterward was that, contrary to what we had been told the prior day, something in writing was distributed to the committee members. He did not know what it was or what it said, and no copy was provided to Reid or his advocate.

Reid had written his statement on his own. It was decidedly the best piece of sustained writing he had done in a long time, maybe ever. Perhaps fear had its effect of focusing his mind. After reviewing what had happened, Reid told the committee:

I understand now the severity of what I did several weeks ago and what has happened in these last few days. I wish I could take it all back and start over. It is true that I gave a boy at this school a small amount of marijuana, off campus and after school and for no money. This was the only incident, but I now realize how actions of this type could have harmed the school in many ways. There really are no words to express how sorry I am and to apologize to the people I have hurt.

When I gave the marijuana to the student, I absolutely did not mean to cause any harm to him or my school. It may be hard to understand, but passing marijuana from one student to another is a regular occurrence at our school, and unfortunately is not regarded as a big deal. This was my first experience doing anything of this kind. I realize that what I did can't be looked at as minor or safe because any circulation of marijuana particularly from upperclassmen who are supposed to be role models creates an unsafe situation because it appears that this conduct is acceptable or will not hurt anybody.

I am very remorseful for having given that student marijuana and I won't ever lose that bad memory. I am completely done with marijuana, and I am glad that my parents and Dr. Jarvis will give me random drug tests so that you will see the evidence of that in the results.

One other thing that really makes me angry and sad that I got myself wrapped around marijuana is that this is now being thrown upon my family members. I really regret the pain that I have caused my sister and that she really doesn't deserve it. The pain that I caused my parents is tremendous. I have caused my mother more tears than I thought were humanly possible. My dad hardly ever gets angry, and he always looks ahead to how we can learn from our mistakes, but I know that he is angry and disappointed.

The pain that I am going through is also the thought that I may never be able to see my friends and my school again. I have put my education and the work that I do with children at risk, and also my future. I might have completely messed up my chances of ever getting into college, with this stupid mistake coming on top of the struggles I have had to get passing grades.

I would like to note that I personally apologized to the parents and student regarding the off-campus incident. The apology was accepted by both the parents and the student.

Finally, I have disappointed everyone who has believed in me, even when I did not believe in myself. I am deeply, deeply sorry. My parents and I have agreed to a series of punishments that I will accept. I respectfully ask you to forgive me, to let me show you that I can put this behind me, that my school means a lot to me, and to give me the chance to graduate with my class. Thank you.

After the hearing, we asked Reid's faculty advocate to tell us what the school's representative had said. To our disbelief, he said that he did not feel that it would be "appropriate" to fill us in. We appreciated that the school's rules had put him in an awkward position, but we were somewhat shocked to learn that, in the end, he considered his loyalty to be to the school, not Reid.

The principal called later that evening to say that the committee recommendation was expulsion and that he was prepared to accept it. In this conversation, the accusation

changed again. This time, there was no claim or proof of on-
campus possession. Reid was being expelled for providing one
joint to the underclassman at the gas station, period. We called
back and stated that we were going to withdraw Reid in the face
of this decision. We sent an email:

> This will confirm our telephone conversation of
> 8:25 this evening. You confirmed that the committee
> action and your acceptance of it were based on one
> incident of distribution of marijuana, off campus, to
> an underclassman. In response, we said that we are
> withdrawing Reid "under protest and under coercion in
> the face of a blatantly unfair disciplinary process."

~

My family awoke Tuesday morning to devastation. Ellen
and I were unnerved by this damage to Reid's future. We
wondered how we could explain to him the incompatible
concepts of plain injustice and picking up the pieces and moving
on. One of my predominant thoughts was that, while parents
and schools preach that actions in life have consequences, the
message from the school was that there are some people who are
so cloaked in rules of their own making and interpretation as to
be unaccountable.

There remained the small voice in my head wondering if
Reid had told us the complete truth. Yet I was highly inclined
to believe him. His confession to us and his written statement
to the committee had the ring of truth. The school had backed
down from its initial, broadside charge about his being a
drug dealer, and had spent days backfilling. At the end, the
school's claim was the one off-campus incident, so its story

had changed, and had mostly aligned with Reid's description. What remained incomprehensible to us was that while others had been spared expulsion for verified on-campus possession, Reid had been expelled based on this one off-campus incident, a first offense, to which he had immediately confessed and to which we as a family had responded promptly and seriously. I understood that private-school families give up some rights so that deans and teachers can protect the environment for which parents pay thousands of dollars, but our conclusion that Reid had been expelled because he was academically struggling and athletically expendable, and because rumor had crowded out facts, left us seething.

On Tuesday, Ellen and I took turns staying home; we were not going to leave Reid alone. Step one was to register him at Town Hall for enrollment at our local public high school. This brought a dose of humiliation, as the school employees betrayed curiosity about why a mid-year senior was transferring. And, of course, we continued to withhold his car keys. We were not about to let him go anywhere. When I made it clear that we were going to keep him home, I offered him a hands-on project that we had talked about before and which seemed like a fitting step at the moment. We went to Sports Authority and bought him a punching bag, assembly required. It would occupy him for hours, and perhaps allow him to vent.

~

As Rev. Miller began to bring his meditation to an end, my recollection brought me to Tuesday night, November 28.

Although both kids were in a funk, Ellen and I decided that a family dinner at a favorite place, California Pizza Kitchen, would get us out of the house and force us, if not to smile, then to stop scowling. Reid was scheduled to visit the guidance office at Conard High the next morning. Dinner seemed like a way to get his mind on something else.

We had a distracting and therefore tolerable dinner. Yet we could see that Reid was chafing and churning. When we arrived home, Reid saw that, in addition to our having his car keys, Ellen and I had installed a club, a locking device, on the steering wheel of his car. We were of course intent that he needed to stay home in his agitated and bewildered state, but we had a faint idea that he might have another ignition key that we did not know about. When he saw the club, he announced that he was taking his car and was going "to see some friends." We told him gently that that was not going to happen.

When I was distracted, Reid grabbed the key to unlock the club, ran outside, and unlocked the club before I could stop him. He separated the two pieces of the club, ran behind the house, and then came back into the kitchen, brandishing one piece of the club and demonstrating that he had gotten rid of the other piece so we could not relock the wheel.

"Give me my f___ing keys," he said, his fist so tight on the club that his hand was red, anger pouring from every limb of his body.

"Reid, put that down," I replied, trying to defuse him.

Ellen came into the kitchen and drew her breath as she realized what was happening.

I started talking, slowly but without stopping. "Reid, I know your school screwed you I know this whole thing is unfair I know you're angry and devastated and you don't want to go to

Conard and…and… and….'' He could see I was running out of things to say.

"Give me my keys now!" he screamed.

I was now dealing with an unknown. I started to talk about picking up the pieces, moving on, dealing with life as it comes—every cliché I could think of. Ellen chimed in.

This went on for about half an hour, but I could see that the conversation was moving in the wrong direction. Occasionally, Reid changed from "Give me my damn keys" to "My life is over!" and "I hate my life" and "I am *going* to see my *friends*!"

Ellen tried to ease her way into the situation, moving closer to him. Reid responded by picking up a large frying pan and holding it over her head. With his other hand, he made a fist.

I picked up the phone, ready to dial 911. My mind was racing. Was my son capable of hurting his mother, or was this his way of acting out, letting us know how angry and scared he was?

Ellen slowly backed away. Reid did not follow. I told Reid that I was ready to call 911 but if I did, it was going to set in motion a whole bunch of things that I could not predict and could make things worse than they were. I asked myself if I was really going to have my son arrested.

I kept talking. I hit upon the idea of all of us going to see Dr. Jarvis in the morning. Reid seemed to relent. Plainly—and to Dr. Jarvis's everlasting credit—Reid viewed him as someone who would understand, who would suggest an acceptable compromise. Eventually, Reid put the pan down, moved away from Ellen, and went outside and stood next to his car in the driveway. My hands shaking, I called Dr. Jarvis's emergency

number. We set an appointment for midday Wednesday. Ellen
and I collapsed in each other's arms, in tears.

The phrase "parent's worst nightmare" flashed through my
mind.

For about two hours after he stormed out of the kitchen
and into an unseasonably warm, almost comfortable November
evening, Reid either sat on or stood next to his car, or curled
up under the front bumper. Every few minutes I looked out
from our second-floor window to let him know I was checking
on him, and he returned my gaze, projecting the defiance and
stubbornness of one for whom a battle has just ended in a draw.

Ellen and I accompanied Reid to our town public high
school's guidance office the next morning. Reid did not tell us
his thoughts, but I suspected they were inaccurately informed in
part by a snobbish private school perspective of a public school:
strict, large, noisy, impersonal, maybe even dangerous. We were
escorted in to meet with counselor Karen Mortenson.

We explained why Reid had to transition. Ms. Mortenson
seemed to understand immediately how devastated Reid was,
how humiliating it was going to be for him to transfer into the
senior class, to be reunited with the kids who had last been his
classmates seven years ago in fifth grade. Properly ignoring
Ellen and me and speaking directly and empathetically to Reid,
she said, "You don't have to explain yourself or why you're here
to anyone. Kids come into this school and leave this school all
the time for lots of different reasons." She moved on to the task,
admittedly difficult, of piecing together enough credits for Reid
to graduate in June. She did her best, but it was obvious that
she had limited choices and that his courses at best would be a
patchwork.

When Ellen and I realized that these courses would be limping to graduation, we got on the Internet and the phone to see if any private-school options remained. We talked to a consultant, who said candidly that an elite private school would only accept a senior to fill a gap on an athletic team, and that Reid's situation would likely make a transfer impossible. Finally, we looked at schools for kids with disciplinary problems. Even making this inquiry seemed unfair, acceding to the view that he was a rotten kid. And when we acknowledged that we were even looking, Reid's look of "You want to send me away?" broke my heart.

Midday Wednesday took us to Dr. Jarvis's office. He was genuinely sorry, eloquent in his empathy for what Reid and we were going through. He talked to Reid privately, then to the three of us together. We all agreed that we needed to go forward one day at a time. I introduced the fact that I was supposed to go to Chicago for a meeting on Friday and Saturday upcoming, that I was willing to stay home, but was hopeful that we could agree on steps and protocols to allow Reid to be with friends, which he seemed to need desperately, while assuring Ellen and me that he would act safely. Our plan also had to include Reid's accepting enrollment at Conard High.

The four of us discussed the terms of another contract. When we arrived home, I quickly wrote it, and Reid, Ellen, and I signed it:

Dec. 1 – 2 – 3

Fri, Dec. 1.

1. Reid will go to Conard
   AM to take tests

2. Reid will go to Dr. Jarvis at 1 p.m., Friday.

3. Reid will not leave house or drive without permission.

4. Reid will leave his key on kitchen counter when home.

5. Reid will be in house by 11 p.m. Friday and Saturday nights.

6. Reid will go to Conard on Monday.

7. Reid will be civil and respectful and helpful to Mom at all times.

All of this seemed to calm Reid down. There was sadness and humiliation, but the unmitigated anger subsided. Wednesday night, we let him drive to West Hartford Center to have a milkshake at Friendly's with a girl who had left his school a few months earlier and was now at our town's other public high school. It seemed like a good way to help Reid see that he could transition and survive.

On Thursday, Reid filled out some paperwork for Conard, finished assembling his punching bag, and talked to dozens of friends on his cellphone and computer. Ellen made his favorite dinner, chicken à la king. Around 9:00 p.m., he said he didn't feel well and went to bed.

Because he was now no longer going to graduate from his private school, Reid took what he had scrawled for his senior page in the yearbook, crumpled it up, and dropped it in the wastebasket in his room. Apparently he had written it in October but never turned it in.

Ellen saw this as she was collecting the trash the next day. Her first instinct was the same as Reid's—that paper was a waste. Then she picked it out and read it.

It was our son in a voice that was barely known to us. To his friend Tom Gersky, "We have had some crazy good times together." And then these entries:

Mike B. – We are bowling champs. Ooh Ahh Ooh

Maddie – We have known each other for like 20 years now and they have been wonderful. Remember those good old days in Voluntown. ILY

Jlamb – Yo son you made my car bump. I duno why we never get in trouble in class but whenever you drive with me I get in trouble.

Martha – You're a real pain sometimes but I've learned to live with you. This Green Day [Martha's favorite band] crap is starting to freak me out. You still have a long time till you get to leave the house. That stinks for you. Don't do drugs or nothing. If you need something, call me and I'll help you. I love you.

Tim and Ellen – I know that you both think I have failed but I have worked hard and gotten better grades than any other year. Thank you for sending me here. I love you both.

Ellen read it over and over, showed it to me. We looked at each other in disbelief.

~

The worship service was coming to an end.

I believe I am on firm ground to say that the death of a child usually precipitates anger at someone. The limits of human judgment are perhaps nowhere displayed more starkly than when a child dies as the result of an adult's mistake. Moreover, how parents handle the anger seems to vary widely. I have read and heard about parents who have accepted the death of their child, in circumstances that would engender hatred in others, as God's will or an unavoidable accident, too remote from other events to support blame. I have seen parents respond with unconditional forgiveness when no one could fault them for considering retribution. And I have seen parents who seek revenge, some blindly, some quite purposefully.

While forgiveness of another's mistake, often to follow religious teaching, can be admired, my own Christian beliefs do not accept incredible human stupidity as God's plan. I subscribe to the belief that God is beneficence, the source of all that is good in the world, but is not and cannot be a guarantor that bad things will never happen. And so my own outlook on life leaves room for anger.

In the days after the expulsion, I was angry at the school, but after Reid's death I was apoplectic. Not that I blamed the administrators and teachers who had participated in the expulsion for Reid's crash. Yet their actions had directly preceded my son's death. In the final days of his life, he had been angry, confused, and scared. The school had imposed on him a need to prove that he was not the dangerous kid that they claimed he was, and now he had been deprived of that chance. In his last days, Reid had been tortured, and because he was now gone and unable to defend himself, I raged.

What, then, could I and should I say in the eulogy about these last episodes of Reid's life? As I sat in the pew at the rear of the church, as Rev. Miller gave the Benediction, I asked myself: Was this my opportunity to describe the struggle that was Reid's final year? Was it my obligation to present a true, altogether human story instead of false appearances? To hold the school accountable? It seemed that to recount Reid's life without referring to the reality of his final weeks would be nothing less than dishonest; it would sweep facts under the proverbial rug. Yet to bring up these realities would have everyone at the memorial service questioning my judgment and indeed my love and respect for my son. I would run the risk of sullying his life by focusing disproportionately on those incomprehensible final events.

I needed to identify what friends attending the memorial service, and posterity, would recognize as an acceptable dose of truth.

As unobtrusively as I had arrived, but now with several pages of notes in hand, I walked out the back door of the sanctuary during the Benediction, mouthing a "thank you" to Sally for not blowing my cover.

~

Driving home, I took a break. I put off the hard decisions in favor of easier ones. If only to collect myself, I returned to other parts of the eulogy.

Humor. Reid Hollister at his zaniest and most entertaining. Here, I was anything but bereft. The problem would be leaving out so much funny stuff. I considered but then rejected what has always been one of my favorite moments of Reid's childhood:

In 1997, when Reid was in third grade, for homework his
teacher asked the kids to write a letter, in cursive. This coincided
with President Clinton's falling down a flight of stairs and
tearing the cartilage in his knee, requiring surgery. I suggested
that Reid's letter be a get-well message to the president. He
labored over the sentiment and the penmanship and then asked
me to mail it. Before I did, I inserted at the bottom: "(The writer
is eight years old.)" A month later, Reid got home from school
and called me at work:

"Daddy! Daddy! It's from THE PRES-I-DENT! 'Dear Reid,
Thank you for your concern following my knee surgery. I am
following the doctor's orders and expect to make a full recovery.
Mrs. Clinton joins me in sending best wishes to you.'"

All of this came in one excited exhale. After catching his
breath, Reid added, "Sincerely, Bill Clinton . . . in cursive!"

On returning home, I began to write, to turn scribbled notes
into text, first haltingly and then quickly—facts, vignettes,
themes, a semblance of an outline. A thought about starting
strongly with variations on angels and then developing a theme
about rivers, based on our walk up the Narrows at Zion National
Park. As I mulled Reid's life and troubles at school, I started to
craft a compromise: a reference to the debacle that would leave
no doubt as to our family's ire, but not a detailed explanation,
attack, or point-by-point defense.

In about two hours, I produced an outline that included a
section about his expulsion, using the words "paying too dearly
for a mistake."

I typed, edited, re-edited, and by Monday morning was
prepared to share two versions—in essence, one taking direct
aim at the school and the other being more oblique about it—

with my ad hoc review committee, consisting of Ellen; Gary
Miller; Peter Grandy; my brother-in-law Steve Boga, who is
a published author; my Pulitzer Prize–winner friend, *Hartford
Courant* reporter Mark Pazniokas; my friend John Boyer, who
had recently left his position as executive director of Hartford's
Mark Twain House; and Wick Sloane, friend, confidant, one-
time reporter, National Public Radio commentator, and father of
Will, one of Reid's best boyhood friends.

John Boyer replied first, by email. His words gave me hope:
"I have read both versions and am speechless. . . . It is always
so difficult being a father, I think. . . . You are still Reid's father,
will always be, and you have yet another standard to set for him
and for all of us." John then advised, "And whatever you do,
do not remove the irreverent story about your walk up the river.
There will be fathers there on Wednesday who will need that
humor and that intimacy between you and your son as they think
of their sons."

Then John weighed in against what I had written about the
school:

> My distance also allows me, compels me, to ask
> you to rescind the very mention of the trauma of Reid's
> last two weeks. I cannot know how bad all of that was
> and the anger you felt, which has now been amplified by
> the cruel loss you have endured.

> But I only ask you to imagine the piece without that
> paragraph.

> As to those last challenging circumstances, let them
> wither. He was not given the time to show us what he
> most certainly would have shown us—that those two
> weeks could not serve to define his beautiful legacy any

more than he would have let them define his promising
future . . . . Do not let them steal anything from him, nor
from you, on a day that should be all about Reid.

Peter Grandy agreed with John Boyer. Ellen was torn. I
don't recall the positions of the others, but I vividly recall Gary
Miller's contrary view: While acknowledging the concerns of
others, he told me, "Tim, you need to say what's in your heart."
He understood, I think, the reality that I needed to define and
defend my son, and that if I did not, if the eulogy was not true to
the facts and my emotions, I might well regret it forever.

So over the next twenty-four hours, I pondered "the
expulsion issue." Ultimately, I concluded that it would be
dishonest, that it would stain Reid's memory to omit completely
any mention of the expulsion, to give the school the slightest
impression that all was forgiven or that its actions had not added
immeasurably to my family's despair. I arrived at a paragraph
that acknowledged the debacle without becoming mired in
accusations.

My advisory committee made many other insightful
suggestions and edits, none more helpful than Mark Pazniokas's
brilliant improvement to the analogy between my river walk
with Reid and my relationship with him. Mark, who had himself
hiked the Narrows, suggested these words: "Our slow progress
upriver was a reflection of life itself: Three steps forward. A side
step to avoid falling. A step back to reassess the path. A yield
of the higher ground for better footing." And then a description
of the flowing water as "the embodiment of our son's spirit, a
bubbling and rushing force that could produce not only gentle
eddies but also roiling rapids."

One critical decision yet unmade: Who would deliver the eulogy? I began to seriously doubt that I was emotionally capable of reading it aloud in front of a packed church, and I soon concluded that this was unavoidably true. Having sweated out the text, I did not now want to dishonor Reid's memory by choking and clutching and pausing over what should be read with passion and precise diction, without error or interruption.

I turned to Wick Sloane, an accomplished public speaker, who immediately understood and accepted the role. He took my draft—and shortened many sentences. "I need to breathe," he explained.

A good compromise leaves no one happy but everyone accepting the result. None of my committee members endorsed the exact wording of the paragraph about the school's disciplinary process, but they recognized the necessity for me to make a statement. As a parent defending his child, I concluded that the final version fulfilled my obligations to truth, judgment, and my son.

6

Hugging Lessons

The Molloy Funeral Home is two blocks east of the commercial center of West Hartford, in the long shadow of the tall steeple of the First Congregational Church, which dominates the center of town.

When we arrived at Molloy, Ellen, Martha, and I and our extended family took in the scene, simultaneously beautiful and incomprehensible. Overlaid on the casket was an enormous bouquet of four dozen yellow roses, arranged in a half-circle, and at the far end, Reid's graduation picture. Around the room were more than a dozen bouquets, from family; my law firm; my alma mater, Wesleyan University; Ellen's Christian sharing group; and several of my clients. On a pedestal in one corner, a soccer ball nestled in a bed of carnations.

The two photo boards stood on easels along the path to the casket. Between the easels and the casket, on a display table, lay the items that we had selected to be buried with Reid. The last was the pencil drawing of Reid that Martha had made on Saturday night, his face surrounded by the words of a song that they had listened to together. The likeness was so stunning— who knew that she had such talent?—that Ellen and I were proud to position it where all could admire it.

It was now time to face the multitude. Outside, we could see, the line extended for several blocks. As those at the front shuffled toward us, their pace slowed decidedly and a backup grew behind them. Standing in front of the casket with Ellen and Martha, I craned my neck to see what the delay was. Martha's drawing—the visitors were stopping to marvel at it and read every word of the song she had chosen to accompany her beloved brother's body. To make the line move better, I took the canvas and moved it to the center of the room, where it could be seen after the mourners had passed through the embraces of our family.

Not long after we began receiving, students began to dominate. About four hundred came to pay their respects. As the kids approached me, a pattern developed. Many looked past me, at the casket, perhaps picturing themselves in Reid's position. I sensed finally that the person in the casket was one of them and they were confronting mortality, probably for the first time.

I did my best to reassure them, encouraged them to remember Reid, reached out with my arms. A master class in hugging.

The calling hours were a roundup, a convention of the constituencies of my life at that juncture. In attendance were colleagues, neighbors, friends, lawyers, judges, church members, teachers, coaches, and confidants. By December 2006 I had lived in Connecticut for twenty-four years, and in West

Hartford for twenty-two of those, and now in just over seven hours it seemed as though everyone whose lives had intersected with mine, even back to college and high school, had come to Molloy.

Jay Sandak is a brilliant lawyer with whom I had worked as co-counsel on several occasions. He is widely known for his ability to settle cases, and this talent stems from his uncanny knack for understanding emotions, motivations, strengths, and weaknesses. Jay is also the father of three boys, slightly older than Reid; when Jay and I had compared notes as dads, his was a sagacious voice.

I turned to greet the next person in line and saw that it was Jay. Unlike just about everyone else in line, when we made eye contact he did not rush toward me with a hug and a backslap. Rather, he continued to lean against the table on which Reid's personal stuff was displayed, cocked his head contemplatively to the left, looked me up and down, pursed his lips, and without saying a word conveyed a bond of understanding between us. By the time he actually said, "I'm sorry," we had already had a telepathic conversation that recalled our chats through the years. We had worked together enough and so respected each other that he knew what I was thinking, and vice versa: Parenting, especially of teenage boys, is perilous, with no guarantees. Jay's two words and the accompanying, simple warm handshake and shoulder clasp said to me that a more extended conversation was unnecessary. Such is what we can do with close friends.

One other moment stands out, because it was less than sixty seconds but repackaged years.

Duane and Mary Lynn are attorneys in Washington, D.C., for a national trade association. Duane was the one I had called

Saturday morning, when he was expecting me at that meeting. After about four hours of receiving, and as the wind chilled the hundreds still waiting to get into the building, I looked to the next in line, and there were Duane and Mary Lynn.

They had gotten on a plane, rented a car, driven to West Hartford, stood in line for two hours in the cold in a place where they knew no one else—to stand with me for about one minute. I was so overwhelmed that I fumbled through trying to explain to Ellen who they were and how incredible it was that they had taken the time to travel from Washington. I will always remember their visit as kindness beyond any reasonable expectation.

As the calling hours came to a close, several of Reid's friends, perhaps prompted by one who had had a similar experience, asked if they could have the casket opened. Recall that Randy Molloy had explained how viewing the body is often a critical step in grieving. It occurred to me that this request highlighted one small part of the process that, temporarily, *was* reversible.

I did not want to see Reid again. I had seen him in the morgue, his skin its normal color and texture. I did not want my last memory—the one I was now tending—to be skin looking plastic, or pallid cheeks that had always been rosy. I was also concerned about what had been done to close that gash on his right temple.

On the other hand, it occurred to Ellen and me that while we had seen Reid at the hospital, his friends had not. After some huddling in corners, we worked out a compromise. Tom, Mike, Lauren, and Maddie, with Rev. Grandy; Maddie's mother, Mary Way; and our friend Diane Beir as the group's chaperones, would remain behind after everyone else had left and say their farewell.

But first Ellen, Martha, and I needed to leave. Ellen bent, then hunched, then sprawled over the casket, kissing it and sobbing, "My baby, my baby." When we judged that the moment was right, Martha and I each took one of Ellen's arms, lifted and led her away.

Months later, Diane Beir explained the viewing to me:

There was a lot of tension in everyone's face, and Mary and I were hugging each other. Randy came around the curtain about two minutes later and said to the group, "Your buddy died in surgery where they needed to pump him up with a lot of fluids, so I want you to be prepared that he isn't going to look exactly the way you remember him." We all gave a look like we understood and then Mary made the gesture for everyone to lock arms for support. We walked to the casket and formed a horseshoe.

Reid didn't look like Reid. He was very bloated and looked heavier than he really was. Then Mary broke out of the circle, went to the casket and started running her fingers through Reid's hair. She did this to show the kids that it was OK to touch him. At that point she signaled to me that we should give the kids some time alone with Reid.

At first there was crying as they inched closer to the casket. Later, I noticed one of the boys bent over so he was looking at Reid at the level of his body and said, "Hey guys, if you look at him from this angle, it looks more like Reid." Then a few of the others did the same and said, "You're right!"

One by one they went over to the side table and got the little wrapped present they had brought and put it in the casket. They were more relaxed now and started telling stories that began with "Remember when . . . ?" and there was laughter.

~

Wednesday we would bury Reid.

The day's first question was what to wear. I could have showed up mismatched and unkempt and everyone would have ascribed it to shock.

It was cold and gray outside, breezy but not frigid and, most important, not snowing. In fact, the forecast was clouds giving way to a blue sky later in the day.

As we drove to Fairview, I was struck again by how close the cemetery is to our house—seven blocks, give or take. The geometry of our town, so familiar to me after living there for so long, had suddenly changed. The north end of Pleasant Street was now the center of town.

I don't recall a debate about whether I, my brothers-in-law, and other family should be the pallbearers or whether it should be Reid's friends, but somewhere along the way we decided on his buddies. We thought it might be beneficial, their final act of friendship.

The grave was remarkable for its symmetry. The excavation appeared to be a perfect rectangle, each corner square. Bright-green carpet covered all four inside walls as well as three feet or so out from the edge. Wooden boards that prevented the freshly dug hole from collapsing protruded beneath the carpet. At the head of the grave sat a large floral arrangement, yellow, orange, and green, with a similar one on the left. On the right were two arrangements dominated by white lilies.

The Molloy staff opened the back of the hearse and with calm and precision talked the six boys and Lauren and Maddie through their task. I recall several "slowlys" and "gentlys." The task was so awkward that I am sure I had the same fleeting thought as all who witness such an exercise. What if they stumble?

They did not. Each showed nothing but poise and courage. Their concentration was unbroken. As they lifted and shouldered, they were the only ones who were not crying. With slow steps they maneuvered their friend toward his grave. They stepped carefully along each side of the green carpet, lowered the casket, and then stepped back and melted into the gathering. The splay of yellow roses that had covered the casket at the calling hours remained in place, already starting to wilt in the cold of a December morning in New England but retaining enough vibrancy to suggest life.

Our ministers, Gary Miller and Peter Grandy, invited us closer. I don't recall a word of what either said. I know there were Bible readings and prayers, but I recall only snapshots: Someone holding Gracie. Everyone's breath visible in the cold. The two grandmothers seated closest to the casket, the disorder of what generation was being buried most illustrated by their presence. Blank faces. The pine tree standing above us.

The contrast from four days earlier was stark. At the hospital it had been just Gary and me, with me flailing in his arms, whimpering about Reid's death being my fault. I had thought at the time that nothing could be more horrible, but now I saw those moments with Gary as only the beginning of the descent. Four days earlier, the mental and spiritual foundations of life had been exploding, shattering, dispersing, and disappearing. Now I was sitting in the middle of the resulting rubble, nothing but destruction in every direction as far as my mind's eye could see.

I was not experiencing the sensation of falling into an abyss while dreams imploded, as had occurred at the hospital; rather, I was aware of my surroundings, comprehending the damage. What I did not know was whether this was the bottom or how or when I would ever, could ever, start to get up, dust myself off, and take a step in some direction with some purpose.

The burial *was* the bottom, however, because although many awful things have happened since, at the end of the service there was a moment of grace that started an upward trajectory.

Ellen was seated in front of me. Martha stood to my right, behind Ellen. To my left was the Rev. Sarah Verasco, the former associate minister of our church. One of Sarah's strengths as a minister is her ability to be direct and forceful yet empathetic when a wandering or grieving soul needs direction or comfort. Sarah is the clergy you want next to you when you confront grief beyond comprehension. She is a shepherd in the best sense of that word.

As I looked at that casket and the hole and vault beneath it, I had the terrifying sensation of joy and hope draining out of my body and into that hole. Several images popped into my head: an hourglass running out of sand, a full bathtub with its plug pulled, a balloon deflating. A part of me was melting into that hole, and I was powerless to stop it.

That was absolutely the worst moment.

Then Sarah took my hand, first palm-in-palm and then our fingers kneaded together. I dropped my head onto her shoulder, and my tears began to drip onto her sleeve. And then a counter-sensation that was palpable, tactile: Sarah started *refilling* whatever was draining out of me. She began replacing the sand in the hourglass, pouring new water into the tub, refilling the balloon. This did not stop the leakage, but the sense of *replenishment* was undeniable. "He restoreth my soul," says Psalm 23. This was not healing, and it was certainly neither closure nor understanding nor anything approaching joy, but perhaps it was the beginning of the possibility of the potential for hope. It was akin to a man wandering in the desert and finding a good clue that he might find something to drink soon.

A sprinkling of grace over the scene at my son's burial, as I struggled to hold myself together.

Gracie pulled on her leash, panting, her breath visible, her coat thick enough to make others feel warm; yet in one of those remarkable moments in which dogs are able to sense acutely and reflect the emotions of their owners, her ears were drooping, her tail was wagging more slowly than usual, she was staring intently at the casket of the boy who had loved her so, and she didn't bark once.

Martha was comforting Ellen, hugging her more firmly whenever the volume or the energy of Ellen's cries increased as if she had just uncovered a new dimension of disbelief. In a way we did not comprehend until months later, Martha was simultaneously trying to understand what grief is and yet containing her own as she bravely tended to her mother.

My dad was stoic, perhaps more than anyone there, a product of a generation and a society in which men do not bare their emotions.

Otherwise, I recall lots of blank stares, faces straining to understand what we were doing.

As the burial service ended, the sense of finality nearly overwhelmed my basic motor skills. It was physically taxing to take one step away from the grave. I was viewing Reid's casket for the last time. Visible from where I stood were the graves of people who had died in the 1800s. There would be a time when no one present at the burial at that moment would be alive to visit and remember Reid.

Yet as we left Fairview, I knew that I would never have any regrets about the burial. With dignity and faith, we had committed Reid's body to eternal rest.

~

The Asylum Hill Congregational Church was built of the same brownstone quarried in nearby Portland, Connecticut, that graces many of New England's churches and academic buildings, as well as New York City's famous brownstones. Its founders laid the cornerstone in May 1865, and dedicated the sanctuary in June 1866. Its steeple, two hundred twenty-six feet high, presides over the area west of downtown Hartford.

The church is best known historically as Mark Twain's church. Samuel Clemens was one of Hartford's most prominent citizens for thirty years, and his pew—assigned on the basis of annual contribution to the church—was the third on the left side of the center aisle. A plaque marks it as his even today. Clemens was a close friend and confidant of Asylum Hill's first pastor, Joseph Twichell—"Uncle Joe" to the Clemens family—and Clemens referred to the congregation as the "Church of the Holy

Speculators" due to the number of prominent Hartford magnates
who were members.

Today the church is a vibrant congregation of about eighteen
hundred, one of the largest within the United Church of Christ.
The sanctuary features soaring stone columns and a vaulted
ceiling, intricate stained-glass windows, and an Aeolian-Skinner
organ widely regarded as one of the world's best. The pews can
seat approximately one thousand people.

I arrived at the church around 4:00 p.m. on Wednesday
afternoon to help Wick Sloane practice his delivery of the
eulogy and to make sure that everything was in place. Not that I
doubted Wick or the church staff, but I needed to go somewhere
and do something. Sitting at home and waiting was excruciating.

I saw that the reception hall had been set up for snacks and
beverages after the service, but not for overflow seating. Steve
Mitchell, the church's minister of music, happened to be the first
staff person I saw. I predicted that we would need more chairs
and a video feed from the sanctuary to accommodate what would
surely be more than one thousand people. He was skeptical.

Our caravan arrived for the service at 6:30 p.m. The
church's parking lots were full but the custodians had saved
spaces for us with traffic cones. We arrived to learn that the
sanctuary seats had been filled by 6:20 and the staff was now
scrambling to—guess what?—set up a video feed and several
hundred folding chairs in the reception hall.

Yogi Berra once supposedly said, "If you go to other
people's funerals, they will come to yours."

We made our way—past about three hundred now seated in
the reception hall—into the standing-room-only church. Gary

Miller, calling us to worship, echoed the obituary and presaged my eulogy:

> He was at times a voice, albeit a tenor voice, crying
> in the wilderness, seeking the right place and fit for
> his skills and interests. With eyes sparkling, a smile
> overwhelming, his whistle resounding, humorously
> present and accounted for, Reid Hollister did the best
> he could in life with the gifts he had been entrusted, and
> we will remember him.

Rev. Miller invited Reid's best friends, Mike and Tom, and our neighbors, Steve and Tom, to speak. Mike Borea started:

> From the moment I met Reid, we couldn't be torn
> apart. I spent so much time at his house, my parents
> had to beg me to come home. Having him around me
> made everything I did feel complete. And not having
> him in my life makes me feel incomplete. Because I
> know that everything I do now will never be the same
> without the jokes, the funny looks, the comforting
> smile. . . .

At that moment, Mike stopped. Everyone present in the sanctuary or listening or watching on the remote video screen could feel their throats tighten—as Mike's had. Mike tried to breathe. He could not. He tried to force the next words out, but they would not come. He started to cry. Everyone else started to or was on the verge.

Gary Miller stepped up and put his arm across Mike's back, just as he had done for me four days earlier. Mike shook the tears from his eyes and pointed Rev. Miller to the spot on the page. In that moment, I suspect, everyone there took stock of the true meaning of the word "friend." Literally and figuratively, Gary carried Mike the rest of the way, reading for him:

> Reid had this way of taking the worst situations and turning them into memories that you will never forget. He was only seventeen years old, but he filled his life with experiences that most people can only dream of. My one wish is that Heaven is big enough to fit Reid's heart.

Our next-door neighbor, Tom Quish, followed:

> Most of you know me and know that I am very shy, and all of you know that Reid wasn't shy at all. That's why you see everybody here today. Many of you who knew Reid knew that he took care of kids, but that's not all. He took care of everybody.

And Tom Gersky, whose comments introduced me to things I had not known:

> Reid and I shared many firsts. He was my first best friend. He took me to my first Red Sox game and my first concert. He introduced me to wings, silly music, mooning, and quoting funny movies. We shared so many good times they all seem to blend together. Sitting in the back of third period science class freshman year and failing every test. Girl problems, JV soccer, basketball. The time he force-fed me Ex-lax and I jumped off the roof. Too many good times to remember, and most of them too inappropriate to tell on holy ground.

> The biggest compliment I can give Reid now is that he changed my life. I met Reid as a shy freshman who was too afraid to be himself. He showed me confidence and formed my whole personality and demeanor. He

was so outgoing that his middle name was Pushing The Envelope. You'll always be my twin brother.

My sister, Liz, was next. She worked for sixteen years as the financial manager of the aircraft-maintenance division at a major airline. From her years of commanding machinists and mechanics to work more efficiently, I had no doubt of her toughness or her ability to speak to an audience. But I had asked her on Sunday if she would speak at the service and she had declined. I didn't question it; I assumed that, like me, she was too choked up to stand before the crowded church. When she called back the next day to reverse herself, to volunteer, we saved a place for her in the program. Given her initial reluctance, her eloquence caught me by surprise:

> Reid was always changing the paradigm and challenging the norm. Never quite sure where he was headed, but it was always to get a big rise and big laugh. And then I thought to myself, Where is all of that energy going when he gets to Heaven?

> Tim, Ellen, Martha, now it's time for us on earth to begin to turn our bad grief to good grief, and transition our pain to healing. When you have those mornings when you are not sure how you're going to get out of bed, Tim, you're going to get up for Ellen. Ellen, you're going to get up for Tim. You're both going to get up for Martha. The rest of the family, we're all going to get up for you, too. And all the people in this congregation, they're going to get up for you every day, one day at a time.

> So as you begin to affirm a new reality, don't fear the world around you. You can live in it again. You can thrive in it again. You can forgive in it again.

You can love in it again. For a time you might think
there is nothing about life you can affirm, but the dark
clouds will begin to break up and occasionally for brief
moments rays of sunshine will come through, and hope
based on faith and God will guide you.

In other words, my little sister stole the show. For months
afterward, friends who had attended the service told me that the
"You will get up" message had stayed with them. In December
2007, just past the one-year anniversary, one of my college
classmates summarized in an email what so many had said:
"The voice I keep hearing is Liz's—Tim, you will get up for
Ellen . . . and so on. Your sister is a very smart woman."

Kathleen Graham, the director of our Sunday school,
probably believed in Reid and his future more than anyone else.
She saw firsthand his gifted way with young children. In four
years she had recruited him, trained him, promoted him, and
infused in him whatever confidence he had in himself:

Was he perfect? Absolutely not. Could he be a
pain in the neck and drive us crazy? For sure. Was he
bigger than life itself? No. Well, maybe. Maybe for the
children who knew him and loved him, I actually think
he was bigger than life.

During church school on Sunday morning, without
any prompting, second-grader Quintin said, "We need to
talk about our sadness." And they did. But as we know,
and I think children know even better, there's only so
much sadness that you can endure, that we can endure.
So they moved to all they loved about Reid:

"He was a funny guy."

"He was my buddy."

"Reid helped me when I was shy."

"Reid helps people understand things."

"He was really fun and he stood up for people if someone was bullying them."

Another child summed it up perfectly. "He was really a good shepherd."

Reid was even one father's idea of a dream date for his daughter. Parents described Reid as charming, precious, loving, handsome, and inclusive.

The Rev. Sarah Verasco was next. She read the poem that Reid had included in "Reid-flections," an eighth-grade autobiographical writing assignment. Sarah began by putting her finger on why the words were so appropriate for the service:

"I Am Who I Am" is the title of a poem Reid wrote in eighth grade, and as you will hear, it offers us a unique glimpse into Reid's self-understanding and a glimmer of his sense of humor:

When I look into a mirror
It takes a while for an image to appear
Waiting watching and standing
I gaze into the mirror and just see the same old thing
As the time passes by
I see something never mind there is just something in my eye
I have a feeling that this could take a while
So I'm going to get through it and smile
I try to concentrate
This mirror is crooked and not straight

I have stood in this place
It's about time I can finally see my face

My black hair is the first thing that I can see
Next comes my contacts (my optometry)
I relax and hope more will come
I turn and walk take one more glance and see if I'm done
I walk back to the mirror to focus, to try
I'm getting off topic, but I can't see why
I have a problem with this not paying attention
It has even caused me a detention
Detention seems to work my problem out
Is it because I have to sit still?
Or could it be my little tiny pill?

It was time for the eulogy. Wick and I had decided that I would introduce it and explain why Wick was going to read it. My heart was pounding. As I approached the microphone and surveyed the room I took a long, deep breath, let it out, and placed the one typed paragraph on the lectern so that my trembling hand would not move it as I tried to read:

> There may be no more important and demanding role for a parent than a eulogy. Which is to say that I wanted to do this myself, to use the love in this sanctuary to propel me past the unspeakable grief that we feel as a family. But the consensus of cooler heads was that you would hear the words better from someone other than me. So our dear friend Wick Sloane, who knew Reid for almost all of his life, has graciously agreed to read to you [at this point I vindicated my decision to delegate—I started to sob] the words that I have written to honor my son.

Wick, slightly rumpled from his day of traveling, tie slightly askew, handkerchief prominently flowing from the breast pocket of his suit jacket, offered his own introduction:

Tim's prominence as an attorney and all is well known; what is less well known is that his writing is absolutely beautiful, and I learned this again the hard way this morning sitting in the back of the shuttle from Washington to Boston, where I said I'm going to read this five times before I get home and practice, and the stewardess kept bringing me more and more coffee and cookies because she could see that I was crying.

As Wick spoke, I stationed myself at the side of the altar's communion table, folded my arms, and rubbed my forehead. Wick paused to elevate his volume:

On this holy night, Reid Hollister is busy in heaven:

- hangin' and chillin' with the boy angels;

- drawing rapturous attention from the girl angels;

- scowling at the midnight curfew that St. Peter has imposed on the teen angels;

- lending his beautiful tenor voice to the Choir of Angels;

- explaining text messaging and MySpace.com to the older angels;

- and giving hugs and high-fives to every little angel who needs one.

So if you need to talk to Reid, hit your cellphone.

On Reid's sixteenth birthday, when he was hiking with the Appalachian Mountain Club, I wrote him a letter: The Very Best Days I Have Spent With My Son Reid. Twenty of them. A copy of the letter is on the back of your program.* I want to tell you about Number 13 and Number 9.

After Reid finished eighth grade in June 2003, I went to Washington on a business trip, and Reid came with me. While I was at my meeting, Reid went to the Spy Museum. We then went up to the Capitol and got tickets from Congressman Larson's office. With the tickets, we watched Congress in action, from the gallery overlooking the House of Representatives. As we sat down, a fierce debate was going on. After listening for a few minutes, Reid turned to me and said, "Dad, is this real, or a show they put on for visitors?"

"Both," I said.

In June 2004, we took a family trip out west that included Zion National Park. Zion Canyon, from the south, is an inverted V—several miles wide at the park entrance, but very narrow at its northern tip. The northernmost section is called, amazingly enough, "the Narrows." It's a high-walled river canyon that starts out fifty yards wide and over several miles shrinks to about three feet. Reid and I took a five-hour walk in the riverbed. Three hours against the flowing water and two hours with the current. Talking, joking, and laughing.

As we walked, I started thinking that the canyon, the river, and our walk were perfect metaphors for our lives and for our father-son relationship: As we went farther north and the walls came closer together, so did we. Our slow progress, especially upriver, was a reflection of life itself: Three steps forward. A side step to avoid falling. A step back to reassess the path. A yield of the higher ground for better footing. It also struck me that the flow of the water over and around those rocks was the embodiment of our son's spirit, a bubbling and

---

* A copy of the letter is on p. 70.

rushing force that could produce not only gentle eddies but also roiling rapids. A flow ultimately, I hoped, headed toward that stretch where the canyon is less confining and the run more peaceful and steady.

When you walk the Narrows, you actually crisscross the water. The bottom is rocky and uneven. The water flows so rapidly that you can't gauge the depth before you cross. Reid and I devised a game: "I can cross this part without getting my knees wet." Or my belly button. Or my chest.

A fierce competition developed. Finally, on one of his turns, Reid said, "I can cross this part without... without getting my wiener wet."

The exchange that followed is not appropriate for church.

When Reid was little, he had his funny phrases. If he wanted to throw a ball, we had to "get-a-ketch." If something was loud, it was "noisy in my ears." Any large vehicle was a "citybus."

We called him "Reidbear." One day, we interviewed him on videotape: What's your name? Where are you from? And later, "Are you a Republican or a Democrat?" "I'm just a Reidbear," he said.

When Reid was older, his humor became zany and unpredictable. During one of our long car rides out west, we asked him, "What's your idea of a perfect evening?" Reid said, "Eating spaghetti ... in the cockpit of an F-16."

There is a sad reality about the end of Reid's life that we need to acknowledge. His passing, in one way, may have been a blessing. The final two weeks of Reid's life were tumultuous. On November 27, he was

forced to withdraw from his school. This is not the time
or place to debate what happened. The truth is that in his
final four days, Reid was angry and scared, seventeen
years old, suddenly without a second chance, facing an
uncertain future. In this sense, he may have been spared
from a rough road ahead.

And so, at the end, Reid's life was questions and
certainties, converging to shape his future:

Why is it so hard for me to focus?

Why am I not more comfortable with who I am?

What am I good at?

What am I best at?

Where is my place in the world? and

Why are there so many rules?

The certainties are that he was a handsome,
charming, energetic, outgoing, funny, and empathetic
young man. In shopping malls and on athletic fields,
at fast-food restaurants and on the sidewalks of West
Hartford Center, his piercing aqua-blue eyes, his electric
smile, and his lanky frame commanded attention. His
attitude was happy-go-lucky. His creed was fierce
loyalty to his friends. He loved his family, no one more
than his sister, Martha. Reid and Martha share the bond
of being adopted. For Martha, Reid would walk through
the thickest brick wall or slay the most fearsome dragon.

Through the inevitable conflicts of teenage years,
Reid loved his mom and his dad. He was a whiz at
electronic communication. And he was "gifted," in
the best sense of that word, with young children.

Effortlessly, magically, Reid turned tears to smiles, fear to trust, reluctance to participation, and confusion to understanding. Reid always had ready a few well-timed and well-chosen words, high-fives, hugs, and smiles.

Ellen and I know that the certainties would have prevailed over time. But with the answers to the questions only starting to reveal themselves, it is clear that when he passed from this life, Reid was a river of promise flowing temporarily through a gully of doubt. We can only take solace from the many memories we have of watching that amazing river run.

Reid now makes his home beyond the stars, safe in God's promise of eternal life. Up in Heaven, the count of devilishly handsome lads is plus one. Until we catch up with Reid, we must emulate his caring ways, practice fairness and mercy and honor. We will carry out his work with children, and recall fondly and often how he enriched our lives.

The poet Alfred, Lord Tennyson said this of faith in God and Jesus:

We have but faith: we cannot know,
For knowledge is of things we see;
And yet we trust it comes from thee,
A beam in darkness: let it grow.

Reid, your life was a warm and shining beam. Wherever you went, you lit up faces, spirits, and rooms. You are not and never will be done. Your spirit will illuminate the paths we walk and the days we live … forever. We love you.

As Wick finished, I was pleased with my decision to defer, to let him do the reading. I was also grateful for his edits, which had made the speech more Reid-centric. I had sobbed during the last paragraph.

Peter Grandy led us in a prayer. Steve Mitchell took the stage and David Bradley took his seat at the piano, for "Bring Him Home." The day before, Steve had asked me if he could modify some of the words to better fit the circumstance of Reid's death. In the original song, Jean Valjean implores God to protect Marius, who is not his son and who is alive and resting from battle on the floor next to him. Steve altered the third stanza to fit Reid.

> *We gave him love and held him close,*
> *We thought our time had just begun,*
> *We never thought this could end,*
> *But now our hearts have to mend*
> *He was our son,*
> *He was our friend.*

As Steve sang, Ellen, Martha, and I were seated not ten feet in front of him. Ellen's crying was continuous, but at Steve's new words, which Ellen did not know were coming, she burst into a new flood of more energetic tears. How Steve kept his composure I do not know.

Rev. Miller stared silently at the congregation, comprehending the moment, communicating its gravity with his somber tone and expression. He did his best to help thirteen hundred confused people make sense of what we were doing and why:

> Tonight is a night when a parent's worst nightmare is acknowledged as reality. Tonight is a night if we are absolutely truthful when in many ways we hurt like hell. And perhaps it is.

Then to what images do we turn? To what promises
do we look to stand secure, blameless and everlasting
as we struggle to live with the painful realities of these
current moments? The Gospel of Mark and from the life
of Jesus, there is an image which is supreme tonight.
It begins with these words: "Immediately he made his
disciples get into the boat and go on ahead to the other
side to Bethsaida while he dismissed the crowd. After
saying farewell to them, he went up on the mountain
to pray. When evening came, the boat was out on the
sea and he was alone on the land. When he saw that
they were straining at the oars against an adverse wind,
he came toward them early in the morning. And Jesus
spoke to them and said, 'Take heart. It is I. Do not be
afraid.' Then he got into the boat with them and the
winds ceased, and they were utterly astounded."

In our time of remembrance and in our time of
painful loss, when adverse winds have come and caused
the journey to be most difficult, our faith teaches us that
Jesus climbs into the boat with us.

Our service tonight is not in an assembly room or
a lecture hall. It's not in a town hall center. It's not in a
gymnasium or a cultural cornerstone of the community.
It's in the church because that's where Reid's family has
found their focus. And it's where Reid found his focus
as well. Where he was a shepherd to children; where he
invited us into his boat even when it listed a bit. Tonight
Jesus gets into our storm-tossed boat to proclaim this
is not God's will. It is not the will, said Jesus, of my
Father that even one of his children should suffer and
die.

Tenor Wayne Rivera, perched in the choir loft that is
cantilevered above the back of the church, filled it to the vaulted
ceiling's top with "O Holy Night." As he sang, I wondered if we

would ever again feel a thrill of hope at the break of a new and glorious morn.

For me, the memorial service was not healing, but it was beauty and therefore it bestowed grace. That is, nothing that was said or sung remotely suggested that what had happened in the previous five days was now comprehensible or God's will or a big bump in life's road. Or even just an accident that could not be helped. Anger was prowling the dark corners of my mind; I wondered what my mental state would have been if I had had *only* grief to deal with.

Yet in the moment that Gary Miller finished the Benediction, I felt a sense of accomplishment. Life had relegated Ellen and me, as Reid's parents, to the task of providing a memorial service that would capture all of the best in him. The tributes achieved that. We needed a dose of reality, and my reference to his school and his expulsion in the eulogy, friends told me afterward, had struck the correct balance. In the prayers, hymn, and Scripture readings, we had invited faith to be present as much as the hearts of those assembled could tolerate. The music had served as our chauffeur, transporting us from segment to segment and providing time for reflection.

For months afterward, people told us that they felt as though they had met Reid that night. We had introduced him even as we remembered him.

Finally, most everyone, I think, walked away with something lasting. On Reid's birthday, in July, we received a card from the mother of one of Reid's friends:

> I often think of you especially when I first awake in the morning. At Reid's service—perhaps it was your cousin who promised that we would get up for you when it

would be so difficult for you. When I get up, I say a prayer for you.

Even now, years later, it is still hard to fathom ninety quickly arranged minutes as the tragic conclusion of seventeen years. I am proud to say, however, that we packed those minutes to the hilt.

7

Him Whom You Cannot Detain

On a day of burial there is no perspective—for space itself is annihilated. Your dead friend is still a fragmentary being. The day you bury him is a day of chores and crowds, of hands false or true to be shaken, of the immediate cares of the mourning. The dead friend will not really die until tomorrow, when silence is round you again. Then he will show himself complete, as he was—to tear himself away, as he was, from the substantial you. Only then will you cry out because of him who is leaving and whom you cannot detain.

—Antoine de Saint-Exupéry, 1942

The day after the memorial service, as family left and silence began to replace commotion, Reid started to show

144

himself complete. That is, I felt an immediate need to confront the debilitating question of "What now?" The shock and despair could not last, because if they did, they would take down my family, my job, and who knows what else.

So during the next several weeks, as friends and counselors pointed me toward what I described earlier as "the Grief Books," and as I soon found those books only slightly helpful, I started, initially out of fear and frustration, to reexamine the life I had given Reid and what he had taken from it. I started to make my way into that fog that had enveloped the end of the tether, flashlight in hand, hoping to discover that to which I was now attached—if not a living son, then a relationship that I could tolerate and perhaps embrace.

~

Because grief was the overburden of my new obligations and part of the maze through which I had to find my way, as a first step I needed to understand it. The books on grief that I started reading came close, but none of them captured how I was feeling, so for lack of a definition that fit, I formulated my own: "Grief is the stream of negative emotions that we experience as a result of the disappearance from our life of someone we loved very much; our continuing thought that everything we do now, our loved one cannot and never will do again; and the fears and apprehensions that haunt us as we try to learn to carry on."

That Reid died a teenager undoubtedly shaped my despair. I had tried so hard to mold him into a responsible adult and then lost him before we could enjoy being father and son as grown-ups. The death of a teen hurts primarily, I think, because adulthood, the ultimate goal of parenting, was within reach.

So that Thursday and the days following were filled with isolation and loneliness, an odd feeling when one has spent the past several days in the company of more than a thousand friends. I began to recognize that I was separating myself from others because I was now a bereaved parent, a tiny minority, and a curiosity to my friends and community. I was quickly becoming convinced that few could understand me. As I set up shop to explore Reid's memory, I began to understand the blunt and subtle impacts of grief.

Four words became a regular presence in my head: *He was just here*. I wandered through the house trying to capture Reid's voice, his smell, the space that his lanky frame had occupied, the sound of his sneakers bounding up the stairs to his room. Each time I said those four words to myself, the emphasis was on a different word, reflecting my thought that if I could simply adjust my approach, tune my mental antennae to the right frequency, I might synchronize with his spirit:

He was *just* here.

He was just here.

He *was* just here.

He was just *here*.

He was just here.

He was *just here*!

Reid's specter was tangible, although by now it was not a benign presence. It was nagging, as if he and I were playing some paranormal game of hide and seek.

~

As I wandered the house, Rev. Grandy called—could he come by with some news? He did not let on what it was or why it should be delivered in person, but I trust his judgment about such things and invited him to stop in.

He had two things to tell us. The first was that "the first person at the accident scene was Jeff Giddings." I recognized the name as that of a member of our church. Peter explained that Jeff had been a longtime member of a nearby town's volunteer fire department, so he knew how to handle an accident scene and a burning car. Jeff had not realized at the crash site who Reid was or that his passenger Jessica and her family are also church members. I felt grateful that we now had an eyewitness.

The second piece of news was a lightning bolt from the past.

"A woman came by the church this morning asking where Reid was buried. She said that she was his birth mother." Peter explained that he had had a warm conversation with her and had provided her directions to Fairview Cemetery and a copy of the program from the prior night's service. She had explained that she had learned of Reid's death too late to attend the memorial.

Peter had also received a call from Mike, Reid's birth father. Laura and Mike had long gone their separate ways. Mike's call, however, provided an eerie detail; he had confided to Peter that he himself had had an accident near Exit 34 on I-84 East, many years ago.

I had no idea how to make sense of Laura's appearance. I was glad that she knew but saddened to learn that had she gotten the word earlier, she would have attended on Wednesday night. How had the news reached her, and where? Had we been remiss in leaving this to the adoption agency? How does a birth mother react to the death of a child she placed in the care of adoptive parents seventeen years earlier?

Ellen and I had met with Laura and Mike in November 1989, after Reid had been in our home for several weeks. After an affirming conversation, our parting words were, "We will see you again, sometime, somewhere." And now the prophecy had come true, albeit under circumstances beyond anyone's contemplation so many years earlier.

Ellen and I asked Peter what we should do now. He told us that Laura had not asked to be in direct touch with us right away but wanted us to know that she knew, and that we would reconnect when the time was right. This was, frankly, a relief. Having learned about the memorial service and found her way to Reid's grave, Laura would give us time to sort out other emotions. We were grateful for her graciousness, even as we knew that she was grieving in a unique way.

That next Sunday, I went to church. At the coffee table after the service, I ran into Jeff Giddings. I was sure we had met before. I did, however, need to confirm that I had the right person. After a moment of silence, I thanked him. Then I stumbled through the question I most wanted to ask, which was, "What happened?"

His explanation was brief. He sensed that I only needed the briefest of recaps. He confirmed that when he had arrived moments after the crash, Jessica was out of the car, crying, trying to reach her parents on her cellphone. The passenger's side of the car had caught fire, so Jeff and others had to approach the car from the upwind driver's side. Reid had been thrown on top of Rachel. With help, Jeff had pulled Reid out through the driver's-side window, and then Rachel.

"Did he suffer?" I asked, in a way that I am sure reinforced that I only needed to hear the basics.

"He was gone," Jeff said.

Good, I thought.

Jeff also confirmed that the accident had occurred at Exit 34, not Exit 33, as someone had told me a few days earlier. The two exits are only about two hundred yards apart, but Exit 33 is a left exit at the end of a long, straight section of highway, while 34 is a sharp, awkward right-side exit at the end of a sweeping turn to the east. It made much more sense that Reid's car had hit the guardrail at 34.

With this verification, a few days later, ten days after the crash, I resolved to visit the scene. By the time I got there, I felt as though I was too late. The Connecticut Department of Transportation had already replaced the guardrail. The exit now sported gleaming new steel; the girders, bolts, nuts, and welds looked as if shrink wrap had just been removed.

I pulled onto the shoulder, got out, and simply stared, tried to imagine, to replay the sequence, to figure out the geometry. I suppose I was practicing again my new habit of trying to make contact with something that wasn't there.

At the bottom of the incline that forms the left side of the exit ramp, twenty feet farther down the highway, just about where I imagined the ambulance had set up, was a single sneaker. A size 11½ D green-and-black high-top basketball shoe. Reid's. It was filthy and wet. I put it in the trunk of my car. When I got home, I put it in a plastic bag and stored the bag on a shelf in our garage—all the while wondering exactly why I was doing this.

A few days later, Christmas now approaching, Mike Borea arrived to say hello. I showed him the sneaker. "Yeah, that's Reid's," he said confidently.

Ellen, who admittedly had paid more attention to Reid's wardrobe and closet than I had, disagreed. "That is not Reid's," she said emphatically. She did not want a moldering sneaker in the garage, and since I had no coherent explanation for keeping it, I got rid of it on the next trash day.

Why did I pick it up? Why did I think about keeping it? Explorer in the fog, desperate for clues, I suppose.

My expedition then took a new turn, two Tuesdays after the accident. Around 9:30 p.m., I was turning out lights before heading upstairs to join Ellen and Martha, who had gone to get ready for bed. It was the night of another day of carrying emotional weight. Then the doorbell rang.

Standing outside beneath our bright porch light was a well-dressed man. His head was clean-shaven. He was well over six feet, with shoulders so broad and a torso so obviously muscular that his frame filled the window screen of our kitchen door.

I was at first embarrassed to be dressed only in a T-shirt and sweatpants for what looked like it was going to be a serious discussion about something. Then my mind began to race about what this gentleman could possibly want. Possibilities sprang to mind: a detective? An investigator? A salesman? An opportunist? A friend or acquaintance of Reid's?

As I approached and opened the door, his size again gave me pause.

"Yes, sir, can I help you?"

"Mr. Hollister?" he said.

"Yes…?" I replied, as if unsure of my own name.

"My name is Robert Jones."

His voice trailed off; he was obviously trying to compose himself.

"I've been trying to find you for a few days. . . . I pulled your son out of the car."

My breathing became labored, and his eyes welled up. While I tried to calm myself, he continued: "I've been having a really hard time these past few days. I haven't been able to sleep. I tried to find out where you live. I've been thinking about how young those kids were. . . ." His voice trailed off again.

"Please come in," I said.

Robert Jones explained that he was from Massachusetts, and on the accident night had been driving along the long stretch of 84 East between Southington and Plainville when he was passed by a Volvo "going really fast, maybe around one hundred."

I swallowed so hard that my throat hurt.

"I asked another guy at the scene if he had seen them going so fast and he said he had seen them as far back as Waterbury. When they passed me, I was worried right away. Then the car got airborne, and rolled over, and then it hit."

Into my head crept defensive parent thoughts: one hundred? He couldn't have been going that fast. Airborne? Rollover? Not my kid. People often misjudge speeds. I tried to avoid the fact that I was dealing with an eyewitness.

Then my need to know took over. I asked for more, "but please give it to me in small doses," I said.

Mr. Jones said that when he had pulled over to the right side of the Interstate, Jessica was out of the car, screaming, crying, fumbling with her cellphone. The car was on fire. He acknowledged that another man had stopped and approached the car with him, from the downwind side, so that the fire was blowing toward them. I assumed that the other man was Jeff Giddings.

My guest explained that they ran to the upwind side of the car, saw Reid in the front passenger seat on top of Rachel, pushed out the remaining glass. He was scared that the gas tank was going to explode but the other man, a retired fireman, assured him that the fire would stay as it was, and so they pulled Reid out, and then Rachel.

Traffic behind them had stopped. An ambulance pulled in, along with police. Mr. Jones complained to me that the state troopers had not asked for his name or for a description of what he had witnessed.

Again distraught, this large, powerfully built man pleaded with me, almost child-like: "They were so young! Why were they going so fast? Why?"

I explained that as best I knew, they had gotten lost on their joyride, trying to get back onto I-84 East in Plainville, and the girls had needed to bc home by 10:30.

"Could I have a picture of your son?"

I hesitated as any parent would with a stranger, but in the few minutes that we had talked, I realized more and more deeply that, like it or not, he was part of my bridge to Reid's last moments.

Momentarily, I had a suspicious thought: Jeff Giddings had said that he was first on the scene and he had pulled the kids out. Did I now have two competing claims? I dismissed the idea. They had gotten there at the same time. They had both helped. Bravery has many fathers.

"Are you a religious man?" I asked this thinking that a prayer might do both of us good at that moment.

"No, not really," he said, putting that idea to rest.

I went into the dining room, where all of the cards, letters, photos, and other tributes and memorabilia were piled, and found one of Reid's school photos. I handed it to him.

Unsolicited, he said, "I still haven't washed my shirt that has your son's blood on it."

Too much information. He seemed to want to retract his words, but we moved on.

"I'm deeply grateful for what you did, sir," I said. "I'm glad that it was a person like you who was there. . . . " My voice trailed off.

I took his address and phone number, not exactly sure why. A warm and extended handshake, a pat on his back that required me to reach up, and he walked out the kitchen door, through an overly bright porch light, into the warm December night.

I stood in the kitchen, stunned and exhausted, not sure what to think.

~

Mr. Jones's visit turned out to be the start of a series of things, large and small, that buffeted us as December and the holidays rolled forward.

On December 14, Reid received a letter from the chief executive officer of the Hospital of Central Connecticut at New Britain General, asking for his evaluation and feedback on his stay on the evening of December 1. "Our mission is to ensure that our patient experiences and our clinical services are so exceptional that patients will always prefer to use us when they need health care. To accomplish this, we need your feedback."

I know they were well-meaning, but is it too much to ask that a hospital take a moment to consider whether to send a patient-satisfaction survey to a seventeen-year-old who had arrived at the hospital unconscious and in cardiac arrest, and had stayed only twenty minutes before being transferred to another hospital to be treated by its trauma unit?

My pique reflected an attitude that was rapidly developing and shaping my outlook as defender of Reid's memory: intolerance. Life had punished my son, my family, and me. So much had happened that should not have. My patience for those who would add misery to my obligations, especially through inadvertence or neglect, was dwindling.

This mind-set began to color my reactions to just about everything. Thankfully, there were moments that reminded me to not let despair rule all the time.

Christmas approached; how in the name of Heaven were we going to get through it?

I could sense that our neighborhood was actively wondering how the Hollister family would fare on December 25. From a few "What can we do?" conversations with several people surrounding us, I pieced together a plan. I told Martha but kept it secret from Ellen.

At 9:30 on Christmas morning, forty of our neighbors descended on our home—in their pajamas—with breakfast. Ellen, Martha, and I went from contemplating hours of awful silence to a parade of welcomes, hugs, and tears. And, oh yes, pastries, muffins, omelets, bagels, melon, pineapple, strawberries, raspberries, bacon, cider, and pie. Our loving neighborhood upgraded the morning from unbearable to slightly tolerable. There is a saying that "Love is what is in the room on

Christmas morning when all of the gifts have been unwrapped,
and we just listen." That morning, presence, not presents,
conveyed the holiday spirit of giving in a way I had never
before experienced.

Four days later, however, reality returned. Just as I had
concluded that I needed to see Reid's body at the morgue
even when I didn't want to, I decided that I had to inspect the
wreckage of his car.

The photos shown on the television newscasts on the night
of December 2, reprinted in the *Courant* the next day, had
displayed a burned-out shell. Over the course of several days,
I confirmed the car's current location, at an auto-body shop in
Plainville, three towns west of ours, the town in which Reid had
crashed on the interstate. The shop owner, the state police, and
Liberty Mutual Insurance agreed that I could inspect the car and
remove the license plate.

I also had another parent job to do, which was to look
for Reid's wallet. Ellen and I had canvassed the police, the
ambulance company, and the emergency rooms at New Britain
General and Hartford Hospital, all to no avail. We assumed it
had been in the pocket of the long, baggy shorts that he had
been wearing on that warm night. An inch-by-inch search of his
room had turned up nothing, so perhaps the car would furnish
the wallet, a charred remnant, or a clue.

By then, more than three weeks after the accident, I
was beginning to see that I was going to be able to survive
physically, day to day; I was not going to suffer an ulcer or
be involuntarily committed to an asylum. I was still in shock,
but I was starting to see that I might be able to manage things.
Of course, I had no choice but to do so; with a return to work

looming the following week, I needed to steady myself. And
I was still a husband and the father of a fourteen-year-old
daughter.

Still, the idea of actually seeing the car made me recoil.

Ultimately, since I had a reason to go—if Reid's wallet or
anything else was inside, I did not want to risk the car's being
towed somewhere else or scavenged by some stranger—the
answer to my angst was that my neighbor Steve Quish would
drive me.

So on the morning of December 29, the two of us went to
Plainville Motorcars. During the fifteen-minute ride, including
exiting Interstate 84 just on the east side of the highway from
the crash site, we made small talk while my mind raced and
I readied myself by remembering that I was doing a father's
bidding.

The shop owner was appropriately businesslike; he did
not offer condolences, and merely acknowledged that he knew
who we were and why we had come and led us down a well-lit
hallway and into a rear storage room.

Because I had seen the news photo, I was prepared to see a
mere cinder. What I saw was Reid's car, plainly recognizable as a
navy-blue Volvo, with severe damage to the driver's side, a jagged
hole where the sunroof had been, and inside, shattered glass
and charred, twisted metal in tiny pieces—thousands of them.
Granules, almost sand particles. No big pieces of twisted metal.

It was immediately clear, as Robert Jones and Jeff Giddings
had said, that the fire had been on the passenger side. The
passenger-side seats were gone, and only the seat frame
remained. The glove compartment was not visible. The biggest

burn appeared to be there, the front passenger seat. There was no sign of any airbags or seat belts, not even the harnesses or clips. The rear license plate was crumpled and muddy but intact and in place.

But the defining characteristic of the car was that the driver's-side door was pushed in about three feet into the car's interior. The crushed metal formed a V, whose inset point was about halfway between the driver's and the passenger's seat.

At that moment, I understood all too well why Reid's death certificate referred to "blunt force thoraco-abdominal trauma with splenic laceration and intra-abdominal hemorrhage trauma." He had hit the guardrail at the midpoint of the driver's-side door, and it had bludgeoned his left side.

The steel reinforcement in the door, for which Volvo is known ("the best tank made in Sweden," they say), was visible, and perhaps the reason that the inversion in the door had not gone farther right and injured Rachel.

Within a few minutes, two other things became evident, one of which will fade from memory, the other of which will stay with me forever. First, we were not going to find his wallet. If it was in the car or in his pants, it had been incinerated in the fire or it was now part of those little shards of glass and metal granules that covered the lower interior of the car. I didn't have any gloves with me, but in any event I was not about to climb in and begin sifting.

The other reality—although Steve and I did not talk about it then or after, perhaps because it was so painful and so obvious—is that Reid was incredibly, maddeningly, stunningly . . . unlucky.

From the location of the V in the door, it was as clear as
the December day outside that if the impact had been *eighteen
inches* forward or backward, Reid might well have been injured
from whiplash or the fire or suffered a concussion, but he would
not have received the midsection blow that killed him. When his
car began to skid, he could have ended up sliding toward any
one of about 270 potential degrees, but the driver's-side door
had hit the guardrail *exactly* at the one worst degree.

When this thought had finally sunk in, I said to Steve that I
was ending the search for his wallet. I suspect that Steve knew
what I was really saying. We retraced our steps through the hall
and the repair areas. I turned to Steve, buried my head in his
shoulder, and began to sob.

~

If grief following a death like Reid's has a conventional
wisdom, it is that the phase of shock and disbelief lasts about six
weeks, after which the feelings change. They did.

Some of my change was force-fed. My wonderful co-
workers covered for me during the month of December, and
many businesses slow down and clients can be less demanding
around the holidays. Certainly, my own clients were very
understanding. Yet as January approached, I had to go back to
work. I considered that doing so might be therapeutic; work can
be a palliative, and if I have any reputation among my peers and
clients, it is for hard work. In any event, I needed to change the
scenery. I had to cut down on wandering into Reid's room to
open his closet, staring at his clothes, and thumbing through his
baseball cards.

My shock was wearing off and reality was setting in. Unfortunately, this did not result in greater clarity of thought or an ability to put distractions out of my mind. I think of the following three months, January through March, as my period of mind games, a time of clumsy steps if not awkward lurches into this new realm of fatherhood.

Before Reid died, my life was busy and full in a good way. Work was consuming and parenting took lots of time, but we had a busy social life with our neighbors, and my extended family was a regular presence in our house. Then Reid's death and its aftershocks laid waste to my daily routines, the cadences of our family and social life, my sleep patterns, my daily attendance to my children's needs, everything. Time slowed, nothing social or personal mattered as much as it had before, and there was less to do. My life became host to what I came to think of as air pockets, empty spaces that discomfiting and sometimes horrible thoughts rushed to fill.

We were tossed and turned. Burnishing Reid's memory morphed into not only defining how he would be remembered, but also tamping down aspects of his life that reared their ugly heads, reminding us of things we wanted to forget.

Throughout December and January and into early February, we received emails from college admissions offices, addressed to Reid, reminding him of the upcoming application deadlines and listing the unparalleled opportunities that awaited him at each campus. Some of the messages were from schools to which Reid had already directed his SAT scores, but perhaps a dozen more were from schools that had purchased his email address from the College Board.

I composed a response that I could cut and paste: "To the
_____ Admissions Office: Please be advised that our son,
Reid Hollister, passed away unexpectedly on December 2, 2006.
Please remove his name from your distribution list. Thank you.
Tim Hollister, father."

Most schools we never heard from again, but a few
continued to send the same email. I will spare them
identification, except to say that each was a relatively small
school from which one would expect better.

We received one message of condolence, from Father
Andújar of Providence College. (Father, thank you.)

~

The inexorable mechanics of death, the steps necessary to
wind up Reid's affairs, continued. On a frigid winter morning,
I waited with about ten other souls outside the Department of
Motor Vehicles, to turn in the license plate of Reid's car. It was
challenging. At a time when I was striving for connections to
Reid's last moments, I was about to discard a significant one. I
was carrying an artifact of Reid's crash, one that signified the
twisting and sliding that took his life. I was unprepared for my
hesitation. How could I give this up?

The office opened, and I laid the grocery bag on the counter
next to the form I had signed, parted the top of the bag, reached
in, and pulled out the plate. The young woman helping me was
taken aback by the dirt and the bent edges. She pinched the
cleanest corner, swung her arm over a box behind her desk, and
clanked in the plate. She did not ask how the plate had gotten
that way, and I was content to be done with this rotten task.

On January 5, our cellphone bill covering late November and early December arrived—a precise digital record of my son's final days, hours, and minutes, courtesy of Verizon.

The entries for the days preceding the crash were about what I expected. Reid had been home trying to manage his anger and distress, leaning on his friends, keeping later nights than would have been the case if he had been in school. In the hours following his Citizenship Committee hearing there was a flurry of calls, I assume him telling friends the outcome. As always, there were lots of text messages. He was in regular contact with his current girlfriend, Lauren; with his sister; and with a few I could not identify.

The bill reflected my final phone call with Reid, when he had called my cellphone at 12:24 on Friday afternoon to check in, as I had asked him to do. Obviously at the time it was a routine father-son call, one that I did not know would be our last and thus did not mentally record. I have since desperately tried to remember our words, to no avail.

The cellphone bill reflects that we talked for five minutes. A call at 9:00 p.m., to Mike Borea, signaled the start of the events leading to the crash. This call was followed by that 9:25 p.m. text message to me, letting me know that he was headed to Mike's house.

Reid left the house around 9:30 p.m. At 10:15 p.m., Lauren called him. She shared with us later that Reid said he was in Cheshire, two towns west of Plainville, and was "headed home."

The bill showed that he was not using his cellphone or texting at the time of the crash. That 10:15 p.m. call from Lauren was Reid's last phone conversation. I struggled to imagine 10:16 to 10:28, what had happened, what Reid had been thinking and doing. The Verizon bill, in a way, placed me inside the car at a time close to the crash but provided no clues as to why his car started to spin. By the time I called his cellphone at 10:40 p.m., he was gone.

~

Parental curiosity took me in several other directions.

Interstate 84 connects Hartford to Waterbury and then to the west, Danbury, and to the south, Fairfield County. These are the areas of Connecticut where most of my clients live and work. Thus, when I went back to work, not only would I be unable to avoid that area, but I was going to have to follow the path to Reid's crash regularly.

When I returned to work in early January, I had to attend a meeting in Cheshire, for which I-84 offers the shortest and most logical return to downtown Hartford. I found myself on that long stretch of 84 eastbound, heading toward that sweeping turn to the right that begins at Exit 33 and passes Exit 34 when the curve has nearly ended.

Compartmentalizing—driving as though this were just another day at the office—might have been possible, but I did not even try. In fact, I did my best to implant myself in Reid's car on that December night with the road slightly wet, trying to re-create what he saw, to imagine where, when, and how he had picked up the speed that killed him. I tried to reinvent the sharp turn, the skid, whatever had rammed the car into the guardrail.

I realized quickly that what I wanted to do was impossible. That section of I-84 is heavily traveled almost around the clock, and it was now midday on a weekday. I had no more than a blink in which to consider where his spin may have started.

I was unable to re-create or imagine much of anything, to understand the mechanics or the physics of Reid's crash.

That brief drive-by, however, did precipitate more speculation and disbelief. I simply could not comprehend the relationship between the geometry of that curve and the crash itself. As I replayed the sequence in my mind, I was confounded by the fact that excessive speed along the long stretch prior to that curve to the right would have made it nearly impossible for a car to hit the guardrail at Exit 34, which is on the far right side of the highway. In other words, I was baffled by how his car could have swerved so far to the right; the car's momentum should have carried it well *left* of and past the right-side exit.

The explanation that made the most sense to me was that along the long I-84 East straightaway that leads to Exit 33, Reid got up a head of steam. He was over the speed limit, but how much is unclear. As he approached the turn to the right, he went too far into the curve, jerked the wheel hard right, went into a skid, lost control, perhaps a 360-degree whip, but enough of a slingshot force to carry the car across the highway, toward the end of the guardrail next to the exit ramp. And then the very bad luck of the exact point of impact being the middle of the driver's side door.

~

Also through those winter months, Ellen and I began to diverge with regard to what Joan Didion has called magical thinking. For my wife, every car door opening and closing outside, every ring of the phone, signaled Reid's return. He was back! It had all been a bad dream, a mere delusion. I, on the other hand, never experienced this stage. I was not confronting apparitions; I was just depressed.

Ellen's state was, if less realistic than mine, probably more comforting to her. She had moments of hope, upticks, while my emotional electrocardiogram was flat and low. Ellen and I were aware of our respective mind-sets because we talked about it, but the recognition didn't make anything easier for us or between us.

Many nights in those weeks I arrived home from work to find my wife, sometimes in the company of a neighbor or two, ensconced in one of the large armchairs in our den, the lights dimmed, soft music playing. On the small table next to Ellen's chair was a box of Kleenex and a burning candle. In her hands, in her lap, or clenched to her body, a framed photo of Reid, and on her cheeks tears, a steady or intermittent stream. I would put my briefcase down, pour myself a glass of wine, sit beside her, and do my best to empathize without disturbing her reverie.

Many nights during that time, neighbors or friends brought us dinner, and so it became part of our evening routine to welcome that evening's chefs, to delight in what they had lovingly prepared, to engage in a few minutes of conversation, and then to eat. Each evening thus featured a built-in reminder of those who were thinking about us.

Arriving home, comforting my wife, checking in with my daughter, and receiving our dinners were the easier parts of each evening. The worst part by far was getting into bed and reaching up to turn out the light.

Perhaps everyone, not just parents, runs through a mental checklist just before trying to sleep: doors locked, oven off, teeth brushed, clothes ready, alarm set. Parents have one more:

kids home, safe and accounted for. This habit, thoroughly ingrained from seventeen years of parenthood, did not abate for Ellen or me and indeed could not, because we had Martha's well-being to consider.

So every evening, lights-out time caused our mental radar to project into our children's bedrooms, and each time the signal came back: ERROR! ERROR! ONE ROOM EMPTY! The message was flashing in red, and mentally I heard one of those awful buzzer sounds. Every time, this distress signal renewed our disbelief and brought tears that postponed sleep, no matter how exhausted we were.

A few times in those months Ellen articulated a frightening vision of Reid, one that was so upsetting to both of us that it took every bit of mental discipline I could summon to get it out of my mind and salvage part of the night's rest. Ellen recalled, quite accurately, Reid's fears. Beneath that cool visage he was scared of so many things: of going away to college, of performing in public, of being on his own. So when Ellen asked, "What if he's here, but just on the other side of a window, crying for us, apologizing for his accident and begging to come back?" I could not say that her conjuring did not reflect who Reid was or how he might have reacted had he known in some way on December 1 that that would be his last day alive. All I could say to Ellen, sometimes with little conviction or persuasiveness, was that our faith had taught us that he was in Heaven with God and the angels, with no pain and only peace.

Our visits to the cemetery, every other day during that nearly snowless winter, brought another battle of mental images. On the winter's coldest and rainiest days, I could not banish the image of Reid's body freezing and decaying, the papers and

mementos we had buried with him disintegrating. Rainwater
seeping around his casket, now enveloped in mud. I fought
to keep in my consciousness the image of my son as cozy,
peaceful, quiet, dry, and warm in his satin bed, below the frost
line and thus comforted by the earth's radiant heat and insulated
from the chill above. I envisioned every memento intact,
surrounding him, accessible to him at all times.

Sometimes I prevailed, but sometimes I didn't.

By late January, when a warm December finally gave way
to frigid days, adding cold to our misery felt like Mother Nature
piling on. Somewhere mid-month, suddenly I realized that
Ellen, Martha, and I had a small window to escape the freeze, to
spend a few days in a warmer place than Connecticut.

In March 2004 and 2005, we had taken a winter family
vacation in Nassau, the Bahamas, at the Atlantis resort. We had
launched our handsome son into a sea of bikini-clad girls. Hard
as it may be to believe, he loved it, so much so that when we
decided to go somewhere else in March 2006, Reid protested,
threatening to stay home unless he could return to the Atlantis.
It was an odd scene: Ellen and I sentencing him to a few days in
the Dominican Republic instead of the Bahamas. Eventually, he
relented and ended up having a passable time—amid yet another
sea of girls.

But this time when the school hiatus presented the
opportunity for a few days in the sun, could we actually *go*
somewhere and enjoy ourselves? Could we really leave Reid in
the frozen ground of Fairview Cemetery while we sat in the sun
in our bathing suits? The idea of leaving, much less leaving to
enjoy ourselves, seemed incomprehensibly selfish. In moments
of what approached appalling rationalization, we told ourselves

that Reid would want us to go; Atlantis was one of his favorite places; we deserved a short break, and a warm one; and given the school calendar and my work obligations over the coming months, this would be our only chance until summer.

Martha did not want to go; Ellen was conflicted. I advocated going, not because I had no illusions about how painful it would be but because I concluded, selfishly, that having experienced three weeks back at work, I needed time away to assess how I was going to deal with work and grief simultaneously in the weeks and months ahead.

So in reality, Ellen and Martha accommodated me, making it clear that this was neither their idea nor their wish.

In retrospect, we were each right and each wrong. The moment our plane lifted off the runway at Bradley International Airport, I was overcome with dread that this trip was a huge mistake. Without even speaking I could tell that Ellen was on the verge of tears as we left Connecticut, West Hartford, and Fairview Cemetery below and behind. There was also a sensation that we were three, no longer four, and that this was wrong.

We arrived at the resort and the dread multiplied. We could only envision our son in a bright-flowered, baggy, extra-long bathing suit, butt crack just visible enough to drive us crazy, cruising the environs of the swimming pools, drawing glances from girls, and collecting friends everywhere he went. We would pass a teenager in the hall and wince. Martha was miserable and lonely, and Ellen was despondent. My efforts to present the brighter side were derided, properly so, as transparently insincere.

Things were so sad that when the weather forecast (mostly to partly cloudy, occasional showers, temperatures in the seventies) turned into cloudless sunshine and eighty-plus degrees for each of the three days, it seemed like God was mocking us—making us more comfortable in our poolside chairs in order to emphasize our self-indulgence.

Still, over the course of three days, we took a few walks together on the beach. We enjoyed two stir-fry dinners, Martha's favorite. I had and took time to think about how to handle work. (Conclusion: Delegate everything possible to others, minimize evenings out, get lots of sleep, keep up with exercise, and talk-talk-talk.)

On our last day, we carried out a beautiful suggestion that our friend Mary Way had made before we left: We took a large plastic bag and filled it with sand from the Atlantis beach—sand to pour onto Reid's grave, to connect that ground to one of the happiest times in his life.

As we filled the bag, Ellen started to cry, but had to choke it down so as not to attract curiosity about why someone on a beautiful beach in the Caribbean on a gorgeous day could possibly be in tears. I said to Ellen and Martha, "We're doing a lot of things I never imagined."

We know another couple in West Hartford who lost a son in a car crash at age seventeen. The wife and mother told me that several months after their loss, she and her husband and their other son took a trip to the Grand Canyon. "We became a family of three," she said.

On our venture to the Atlantis, we did not become a family of three. We merely added to our understanding of our loss. Certainly the fact that we were less than two months from

Reid's death played a role in the constant, debilitating presence of these feelings of loss, and the absence of any sense of justification for our trip or realignment of our family.

Was the trip an outright mistake? On the day we returned to Connecticut, I would have said yes. But we had gotten a taste of three-person reality, even if we had recoiled from it. And we had our bag of sand to further sanctify Reid's grave and infuse it with a family memory.

~

Consecration of Reid's life continued in ways large and small, expected and unexpected, through those winter months.

In my twenty-five years as a member of the Asylum Hill Congregational Church, I have participated in and admired its rituals and traditions. One is the Annual Meeting, held in late February, when the church takes stock of the year just ended. One component of this annual event is the reading of the Necrology, the list of church members who have passed away during the preceding year.

Sometime in early February, it dawned on me that for the 142nd straight year there would be an Annual Meeting of the Asylum Hill Congregational Church and the Necrology would be read, and this time Reid Samuel Hollister's name would be on it. I discussed with Ellen whether we should or even could attend. Ellen, who as a member of the church staff had overseen the preparation of the Annual Report, which includes the Necrology, decided that attending would be too painful; and in helping to prepare the report and the list, she had paid her homage.

I decided to attend, to be present to hear Reid's name called. I knew that I was walking headlong into a gut-wrenching event, but having the vice moderator read his name with no family attending didn't seem right either.

The list was even harder to bear when I reviewed the names. I knew most of them and, roughly speaking, Reid was the youngest by fifty years.

As the meeting began, I made strategic use of the architecture of our church. From left to right facing the altar, the sanctuary contains three aisles. Just inside the right and left aisles, Gothic-style stone columns every four pews leave one seat set off from the rest. I parked myself in the isolated seat, three rows back on the right, where I could see the vice moderator but could, if need be, bawl without disturbing anyone else.

Listening to the start of the call of the names was a strange experience: Tim, you are going to cry in approximately ninety seconds. Forty. Fifteen. Several names before Reid's, my breath became short, my shoulders began to heave. I tried to keep quiet, if only out of respect for the reading of the other names. The reader's voice cracked—her son had been a friend of Reid's—and she still had fifteen or so names to go.

As I tried to choke down my noise, one member slipped in behind me and wrapped his arms around my neck. Another pushed himself into my pew—the one that is only supposed to fit one person—and took my hand while I laid my head on his shoulder.

I guess I made quite a scene. At the end of the meeting, I was surrounded. Several others were crying. Hands patted my back and shoulders. Jeanne Grandy, the wife of our associate minister, summed it up by saying, "Every day, Tim. Every day."

~

Anguish continued to propel me forward. Day by day I learned new dimensions of my new and ongoing role as Reid's father, and how to comport if not comfort myself. Meanwhile, I began to learn more about the boy to whom I had been tethered.

For most of seventeen years, my focus on school and my insistence on effort had put me in regular conflict with Reid's limitations and fears. Suddenly, with Reid gone, his education mattered to me only as a past misgiving, and not at all to anyone else. Now front and center, alone in the spotlight, were his personality and his character. I felt somewhat embarrassed that I had been so myopic, so fearful that if he did not study and perform—especially on some par with his peers at school— he would be consigned to an unfulfilling life. I consoled myself by recalling that I had told Reid regularly that what mattered was effort, not grades, but I did not entirely believe that, and Reid had known it.

But beginning on December 2 and continuing for months, praise and stories reprogrammed Ellen and me to appreciate Reid the person rather than bemoan Reid the student. One could say that we received his final report card, not on his academic ability, but on his character. What was said about Reid stunned us with its fervor, its consistency, and its details.

The testimonials to Reid's character, conveyed in handwritten and online messages, were not tepid adjectives— "He was kind/good/caring/funny"—but compelling eyewitness accounts of unusual kindness, empathy, and caring. There were appraisals of his gift for working with young children:

~   If he was ever late to church, all the kids would start asking, "Where's Reid?"

~   He was the kindest and most gentle of shepherds. When a child would become a bit disruptive or cry at the prospect of being left in a room full of strangers, Reid would stoop down and gently embrace the child—speaking in a very soothing tone until the child was calmer. The children loved him, flocked to him, and hung on him like he was the Pied Piper.

~   Yesterday, as I walked my six-year-old daughter Anna up the steps to church, she proclaimed, "I *love* this church!" It was a happy moment for me, because I had not found a community of faith where I felt I belonged until much later in life, and because Anna is shy, and embracing Spirit Hill was a leap of faith for her. Reid was the true shepherd Anna needed to feel safe and loved as she began that journey.

~   Our first graders didn't just respect him—they loved him. Whenever a child was too nervous to leave their parents, Reid could talk them into joining the circle. One time, a kindergartener in a pirate hat came in glued to his mom's leg, and Reid kneeled down to talk to him. The little boy spent the next twenty minutes singing with Reid, and next week he made a beeline for Reid the second he saw him. Reid would always compliment him on his hat.

Other comments illustrated his empathy and energy:

~   I'd like to share a memory about my daughter, one of Reid's classmates. A few years ago, a diabetic

came to school to speak to the students. Part of his
talk was to explain what it was like to face every
day with a chronic illness. After the assembly
concluded, my daughter [a diabetic] felt a hand
on her shoulder. It was Reid, who said, "I never
knew what you go through every day, I'm sorry."
She came home from school and shared that story.
Reid's words were so supportive and kind.

~   I rarely give people hugs, but one time this fall
everyone was meeting in the parking lot and Reid
was there. Upon greeting everyone, he embraced
each person in one of his famous hugs. When he
turned to me, I smiled awkwardly, wondering if I
was going to be next. I had little time to wonder,
however, because Reid looked at me, grinned,
raised his eyebrows, and gave me a big hug. Even
though I thought I would never admit it, I secretly
like hugs.

~   Do you remember . . . his pink collared shirt,
his blue eyes, his warm enthusiastic hugs, his
fascination with squirrels, his two fingers tapping
his cheek . . . waiting for a kiss, his red Velcro
shoes, the overwhelming excitement he had for
just about everything he did, whether it be 3rds
basketball, bowling, soccer, singing, lacrosse, or
making other people happy.

Others described an effervescent personality:

~   Reid lived in the moment, always convincing me
that whatever I thought I had to do, whatever was
stressing me out, could wait just a minute or two.
He knew how to relax and just smile a smile that, no
matter how upset you might have felt, would make
your face light up just like his. He was the kind of
person you should find yourself lucky to meet in
your lifetime.

~ Reid was incredibly open-minded and accepting.
  He has so many friends because he had an innate
  inclination to be kind to everyone.

~ You knew there was something magnetic about his
  personality, but you just couldn't put your finger
  on it. Perhaps it was just a combination of his
  unbelievable sense of humor, his passion for life,
  and his care for others.

~ It was amazing that even on the darkest of days he'd
  always put a smile on your face.

~ He's the only person I've ever known who was
  constantly surprising himself and others with
  everything he did. He lived at the absolute end of
  his tether, and I never saw him do anything that
  wouldn't make a good story. He was a character in
  his own life.

Finally, the director of the summer sports camp that Reid
loved so much, the man who gave Reid his first job and became
a mentor and fan, posted this on the Molloy Funeral Home's
online guestbook:

Over the last decade, and with great distinction,
Reid Hollister participated as a camper and as a highly
respected member of our summer camp staff.

In the days since Reid's passing, I have received
innumerable calls from parents, staffers, and others who
shared their poignant memories of this remarkable boy.
Their messages of support and affection confirm what
all of us who had the privilege of working with Reid
knew—he was a very special young man who had an
extraordinary ability to connect with children.

These many messages, along with my personal
knowledge and great fondness of Reid, make it clear
to me that his keen wit, his remarkable ability to
make friends, and his many acts of good deeds were
felt by enough people that Reid Hollister will never
be forgotten by all of us who were privileged to have
known him.

This remarkable boy.

These messages, which arrived daily during those first three
months, traced the outline of three phenomena, three shapes that
were becoming visible through the haze, and the bases on which
I could construct a durable relationship with my son.

First, in retrospect, I had been frozen in my decision-making
about Reid's life in general and his education in particular by
conflicting evidence, emotions, and hopes. Intelligence tests
and psychological evaluations had documented his ability to
succeed in school and pointed to the ways he could overcome
his learning challenges, but in retrospect, long after it was
evident that he was failing his school and vice versa, I allowed
the pull of his social rootedness, the aphorism that "kids
mature at different times," the advisors' promises to work with
him, and that long series of teacher comments about what a
delightful presence he was in the classroom to constrict my
judgment about whether he was in the right school. Ellen argued
for a change while I hoped that the current situation would
improve. It would not be correct to say that I "won" the debate;
more accurately, intermittent rays of hope and thin hopes for
improvement prevented us from acting on mounting evidence
that in another school, he might have developed a better sense of
self-worth and overcome his fear of failure.

Second, it is well known that teenagers are often disrespectful to their parents, deriving a perverse pleasure from being irksome if not infuriating. They like to get under our skin. It is their way of breaking out of the shackles, real and imagined, that we impose on them. This disrespect, of course, is specially reserved for parents; it is not visited on grandparents, aunts and uncles, neighbors, teachers, coaches, employers, or any of the other innumerable people who help our teens as they make their way toward the adult world. To these others, teenagers are capable of politeness, respect, kindness, and thoughtfulness. It is for this reason that a common experience for parents of teens is to listen with a mix of joy, bemusement, and disbelief to compliments about Joe or Jane and to respond by saying, "Are we talking about the same kid?" They are often better than we realize.

Lastly, if there is a life that demonstrates the importance of expressions of love—what will remain after we are gone—it is my son's. Think about it: Reid and I were at loggerheads for years, and we had a potentially violent confrontation three days before he died, and then *on the evening before the day of his death*, Ellen serendipitously retrieved from a wastebasket a piece of paper on which Reid had written to us, "I love you both." Without that one sheet, that one entry, my emotional journey after Reid's death would have been profoundly different, probably more defined by guilt than pride.

As a student, Reid had many capabilities but was unable to sustain the coping skills and strategies necessary to counter his learning disability. As a result, for most of his years in school he resigned himself to failure and internalized the fear that this generated. He fought his way through an academic environment into which his parents had placed him and for which, in retrospect, he may not have been suited. What I had failed to appreciate, and what emerged as I began to see him complete, was that he was handsome, energetic, funny, polite, friendly, empathetic, and gifted with children.

As this composite came into focus, I began to wrestle with the fact that when Reid was alive I struggled with him so, focused on his education and behavior, while underappreciating who he was as a person. Through the travails of education and behavior and all else, I loved my son with every ounce and fiber of my body and soul, and yet it was the challenges that predominated. In death, for Ellen and me, Reid Samuel Hollister stepped into the light. He showed himself to be better than we knew. My retracing illuminated a depth of character that I had not appreciated and that I could not have predicted when he was alive.

Thus took shape a critical piece of our new, sustainable relationship: my solace as a parent. A discovery that he was better than I thought, and pride in the revelation.

8

Our Electronic Funeral

Caring communities focus lots of attention on bereaved parents. Words came hurtling at us from many directions.

Not so long ago, news of a death and the conveyance of condolences to the bereaved family followed a pattern that had been unchanged for decades: Word spread by telephone, face-to-face conversation, and the mail, and, if the person had achieved some prominence or the death was in some way remarkable, through the news media. Funeral arrangements and the family's wishes appeared in an obituary in a newspaper. Barring exceptional creativity or a disregard of social norms, there were no other options.

Reid's crash and passing coincided with the advent of Facebook and texting. In 2006, both were new technologies. At that stage of my life, I had given not a moment's thought to how our society communicates a death, nor had I ever considered condolence as anything other than one individual's expression to another, in person or by phone, card, or letter. Nor had I pondered the language of condolence. On the few occasions in my life when someone I knew well had suffered an unexpected and devastating loss, I had prided myself on sending a handwritten letter instead of a commercially printed card, and I had tried to personalize the sentiment by avoiding clichés.

Quaint though it may sound today, I was unprepared and then flabbergasted, irritated, and confused when Reid's death intersected with and played out in cyberspace. While personal touches, phone calls, the mail, and the newspaper played their traditional roles in his passing, social-networking sites, online guestbooks, and even Reid's cellphone account with Verizon became a surprisingly integral part of his passing, his memory, and then my further insights into his life. In retrospect, I suppose I should have recognized earlier that technology had so altered human communication in recent years that it would have been strange if remembrance of Reid had not been caught in this updraft, but I did not.

That is, during that December and January, I didn't just learn about a new way of communicating, the adaptation of the Internet and social media to grieving, but I witnessed and lived it. Ultimately I realized that this was coincidence, but initially I felt as if my son was being shanghaied by geeks and dragged into a forum that was public, beyond my control as a parent, and at odds with those decisions through which Ellen, Martha, and I had sought to guard Reid's reputation. My perspective evolved. What I now call Reid's "electronic funeral" was an unexpected but ultimately valuable source of information, another front in my paternal campaign to monitor what was said about him in death and to counter inaccuracy or disrespect. The Internet turned out to be the realm I could least control, but I came to terms with it.

It may be that the way Reid's death played out in electronic messages less fits the term "journey" than the other happenings I have described here, because this part of my fatherhood occurred entirely with me sitting at home, transfixed, my only physical activity being to focus my eyes on the screen, click the mouse, and alternately nod in agreement and shake my head in disbelief over what I was reading. In the weeks after Reid's death I went there regularly, seeking comfort while confronting a new social phenomenon on which I had to reflect before I could appreciate its promise.

To provide an accurate context for the role of technology in my inquiry into Reid's life and memory at that time, I need to confess that my starting point was (and remains) a relative lack of sophistication regarding electronics, computers, and social media. I would not describe myself as an ignoramus, but there are some, including my wife, daughter, and assistant, who would, with some justification. I have worked hard to use email, online research, Facebook, LinkedIn, and Twitter to manage my life, and I know enough to get by, but advanced techniques remain dangerous undertakings likely to result in a frozen screen, an error message, or a call to my firm's help desk. Thus, the e-life is a phenomenon into which I have been dragged and to which I have adapted with only partial success.

This experience began inauspiciously on Sunday afternoon, the day after Reid's death. Amid a house overflowing with visitors, one of Reid's classmates, whose name I did not know, came up to me in our kitchen and said, "My friend just sent me a text message asking me to tell you that he's sorry for your loss." (Again, the extent of my knowledge of texting was Reid's tutorial three days earlier.) This young man did not tell me his name, nor did he say who had texted him, and that was the end of our conversation.

Then, about ten days after Reid's memorial service, my niece Emily, a 2005 college graduate and thus a pioneering Facebook user, told me that "there's this amazing group on Facebook about Reid." This sounded interesting but I had little concept of it. My expectations were low, but with the house now quiet and the enormity of our loss beginning to sink in, I was desperate for anything that might reveal a new dimension of Reid's life or even his crash.

Emily needed to advise me how to log onto Facebook and to navigate, but her direction led me in mid-December to what were three groups. Unfortunately, my first Facebook foray was the wall of a group entitled "What Happened?" It contained sixty-four posts that began just before noon on Saturday the second, when Reid had been declared dead for not even nine hours, and ended four days later, December 5.

Below are some of the posts, exactly as I read them in mid-December. I have substituted letters for names; my purpose is not to chastise or upbraid. The spelling and punctuation, or lack thereof, are as posted.

The first post, by A. at 11:53 Saturday morning, was from a student who I assume was the group's originator:

what exactly happened to him? does anybody know. . .i know the basic stuff but yah...

Here is *some* of what followed:

B., Dec. 2, 2006 at 3:17 p.m.

> I was driving home from my girlfriend's house on the
> highway and before I went under the tunnel I saw that
> traffic was all backed up, and I thought it was really
> weird that there was a major traffic accident at 11:30 at
> night. I saw an ambulance rush through all the cars but
> I didn't think much of it, but this morning I found out it
> was him.

A. at 6:51 p.m.

> omg that awful..yah I knew it was a car accident and
> there were two other girls.. are they okay??

C. at 7:21 p.m.

> I was told that he was speeding on the high way.. and it
> was druing that storm last night. and the two girls that
> were with him were fine. But i guess he wasn't as lucky.

D. at 7:25 p.m.

> the two girls are both in the hospital in serious
> condition...I know that one has a conclusion and a
> broken collar bone and the other has a concusion

C. at 7:29 p.m.

> oh wow. That was such a bad accident

> :(

C. at 7:32 p.m.

why would she get charged for manslauter if it was an accident?

C. at 7:34 p.m.

oh oh never mind I was thinking that meant murder..but it dosnt.

B. at 7:55 p.m.

At that time of night, the roads were surprisingly dry even though there was a huge storm. It cleared up a lot by 11:00pm on the highway.

F. at 7:55 p.m.

Their names haven't been released, but we know that they were both freshmen.

G. at 8.03 p.m.

hold up, one of the girls was driving? on the highway?

H. at 8:04 p.m.

noo reid was driving

G. at 8:08 p.m.

reidy wasn't driving, one of the girls was and now theyre both hurt too but they are alive as of now, but the driver might get charged for manslaughter

I. at 8:12 p.m.

yeah why would 2 freshman girls drive, they arent retarded especially if it was on a highway

J. at 8:13 p.m.

thank you. Was reid speeding?

K. at 8:15 p.m.

he was going 80+ on a sharp turn lost car and hit the guard rail in the plainville area....the two girls in the car were froshs and they are in the hospital but will survive...they have nasty injuries

G. at 8:21 p.m.

in response to this,my information is fully based this thread, so if someone posts' no raid wasn't driving, the girl was', I have nothing else to believe, but we shouldn't be arguing over such, minute details if you may

I. at 8:23 p.m.

I don't want rumors going around,

L. at 9:32 p.m.

after the car crashed someone pulled them out of the car, which is what saved those two girls lives

M., Dec. 3, 2006 at 6:31 a.m.

so he wasn't driving drunk

N. at 6:43 a.m.

No, he wasn't

M. at 6:56 a.m.

yeah good. that's what i thought but people told me otherwise

I. at 7:01 a.m.

then they don't know shit

K. at 12:28 a.m.

no alcohol and/or drugs were involved...he juts lost control of the corner on a sharp corner in the wet conditions and crashed!

K. at 12:29 p.m.

the news paper and new website had 2 diff storys about different times and all that....soo don't rely on those articles

O. at 1:36 a.m.

thank you D. for setting pople straight in here, im sick of the rumors going around about it.

B. at 5:36 p.m.

[the school] feels like shit

P. at 6:17 p.m.

how did reid die? mainly from the impact?

L. at 6:49 p.m.

yes. have you seen the picture of the car?

Q. at 8:10 p.m.

[the school is] not gonna brush this under the rug and pretend he didn't matter because he got kicked out

R., Dec. 4, 2006 at 1:30 p.m.

he did not die inthe car. he was rushed to new britain hospital, then transferred to hartford hospital where he died on the operating table due to severe head trauma

O. at 2:23 p.m.

he actually was pronounced dead on the scene but they revived him, then he went to the hospital

S. at 3:11 p.m.

Reid died on the operating table at like 3 AM yesterday morning or something.

I then discovered, to my horror, a post from Martha, demonstrating that she had been monitoring all of this. To her credit, she stepped in with a firm and touching response. Perhaps because she was a teenager and herself a regular participant on Facebook, she did not scold these online speculators; her post—albeit with a few inaccuracies of her own—was to the point:

> The accident was because of the weather. Reid was speeding a little, but not too much because there were other people in the car. He was knocked out almost immediately, so he didn't feel anything. He died before 3 in the morning, because that is when I got to the

hospital. It was painless for him, and the doctors said he didn't notice anything. He sustained no external injuries except for a burn on his hand. There was internal bleeding that stopped his lungs, and even if the doctors could have stopped it, there was too much trauma on this body. I'm just glad that I got to spend Friday night with him.

I was proud of my daughter for trying to put a stop to this ghoulish speculation. But some remained undaunted:

U. at 5:47 p.m.

i cant say for sure if its all true

. . . he lost control of the car (wasnt drunk or on drugs) and hit a guard rail and bounced back into the road the car caught on fire, those in the car behind them were able to pull [the girls] out but reid was stuck, they had to wait for the ambulence to come to get him out

30-60 minutes after the accident he was declared brain dead he needed to get his spleen taken out and had internal bleeding at 3 in the morning he was declared dead

V. at 6:32 p.m.

that doesn't at all sound like what really happened tho... like he didnt have barin trauma... he had internal bleeding and fluids stopping his lungs... nothing to do w/ his spleen...

W. at 10:31 p.m.

im pretty sure martha knows what happned, dont listen to the rumors of all that was going on...its disrespectful, for the most part their completly fabricated.

Then Martha intervened again:

> Thanks, W. Reid was never declared brain dead, he
> went into a coma right away, his brain shut down after
> he died. Rachel didn't sprain or break her ankle, just
> her shoulder. Jessica and Rachel are fine, I saw them
> yesterday. The rumors about drugs or alcohol are untrue.
> The car hit the guard rail, it did catch fire, but it didn't
> move much after it hit the rail.

O. at 2:45 p.m.

> by the way martha im so sorry about all this, i don't
> know what i would have done if i lost Rachel. your
> family is in my prayers, stay strong.

X. at 4:36 p.m.

> I agree martha knows the truth.
>
> . . . don't start any rumors.

E. at 5:37 p.m.

> I think we neeed to seriously stop arguing about what
> happened to reid, its so selfish theres no rumors going
> around, just talk about the good times or wat you liked
> about reid, honestly this isn't a place for fighting and
> bitching im sick of it.

And that was the last post for this group.

This was my first, unfortunate exposure to a social-
networking site, and when I read these entries I was—no other
way to say it—furious. The speculation was disrespectful and
the fact that it was public made it unbearable. I felt as though
Reid's image had been spray-painted.

What somewhat ameliorated my initial reaction was the second Facebook group, also formed on that Saturday morning: "Reid Hollister, Rest In Peace." The originator was one of Reid's classmates. By the time I saw this group and its messages, there were nearly seven hundred fifty members, more than four hundred posts, and almost one hundred photos.

To my relief, I quickly saw that this group and its posts were qualitatively different from the "What Happened?" group. This site did not make me angry as the first had, but neither am I prepared to say that I found its content uniformly comforting or appropriate. It was clear, as soon as I began scrolling, that these were messages conveying grief, recalling memories, plumbing the dimensions of what a community of friends had lost. But it also became clear that these entries were *not* messages of condolence to Ellen, Martha, or me, and this was difficult to understand. In my grief, I had put myself and my family at the center of the universe, and I now expected that if anyone was going to express his or her sorrow it would be directed to the three of us. Firmly implanted in my mind was the traditional diagram of how grief is communicated in our society, with the arrow pointing from the community to the family, but what I was reading on Facebook was a bright new line that connected teens to each other with laptops.

In retrospect, of course, I was wrong in evaluating and judging. Wrong in considering my family and myself as having exclusive rights to receive expressions of sympathy, and wrong to expect that a mode of communication by then as familiar to teens as breathing would be anything but their chosen way to grieve. Thus, in reading Reid's wall, seeking to learn more about my son and comfort for myself, I was looking in the wrong place for the wrong thing.

Here is a sampling of the entries from the Rest In Peace group. Each entry is complete and exact. In the first dozen entries—again, posted not even a day after Reid's death—"Rest in Peace" and "RIP" predominated:

> You will definitely be missed

> RIP . . . we will miss you at camp!

> RIP dude

Brevity, of course, is the soul of wit, but it is not the soul or the heart of condolence. Thus, these entries, which gave the appearance of being tossed off in class or while engaged in some other activity, struck me as less than thoughtful:

> Duffy [elementary school] memories along with the fun block parties and everything else we did, it was a fucken blast

> Today was rough

> rock da heavens!!!

> good luck coping hollisters

> Reid bit me once when we were babies

> sux it had to end like that

> this whole thing was just a huge reality check and its sucks

I saw a stop sign with part of the P missing, and thought of you.

Anyway, when you commin back? I'm tired of this whole, "Reid isn't here" game. I'm gonna have to take that up with you when I finally find you.

Some described the calling hours or the memorial service:

Reid it was so hard to go to your wake tonight but I'm almost positive that you were up in heaven laughing ur head off at all the silly people standing in the freezing cold weather because they love you so much!

If you could only see the number of people that you touched. The funeral was amazing and lifted everyone's spirit.

that was really, really nice. and really, really sad.

We know it was you who broke our pew during tom's speech. very funny.

Predictably, I suppose, there were sweet nothings from girls:

I can't wait to meet up with you in heaven.....first day i'm there we have a date alright.

You always had the best entrances and I miss sitting next to you in Stats and you trying to hold my hand

hey hun, just wanted to let you know you know i brought you some flowers today. They didn't have any more pink roses that i usually bring you. We will play again some day aright?

Some messages starkly illustrated friends addressing themselves
only to Reid, such as:

> I have like a million memories of us and all of them
> are of us laughing. ALL. Remember when we did CPR
> training and you were like omG, you're gonna kill
> that baby and you were laughing at me for putting that
> mouth guard wrong, and then when you pretended to be
> kissing that dummy while training and I was on the floor
> from laughing. And then the whole ADD pill which is
> like so illegal to write about but I'm sure you remember.
> And you making fun of me like all the time or telling
> me some crazy story of you getting arrested or almost
> getting arrested. Crazy Reid. I know you're probably
> looking down on us and thinking, haha, those loosers
> they're still down there while you're up on cloud nine.

From our neighbor, Steve Quish:

> Im gonna miss waking up in the morning and seeing
> you outside on your roof bending over and mooning the
> entire neighborhood which was absolutely hilarious cuz
> the little kids told on us. You were such a good friend
> that you even took the blame for when *I* broke the
> neighbors window hitting golf balls in the front yard.

Reid's classmates posted reports from school, some of them
bordering on the belief that he would be coming back soon:

> We spent the whole time singing off key just for haha's.
> When I sing, I sing for you.

> we had our physics exam and you wouldve roasted it
> because it had a lot of dropped object problems..and you
> were gangster at those.

> Since you left . . . school's been a drag

Reid, I missed you in marine bio and stats class today. .
. so did everyone else.

Our entire class misses you (including killer). [Killer
was a tropical fish in the marine-biology classroom's
aquarium.]

It's hard to be sad for long periods of time because we
all remember a story about you and end up laughing
hysterically.

I still really want to call you and expect you to sneak up
behind me and scare me or just wrap your arms around
me. . . your wonderful self wont beable to continue
to spread that laughter down here, but i'm more than
certain you're doing it up there.

There were thank-you's and characterizations of his impact on
others:

thanks reid . . . for always dissapating those awk
moments. . .

martha spoke so highly of you all the time and made
you sound like such a great brother.

the effect that you have had is everlasting

You know you really did a pretty great job at leaving
you're mark on everyone I mean pretty much everything
reminds me of you.

Martha monitored the wall and stepped in:

I want to thank everyone for their support. You were
what made his life great.

And later:

Reid was a great brother and friend. I want to thank
everyone who stood in line for 2 hours in the freezing
cold to say goodbye to him. 932 lines in the guest book
were used. [She counted!] That's over 1,000 people
because many people doubled up.

Almost every message was addressed directly and
intimately to Reid, as though he were still ensconced in his
bedroom, typing away in a dozen simultaneous conversations,
the only light emanating from his laptop screen. Contrary, again,
to any initial expectation, almost none of the messages were
directed to Ellen or me, nor were they, on their face at least,
intended for Reid's classmates and peers. There were no "Hey,
everyone" missives or announcements, just teens conversing
in what had become the ordinary way of instant messages and
texting. Those posting on the wall preserved Reid by uploading
intensely personal communiqués to a place where eight hundred
others could see them.

~

The Facebook memorial continued into 2007. Posts referred
to Reid as if he were still alive or had died last week. Friends
reported their lives to Reid in a matter-of-fact tone, as if they
were chillin' with Reid outside a movie theater.
On Valentine's Day:

~   i went to the dance this saturday and i didn't get in
    trouble for my dancing with you this time haha...
    guess it really was just how you and i danced...oh well
    haha...it felt weird tho because this was the first dance
    that i didn't get to dance with you at, plus i remember

freshman year valentines day dance haha that was an
interesting night and so was this upcoming week

~   happy valentines dayy. make sure you're holding down
    the fort. i'm sure your celebrating up there.

Predictably, the continuing messages that year were
clustered around events and anniversaries—his class's
graduation in May, Reid's eighteenth birthday in July,
and another flurry at the one-year "anniversary" (what an
inappropriate word—is there a better one?) of his crash:

~   I think about you every time i pass by the funeral home,
    on my way too and leaving from school. fuck, its late.
    I'm gonna hit the sack, but uh, don't forget us man
    because we haven't forgotten about you.

~   i'm certain that you are having the best time where you
    are because you always knew how to make everything
    the greatest time no matter where you were or what you
    were doing.

~   hope your lighting up heaven just as much as you lit up
    the world and everyone u knew in it.

~   Also, I miss you soo much, tonight was one of those
    nights you know when we use to go driving haha god i
    wish we could do that right now!!

~   you being done is still pretty damn hard.

The December 1 and 2 messages, about two dozen, began
in words or substance with "I can't believe it's been a year,"
but some said the year had flown by while others called it the
longest year of their lives.

On New Year's Day, six friends wished Reid a happy 2008.

As months passed, I began to realize the context of what I had read: Reid's online funeral was one of the first. Reid's death occurred in December 2006, and that calendar year is verifiably when Facebook came into its own among teenagers. Someone had invented the technology, and Reid died while users were first developing protocols for discussing tragic, fatal accidents. Reid's death was one of the first in which hundreds of teenagers coalesced online to mourn one of their own. That is, my first angry reaction to the "What Happened" group in time was tempered by the realization that that group's participants were drawn to a new technology with which they had become comfortable, and their mistake was in not considering who might be not just reading their speculation but indeed hanging, while in emotional shock, on every word.

~

If the Facebook groups and walls were emblematic of a new technology of grief, then the online guestbooks (another new phrase) of the Molloy Funeral Home and the *Courant* were the adaptation of an existing technology to convenience. The guestbooks were nothing more or less than an email address to which mourners could send Ellen, Martha, and me messages, and that is indeed what happened: The Molloy site began December 3, the day Reid's obituary appeared in the newspaper with directions to send online messages, and ended in mid-January. The *Courant*'s spanned six weeks.

Parents empathized:

~   I have a son the exact same age and cannot imagine the depth of your grief.

~   My husband and I have 17-year-old twins so the sting is especially acute.

~   I know how much your children mean to you—you've always shared so much about your family with me that without having ever met them, I feel as if I knew of their special light in the world.

We found additional evidence that as a teenager, Reid made a memorable first impression on those he met:

~   I only knew Reid for a few minutes but when I heard the unfortunate news, I was extremely saddened and felt a great loss.

~   Reid had the special quality of being able to connect, if only for a moment, with those whose paths crossed his.

I heard from friends and colleagues who spoke to me directly, in an effort to boost my battered sense of self-worth:

~   The tragic death of Reid has touched not only your immediate family and friends, but has reached out to draw the prayers of your nationwide circle of friends.

~   Tim, I have seen you accomplish the impossible many, many times before. You will persevere and you all will continue to be loved by many.

~   Take comfort knowing that you raised quite an amazing young man.

This message, if from a teenager, might have been regarded as ordinary, but it was written by a man in his sixties: "Save me a place Reid. I'll see you when I get there."

Our electronic funeral had two other components. Through the end of 2007, we paid to preserve Reid's cellphone number and his voice mailbox. Ellen and Martha liked being able to call and hear Reid's voice. I called a few times myself. We discovered that several kids were continuing to leave messages, sometimes "just to say good night."

During the weeks following the crash, my cyber-inspections took one other strange turn that illustrates one more dimension of living on in cyberspace. As I periodically checked the online guestbooks of the *Courant* and the Molloy Funeral Home, I ran a search of Reid's name on Google. For the first several tries, the Google search brought up only Reid's obituary and our church's website, which listed him among its Sunday-school teachers. Then in late January, a link appeared to an art gallery. I thought at first that this was a mistake. But I clicked the link, and there it was: "Reid Samuel Hollister," a portrait of my son. The artist's last name was an uncommon one, and I recalled it from Reid's Facebook site.

Before tracking down the artist, I sat glued to the computer screen, staring at the bold strokes and colors that had been used to re-create Reid's face. I am barely conversant in the language of art, much less the finer points of painting, so I am not able to describe a style except to say that it was an oil painting that accurately captured the shape of his face, his coloring, and most of all, his eyes.

I wrote down the phone number and called the next day to inquire. Without my having to explain why I was interested, the gentleman who answered politely offered to have the artist call me. He also said that the price was $2,500. Because I surmised some personal connection between the artist and one of Reid's friends, I suspended judgment.

A few days later, the artist left me a voice message, in part as follows:

Hi Tim. I painted the picture of your son Reid, and the gallery contacted me. I just want to say, Tim, I hope that picture didn't upset you. I did it as a gift for my niece. Anyway, there is a whole story behind it as your son trickled through many people's lives, as you can see, and I didn't even know him, but I loved painting it. It was really a pleasure, and I painted it before Christmas, after December 2. I know all the dates. I know a lot about your son. It was important to my niece because she really cared for him. She was upset, and I wanted to do something special. I just want to tell you that you had a beautiful son, and I learned a lot about him. It was a pleasure to paint him. Thank you.

I called her back. She further explained that she had done the painting as a gift, that there really was no price tag or intention to sell it. She reiterated that Reid's passing "had been felt far and wide." She asked if I was upset or concerned, and I replied that when I had first seen the link on the Internet I had not known what to think, but now having seen the work and heard her explanation, I was grateful that Reid had been honored, albeit in an unusual way. I was satisfied that her motive was compassion.

I thanked her. Not in a bad way, I shook my head in disbelief. I never did understand why the painting had been on the Internet, but now Reid's friend had it as a gift, and I did not need to know more.

~

I am not certain that seeing the online assemblies who mourned Reid as emblematic of technological adaptation made me feel better about what happened, but it did make me realize that I was probably being too harsh on the teens who were the figurative pallbearers of this cyber-funeral. I see now that they were feeling their way with a new technology whose best practices had not yet become apparent.

The model in my head in December 2006, of news conveyed by phone and email, obituary in the newspaper, and condolence in person or in a card or letter, was outdated then and is even more so now. How we communicate a death and support the bereaved is contemporaneous with how we communicate as a society. For the last two to three years of his life, Reid lived online, and so it was inevitable and unstoppable—and therefore fitting—that his friends grieved and preserved his memory in precisely the same way.

But the use of Facebook to express sympathy ultimately left me, if not cold, lukewarm and puzzled, and that feeling persists today. The bereaved work through emotional devastation; dealing with grief is hard work. Facebook on the other hand is easy, a few strokes on a keyboard. Perhaps too easy. I saw few posts on Reid's wall that suggested contemplation. In fact, many entries evinced a quick message sent while multitasking.

Facebook originally was supposed to be online theater, a medium whose original currency was mostly fake, entertaining personal information. If we extend this analogy, then social media's adaptation to grief constituted its transformation from comedy to tragedy and fantasy to reality. These changes altered not only the lines spoken but also who constituted the audience. Had those who sent messages in 2006 stopped to think that "the Hollisters are going to read this," as well as who knew who else, many entries would have been stated differently and perhaps not posted at all. As parents, Ellen and I were logging in out of desperation; once our visitors went home and the mail slowed to a trickle and the house became deathly quiet, those posts were all we had. Yet we were invisible to the network.

As noted, many impossibly short entries were posted, such as "RIP" or "sucks." Those brief posts, three-second efforts, conveyed a lack of caring. "RIP" and nothing else suggested a person who was either doing something else while purporting to be concerned about Reid's demise, or sending out one short message after another while doing so, or both. Sympathy should not connote haste. (There is a way to test this. Take the shortest messages posted on Reid's wall—"RIP" continues to serve as a good example—and envision it as the full text of a handwritten letter to the deceased's family. Would anyone send *a card* that said only "RIP"? Hopefully not.)

Electronic communication speeds up life. For those in grief, not only does life slow down, but we want it to stop in its tracks. We want to turn the clock back to when our loved one was alive, or linger indefinitely in the present, with our memories as fresh, detailed, and vibrant as possible. Movement is painful. Forward progress is agonizing, because it forces us to leave things—memories—behind. People in grief read more slowly, think more slowly, and act more slowly than they did before. Thus, "RIP" and "So sorry" and "That sucks" and "Good luck" did not console anywhere near as much as a few sentences that conveyed time spent contemplating the loss and empathizing.

When I first read those posts on those dark December and January nights, I wanted to hover over each word, to digest what the message was telling me about Reid. But it was difficult to linger long over "RIP." I was, I suppose, grateful for the attention and the ease of communication, but perplexed by the disconnect of expressing sympathy by hitting "Send," and worried about the next online gatherings arising from a tragedy. Online messages were hurled at my family, and it took considerable time to separate the gratefully received messages from how they were delivered.

9

Memory Posts

*"Strengthen me by sympathizing with my strength,
not my weakness."*

—A. Bronson Alcott, *Table Talk*, 1877

The doctors declared Reid dead in the early hours of
Saturday morning. Cards and letters began to arrive by hand
delivery on Sunday and by mail on Tuesday, first a handful,
then a bigger pile on Wednesday. Thursday afternoon Mike the
mailman arrived with one of those U.S. Mail crates that requires
two hands. It was filled with about two hundred envelopes.

I stared at Mike in disbelief, and he seemed to acknowledge
that this was beyond his experience as a letter carrier.

"Thanks," I mumbled.

"It's nice to see that you have so much support," he replied.

From that day and in the months following, fairly or not, reading condolences became a kind of accelerated, unintended peer review of my parenting of Reid, of what I had done well, what I had lost, and what in the past seventeen years I should revisit. Every communication, if not consciously directing my new role as custodian of Reid's memory, highlighted some aspect of my life with him and thus provided more material for my reflections about his legacy. In a few weeks, hundreds expressed why they were sad that I was not still Reid's father. As it developed, the experience added to the framework by which I reconnected myself to Reid.

~

Many of the cards and letters were a response to seventeen years of holiday-season letters that Ellen and I had sent to several hundred friends. Over time, many had paid us the highest compliment—that our letters were "refrigerator material." For example, in 2004, we capitalized on our region's euphoria over championships achieved by the Boston Red Sox and the University of Connecticut basketball teams. Tongue firmly planted in cheek, on paper adorned with a border of gingerbread houses and candy canes, we wrote:

(The Hollister Family Dinner Table, late November 2004)

Tim: I have an idea for our year-end letter, and I'd like your comments.

Ellen: . . .

Reid: . . .

Martha: . . .

Tim.	I thought I would write an essay reflecting on how the Red Sox winning the World Series, along with the UConn men's and women's basketball teams winning national championships, have caused people all across Connecticut to believe again in the goodness of mankind, to appreciate the resilience of the human spirit, and to have hope that there are better days ahead . . .
Ellen:	. . .
Reid:	. . .
Martha:	. . .
Tim:	Okay, if you don't like that, then I need your suggestions about what to put in our letter.
Reid:	Why do we even have to do a dumb Christmas letter? They're so stupid.
Tim:	This will be our 17th annual letter. It's how we tell people what is going on in our lives, and how we send them our best wishes for the holidays and the New Year. And we enjoy getting other families' letters.
Reid:	Who . . . cares . . . !!!???
Tim:	Excuse me, the subject on the table is not WHETHER we are sending a letter, but WHAT is going to be IN IT.
Ellen:	Well, we should mention the kids' activities.
Tim:	Correct. Martha, this year, you sang in the chorus, did field hockey and swimming, played softball, and went to Jen Rizzotti's basketball camp.
Martha:	Yes, Daddy.
Tim:	And you made the Hon—

Ellen: No bragging.

Tim: Okay, okay.

Reid: Can I leave?

Tim: We're not done yet. Reid, you are now 15 years old . . .

Reid: And a prisoner in a psychotic family . . .

Tim: . . . and you played soccer, basketball, and lacrosse, you worked with four-year olds in the church's day care center, and you were in that excellent a cappella singing group, what was it called?

Reid: I can't believe this.

Martha: "Spartan 7," and Reid was one of only two freshmen, and they sang a drinking song.

Reid: I'm out of here.

Tim: Sit down!! . . . Ell, I'd like to put in that you're in your 19th year at Asylum Hill Congregational, and you're overseeing construction of a new addition to the church.

Ellen: We need to mention our trip out west in June.

Tim: Right. We started in Las Vegas and then visited six national parks—Zion, Bryce, Capitol Reef, Arches, Grand Teton, and Yellowstone; and we went white water rafting and horseback riding.

Martha: And to rock-climbing school, where we finished the day with a 70-foot rappel over a cliff. In Grand Teton, we saw a moose, a marmot, a herd of bison, and a mule deer, but no bears.

Tim: And Reid, remember during the trip when I was giving you hints that Father's Day was coming up, and I said, "Next Sunday is F Day," and you said, "I'm getting my report card?"

Reid: Can I go now?

Tim: Why are you so anxious to leave the table?

Reid: My game is paused.

Tim: Have you finished your homework?

Reid: I'll do it later! Now will you leave me alone?

Martha: Daddy, what about your getting a 3 on the par 5 fourth hole at the Tobacco Road Golf Club in North Carolina in October, your first eagle after playing for 38 years? What about that?

Tim: No, sweetie, we'll leave that out. But thanks for bringing it up.

Reid: I am DONE with this dinner and this family and this _____ letter!!!

Tim: Watch your language.

Ellen: Reid, you need to learn to be more respect— !!!!!

Reid: *@&%$#&@*#!!!!!!

Gracie: Woooooooofff!!!!!!

Martha: May I clear your plate, Daddy?

Happy holidays to all!

Similarly, as 2005 came to a close, our letter again became our way to smooth over the bumps in our day-to-day life. Mirroring the fact that a growing source of angst was the SATs and college applications, the Reid part of our letter that year said:

Mathematical Application

Reid is the third party beneficiary of a contract for cellular phone service between his father and a company called Verizon. If the monthly service charge for Reid's

phone is $19.99, he has unlimited text messaging,
but his hours are restricted and he must pay $.99 for
downloads, and has 32 downloads, but is able to reduce
this cost through rollover minutes from a prior month,
and 18 percent of this cost is covered by his monthly
allowance, but the allowance was withheld because he
forgot to take out the garbage twice, how much does he
owe his parents at the end of a typical month?

> A. $34.92
> B. Nothing because he talks his way out of it
> C. We couldn't figure it out either.

Thus, our holiday letters, 1987 to 2005, undoubtedly
contributed to the huge counter-flow of December 2006. In an
unquantifiable yet undeniable way, the letters and messages
we received after Reid died were a response to how we had
annually shared the triumphs and travails of bringing up our
kids.

~

In *Letters From the Earth*, Mark Twain observed: "Where
a blood relation sobs, an intimate friend should choke up, a
distance acquaintance should sigh, and a stranger should merely
fumble sympathetically with his handkerchief." How and what
one says to the bereaved, especially a parent, depends in part on
one's relationship to the person who died and his or her family.
Degrees of separation need to be considered. Fair or not, as
the condolences swelled from a trickle to a stream to a flood,
I started to notice, among other things, some who fumbled
with their handkerchiefs when perhaps they should have been
choking up.

After my multifaceted first encounter with Facebook, I ultimately blessed electronic messaging for the speed and convenience that it provides when one wishes to be in contact quickly with a family in tragedy. However, the emails we got laid bare another consideration: I received a condolence email, and nothing else, from a neighbor, someone I saw regularly mowing his lawn, raking leaves, and shoveling snow; I have no doubt that his sympathy was sincere, but it struck me that because he was so physically close, his disembodied email created emotional distance—cyberspace—where it need not have existed. If Twain were alive today, perhaps he would restyle his quote, "Where a relation sobs in our living room, a neighbor should visit, an acquaintance should send a card, and a stranger may send an email." The email from my immediate neighbor arrived with a thud.

Then there were the dozens of messages that said, in so many words, "We can't imagine what you are going through." I took these as neutral, a straightforward acknowledgement that our loss was so great as to defy efforts to select comforting words. Some boiled down this dilemma to its essence, saying only: "There are no words." Jess Decourcy Hinds once counseled her readers in *Newsweek*: "Never say 'I can't imagine what you're going through.' To me this translates as 'This is too hard for me, I don't want to think about it.'" I saw her point.

My view of one other category changed over time. Two people whom I had known for a long time and considered to be more than passing acquaintances, closer to good friends, said nothing after Reid died. I did not ask them about this or confront them. I asked myself if I had done something to so offend them as to be unworthy of a condolence. It may have been that they

were unable to figure out what to say, and then when weeks
and months passed, it became more embarrassing to send a late
condolence, and maybe they hoped that in the tumult I hadn't
noticed and had forgotten. Not so. Perhaps there was something
in their own makeup that made Reid's death unbearable to
confront.

Which leads me to the letters and cards that truly *consoled*
me, both in the sense of making me feel better and helping me
reposition my son, realign that tether, in my new reality.

I came to learn that an almost universal warning for those
expressing condolence is to either avoid or to be extremely
careful in claiming that "I know how you are feeling." Such
words invite a comparison between the writer's loss and the
newly bereaved's, an exercise that has no benefit and the
potential to make things worse. (Yes, I acknowledge having
done so at times.) Those who ventured such a thought succeeded
only if they were factual and made their claim obliquely:

~   My own brother died when he was 24 and I was 20.
    The grief was overwhelming and I was only his kid-
    sister. I have watched my parents suffer for years.
    I can only tell you that the passage of many years
    does dull the ache.

~   If you ever need to talk to another parent who lost
    a teenage son in a similar way, I am completely
    available to you—day or night—for as long as you
    need. You have a long journey ahead and you are
    not alone.

~   We share membership in a terrible group, and I
    know only too well your misery. My 24 year old
    son died suddenly three months ago. Many people
    have offered me comfort. I have found helpful the

company of those who are also trying to cope with
the same devastating loss.

As I began in mid-December to reflect upon those blinding
five days from crash to burial and those decisions we had
made, compliments for our choices and arrangements became
cherished affirmations that we had appropriately preserved
Reid's memory:

~ A good friend was in West Hartford last Tuesday
evening. She saw the long line of people around
Molloy and she said the traffic was so backed up
she had to sit through two green lights before she
could get going again. She told me her reaction
was—"this must have been an exceptional person."

~ The Memorial Service cut deep into my soul,
allowing the love and warmth of the community
that has come to know you all and love you all so
deeply to pour in and to cast its glow to warm my
heart. I believe I met Reid last night during this
incredible service. None left unaffected by the
surrounding love.

~ It was truly a "Holy Night" and the angels were
singing. I commend you for arranging such a
beautiful service and yes it was the start of healing
for your broken hearts.

~ As you promised, Tim, Reid had the most special
tribute to his life that could be done. For those of
us who did not know him well, a vivid picture of
a carefree and caring young man was detailed in
everyone's remarks.

~ Tim, your eulogy meant more to me than you will
ever know. I found myself instantly transported to

the same lectern in the same pulpit some 14 years
ago, when I gave a eulogy at my father's memorial
service. While my father didn't die until 1992 when
I was 22, the last time I really remember him in full
health and fully engaged as a father was the summer
of 1986, when I was 16 years old. That summer
we took a father-son trip to the Southwestern U.S.
Our desert rambles took us to Zion for a few days,
where one afternoon we hiked, waded, then swam
in "the Narrows." It is a poignantly fond memory
that I have of time with my Dad, and one of the last.
I have never thought about that meandering river
metaphorically as you did so eloquently tonight,
but I couldn't help but be struck at the parallels of
our father-son moment in that unique place. I also
couldn't help but relate to the agonizing pain of
experiencing a father-son bond broken before its
time.

We received religious messages, beautifully stated:

~ I don't know why, but God seems to test the faith of
   the most faithful; and although you won't know it
   (because you can't know what you would be feeling
   now had you no faith), your faith is what will make
   this terrible loss bearable in the end. I hope you
   believe that God must want Reid with Him, and as
   enraging as that thought must be, after reading all of
   the wonderful qualities Reid held, I can understand
   the strengths God sees. Reid's goodness will be so
   much more vast in the hands of God.

~ I thoroughly believe that God has taken Reid to
   other happiness and understanding and that we are
   the ones who are robbed of knowing his life's work,
   and his wife, and his children and finding out how
   that wonderful friendliness and extroversion and
   gentleness and mischief was going to play out.

~ I feel compelled to share my thinking on the loss
of loved ones—they never leave you, they hear
everything you say and know all of your thoughts—
love is a strong bond—the only absence is physical.
There's a big balcony in heaven and Reid has a
front row seat. He's watching you from above—
probably making some choice comments here and
there.

~

Consolation, then, came less from expressions of sorrow
about our loss, and more from those who strengthened us for the
days we were living and those upcoming. Those who could truly
empathize because they had suffered a similar loss and were
still standing; those who reassured us that amid our free fall,
shock, and despair, we had managed to make correct choices
that would preserve Reid's memory appropriately and for a long
time; and those who recognized that, while faith is individual
and idiosyncratic, it penetrates most when we are figuratively
flat on our backs, struggling to get up. A common denominator
in the words that worked directly on the pain was that they
strengthened my connections to Reid, by showing me that I
could reattach, by commending me for the steps already taken
to do so, and by reminding me that a Higher Power was ready to
help, should I be receptive or needy.

In late December, three weeks after the crash, Ellen, Martha,
and I felt compelled to thank so many who had supported us by
continuing one of our most precious family traditions, our year-
end letter. We composed a piece that was part report, part thank-
you, and part memorial; a combination of news, gratitude, and
the best of snippets from the cards and letters we had received

up to that time. We quoted from the cards and letters that had
propped us up:

~ He was a young man who would give of himself on
Sunday morning instead of sleeping late.

~ My son, Alex, age 7, offered that God must need
Reid for something very important.

~ The Reid Hollister we knew would burst through
our door full of fun and laughter.

~ [My son] Kevin also told me how protective Reid
was of Martha. So often teenagers create distance
from siblings as they figure themselves out. Reid
seems to have been mature in ways other kids
hadn't achieved.

~ He never left our house without saying, "Thanks for
having me"—something most kids don't do.

~ He was a catch.

~ The resulting ripples of Reid's passing are
widespread and immeasurable.

~ He wasn't scared of having a good time or being
just totally ridiculous.

~ Why God takes a young man of character and
promise on the threshold of his most productive
years, who has already shown an affinity for helping
others, we cannot know.

~

The flood of December and January abated, replaced by a
small, steady stream. Letters that came later in the year stood

out not only for what they said but also for when they were sent, for their affirmation that others were still thinking about Reid. This one came in June:

> Every time someone tells a funny memory of
> something that's happened, it's interesting how my
> mind immediately jumps to a story with Reid in it. It's
> still not programmed into me that Reid's no longer
> here with us, but that's probably because I know deep
> down that he really still is here with us. Although we
> no longer get to see his beautiful eyes and charming
> smile, or hear his contagious laughter and inappropriate
> comments, I know he's still there, he's there for all of
> us, helping us make it through the day. Everything we
> say or do somehow brings our minds right back to him,
> but I guess that's how it's supposed to be when you're
> blessed to have someone so wonderful be a part of your
> life. I don't think those people ever really leave.

One July 22, Reid's eighteenth birthday, the mother of one of Reid's best friends, one of his pallbearers, wrote:

> I don't call you because I will not be able to speak
> and that will be of no help to you. I want you to know,
> however, that I think of you, pray for you and appreciate
> my own son a little bit more because of you.

Also in July, I sent a note to Karen Mortenson, the high school guidance counselor who had handled Reid so soothingly in those four days between his expulsion and his crash. In response to a short thank-you email, we received this:

> As for Reid and your comment that I was a bright spot
> for him during a tumultuous time, I must admit I did
> feel then like perhaps I had done some good, which is
> a rare occurrence working in education, at least in the

short term sense. So often, much of what we (those
who work in schools) do or say plays out (or not) in the
long term. We hope that our words and actions have
some positive impact, but it's usually uncertain or the
answer(s) comes at a much later date. As a counselor I
strive to be effective in "quick hits" because that is my
typical interaction with kids. When necessary, I hope
for a cumulative effect. With Reid however, I felt like I
struck some chord and in turn, he resonated with me.

I had no doubt that Reid was going to be successful
finishing the year and beyond, and my confidence came
from my dealings with him and you. Reid was certainly
charming and charismatic, but not disingenuous.
Although the situation wasn't what he would have
chosen if given the opportunity, he was making a
concerted effort to transition academically and socially.

My last meeting with him after we had discussed all
the academic details, we briefly talked about what
had happened and his family. Tim and Ellen, it was
clear to me he knew how hurtful the situation was.
Yet, from the way he talked, the love between you was
just as obvious. It was evident that Reid appreciated
your support and that he was a young man who was
"grounded" in his family.

One letter addressed directly the construct rising in my mind
about my relationship to Reid, before and now, as a tether:

Being a parent is probably the most difficult job in this
world. We do everything we can to protect our children
and to prepare them for the rigors of life, but there is
so much that is beyond our control. Reid was taken
from you during the time in a child's life that is the
most trying for caring parents. From the time they enter
their teens until some time in their mid to late twenties
they simply have to test limits, and they lack the fully-

developed reasoning power to make good decisions
And yet we must give them the freedom to learn things
for themselves that we, in our own time, learned from
experience and have tried to pass on to them. To do
otherwise would be to dampen the emergence of what
makes each of them unique.

~

As alluded to earlier, out of so, so many messages, two
stood apart from the others for their intuitive and beautifully
expressed understanding of Alcott's point that we most console
others by dispensing stories and reminders of love achieved,
compliments about deeds and strengths, and affirmations that
loved ones endure. From one of my colleagues at work, the
mother of four grown children:

> [Hiking the Narrows in Zion National Park] is a
> metaphor for all parenting. As inviting as the Narrows
> are, we know that there is risk in venturing there—of
> an upstream cloudburst, of the flash flood that sweeps
> us off our feet and leaves us gasping for breath. But if
> we never took the tentative steps, risked the slippery
> footing, and got wet, we would never notice the way the
> rays of light slant into the canyon, or know the sound of
> laughter reverberating off the canyon walls.

From the mother of one of Martha's classmates, a few lines
that captured every aspect of our despair and hope as parents:

> As we light our Advent candles, our family prays for
> yours. We ask God to give you:
>
> • Courage – to bear the unbearable
> • Strength – that comes from so many people sharing
>   your grief and pain

- Peace – that comes from knowing that Reid knew he was well-loved and that he lived his short life to the fullest
- Hope – that while there will never be a day you won't miss him, one day you will again smile and laugh and enjoy life as Reid did
- Remembrance – of the joy that was Reid and the special gifts he brought to your family
- Faith – that God will never leave your side; certainly not when you need him most
- Patience – with yourself and each other as you adjust to a different world than the one you knew before
- Comfort – in knowing that families are forever
- Love – because in the end, that's all there is.

The condolence messages we received in 2006 and 2007, including hard copies of the electronic ones, are now packed into two large cardboard boxes that I keep at home in a corner of my study. Sometimes I am comforted simply by the size of the boxes. When I need to count my blessings, they provide a visual aid. At other times, I leaf through them, recognizing that they represent a community's outpouring to parents coping with a broken bond. They are the building blocks on which my ongoing role as Reid's father now stands. I marvel continually at the phenomenon.

~

Though cards, letters, and emails rained down, there were also conversations.

In 2007, I did not see a therapist. Instead, what was most helpful to me was regular, sincere, and extended conversations in which friends and acquaintances would ask, "How are you doing?" and I would not hesitate to answer at length, and they would listen attentively. Many would ask about Ellen and Martha, and I was never reticent or bashful about providing a complete and candid answer. I also do not doubt that I regularly tested the patience of my questioners, providing more of a response than they wanted to hear. But I got my point across, that I was at all times ready, willing, and able to talk about Reid's memory and needed to do so.

Two categories of talks and one particular encounter stand out. The first was dozens of interactions with men who in one way or another avoided the subject of Reid. As a man, I understood what was going on and I knew that it was not insensitivity or lack of caring. These men were trying at all costs to avoid breaking down themselves while talking to me, especially if our conversation was in the presence of others.

A second, smaller batch of conversations became memorable as I wondered about perspective and distance. On several occasions, other parents, aware of who I was and of Reid's death, complained out loud about their own teens or young adults. They lamented laziness, lack of focus, rudeness, ingratitude, poor grades, disrespect, alcohol or drug abuse—the litany of parental angst. And all the while, I longed to be in their shoes.

As face-to-face conversation was at best a mixed blessing, it is odd and slightly funny to say that the most therapeutic talk I had during that first year after the crash was in a bar with a woman I was meeting for the first time. I had to go to Washington again for work, and when I was done, three hours before my flight, I called my law-school classmate and close friend Donna Thiel to see if she had time to say hello, and she suggested a bar near her office. When I arrived, Donna introduced me to her co-worker Celeste, who had been a hospice worker in a prior life. Donna had told her about Reid.

As we settled into our barstools, for some unexplained reason I mumbled something about this being "my first time at a bar" since Reid's accident, and that I "might not be on my game" where the situation called for light, witty banter. After a few minutes, Celeste began to ask me questions. She did not ask for permission to change the subject or apologize for doing so; she just did it.

"How are you doing?" she asked somewhat sternly. I responded by talking mostly about Ellen and Martha and what I was doing to care for them.

This was not a satisfactory answer. "No, how are *you* doing?" Celeste politely but firmly insisted. Was I sleeping? Exercising? Reading? Meditating? Seeing a therapist? Donna listened attentively, but this was now a two-way conversation.

Celeste not only refused to accept self-deprecation, understatement, incompleteness, or avoidance, but she nearly read my mind, discerning not only that I wanted to talk about the accident and the five months just past, but also that she could and should probe deeply.

"Tell me about the accident night," she directed. "What was going through your mind when you were driving to Connecticut?" and I explained the mind games that had occupied me as I sped north along Interstate 95.

"What did Reid look like in the morgue?" by which I took her to mean whether I considered him a soul and spirit at that

moment, or just an empty shell of a body. I talked about his chin
and our conversation about the Very Best Days With Reid letter.

"What do you miss most about Reid?"

"What's your happiest memory as a parent?"

"What's your greatest regret?"

It was a gentle grilling, but Celeste challenged me as no one
before.

I had to leave for the airport, but as I sat in the taxi,
contemplating a late-spring sunset over the Potomac River and
the Lincoln Memorial, I felt as though my soul had received
a tune-up. I was grateful for having been so thoroughly
engaged and for a questioner who refused to take my answers
at face value, lest some emotion or perspective that should be
brought out be allowed to linger beneath the surface of my
consciousness.

More than a year later, I had the chance to talk to Celeste
again, and we shared our recollections of that conversation.
"It just poured out of you," she said. She agreed that she had
brought to her questioning her experiences as a hospice nurse
and as a mother who had lost a baby, born prematurely in a rural
hospital in the United Kingdom. A moment of grace over drinks
in a bar, with a stranger.

~

All in, being on the receiving end of hundreds of condolence
messages was both a tutorial on interpersonal relationships
and the mortar for building a new relationship with Reid. The
messages that complimented Reid, especially by sharing a
recollection or affirming what Ellen and I had done or were

doing to preserve his memory, or otherwise explaining how he will endure, were not only comforting but also the process by which I defined and shaped the memory I would carry, proclaim, and defend thereafter. In those condolence messages I found in full the boy with whom I had had less and less contact, and what I found was not only agreeable but a source of considerable pride.

I learned how to be a better friend to those who have lost, especially a child, but anyone in grief; we need compliments, not reminders. There is no better time to repair a frayed, broken, or dormant relationship or to ripen an acquaintance into a friendship than by reaching out when another has lost a loved one. When a loss calls for sympathy, carefully measure your degree of separation from the deceased and the family and act accordingly. When a loss occurs, make a calendar note of birthdays, anniversaries, any upcoming dates when being in touch again will demonstrate caring and support. And absent a clear signal that someone in grief does not want to talk, engage actively, listen intently, and react supportively.

In those messages and lessons, I found a way to reattach myself to my son—not just his memory but his spirit. He became not a loss but a presence, albeit ephemeral, with which I could have an agreeable and therefore continuing relationship.

~

Given that the most insightful source of empathy for bereaved parents is someone who has experienced a similar loss, Ellen and I should not have been surprised that the most remarkable letter we received was from the mother of a young woman who had taken her own life, in 2002. Her daughter had been a teacher at Reid's school. She reinforced, better than anyone, the idea that we could and should build an enduring connection with Reid, by painting for us an image of her daughter comforting our son upon his arrival in Heaven:

Ellen, now I need to share something that happened . . . .

The night Reid died, about 2:45 or 3:00 a.m., I woke up with a feeling of alertness. Sometimes I feel Kristina's spirit reaching me and this was that kind of feeling. A little wake-up-call by her spirit coming to me. There was no sense of urgency, yet it was a compelling feeling. I decided to get out of bed and go into the family room where I sat by the fireplace. I wrapped myself in the prayer shawl you had knitted for me when Kristina died. As always it both warmed and comforted me. So I sat there in the quiet and heard Kristina's sweet gentle voice in my head, "It's all right, Mom. Everything's fine."

Since I wasn't troubled or disquieted about any problems or thoughts, I didn't understand what she meant. She didn't sound unhappy herself or distressed. It was a peaceful reassurance meant to comfort, but clearly the message was not meant for me. So I went back to bed pondering one of life's little mysteries that I accept and know will take time to figure out.

The next morning we had an early telephone call from Rev. Gary Miller letting us know about the tragedy. Reid in an automobile accident. He has died. Would we help the Hollisters?

Before going to your home, I first wrote a letter to Kristina. Writing letters to her has become my favorite way to ease my mother's heart that grieves deeply for her in the four years since her death.

So I wrote a letter that morning . . . .

> *Dear Kristina,*
>
> *I don't know how these things work in Heaven, but please embrace a new soul who has joined you, Reid Hollister. You may have met him at church or at school, where he was a student. He was in a car accident. It happened so fast. He didn't want to leave here. He is young, possibly afraid. You know how that was. Please help him find his peace and his new place in God's home.*
>
> *Love,*
> *Mom*

10

Hawks, Crosses, Polos, and Angels

The physical spaces that Reid had inhabited were now empty, but they began to exert a magnetic force. I was now a parent who had lost a child, and his haunts—his room, the basement, the couch in the den—became black holes, voids begging to be filled. Another dimension of my search was for symbols and signs of his presence, a connection between the emptiness on earth and Reid's spirit in the heavens.

The first connection arose when Ellen went back to work as administrator of our church. There, Mary Way, a longtime part of the office staff and one of Ellen's closest friends—she had been with Ellen and then me throughout the accident night at Hartford Hospital—took the initiative, asking aloud for Reid to "give me a sign" that he was okay. (Actually, in Mary's authentic Roanoke, Virginia, twang, she said, "Raid, gimme a sahn.")

Reid heard, understood, and responded. I have witnesses, and my witnesses have photos.

Just days after Mary's plea, a visitor came into the church office and asked if the staff was aware of the very large bird that was sitting on the ground just outside the vestibule of the entrance to the parish house. Mary, Rev. Grandy, and Ellen went to investigate. A hawk was just standing there, looking inside the building.

Its left wing was injured, crumpled in contrast to the right wing, which was straight and smooth. (Recall that Reid had been injured on his left side.) Mary said, "It's Reid." She encouraged Ellen to talk to him, which she did. Mary took a picture.

Peter Grandy, who has been at Asylum Hill Church for thirty years, said that he had never seen a bird of that size sit so close, so still, for so long on the church's grounds.

As Mary, Ellen, Peter, and other staff now gathered stared back, the hawk did a very Reid-like thing: It pooped.

This visitor lingered for about ten minutes before slowly flying away.

Fade to the campus of Reid's school, later on that same day. In the middle of the grounds is "the Green," an expanse of grass on which only seniors and those accompanied by them are permitted to walk. One of the highest honors that a senior can bestow on an underclassman is to provide an escort across the green while others take the more circuitous route, the sidewalk.

Just hours after Mary's request had brought a hawk to Asylum Hill Church, Mary's daughter, Maddie, saw a hawk walking across the Green.

At the top of the stairs in our house, on our second-floor landing, we have displayed for years Reid's and Martha's artwork from elementary school. Twelve pictures in all. The drawings and paintings have been there for so long that we barely looked at them—until, sometime in February, Ellen and I noticed that the first drawing at the top of the staircase, drawn by Reid in fifth grade in 1999, is of a hawk.

March 14 was the first day of 2007 that the temperature broke sixty degrees. It was the first beautiful day of the spring. As Ellen and I were getting ready for work, a hawk settled into the oak tree outside our bedroom window.

The earliest of these hawk sightings coincided with one of the most important emblems of Reid's memory, our choice and design of the headstone for his grave. We became clear about what we wanted on the headstone's face: a cross and a hawk; Reid's name in block letters running straight across the slant face; his birth and death dates; and a smooth area for the letters and numbers, with a rough texture surrounding the plate. As with his casket, the headstone needed to suggest an unfinished life, not a polished one. And so we commissioned Reid's permanent marker with a hawk and a cross.

The hawk legend grew. Reid's crash occurred on Interstate 84 eastbound, in Plainville, at Exit 34, just after the highway bends to the right after a straightaway that is almost two miles long. On the right side of that long section of the road is a golf course. I had driven by it many times but never knew its name. Part of the course is less than a mile from where Reid died. In the spring of 2007, the owners posted a new sign, visible from the interstate, with the course's name: Hawk's Landing.

The hawk sightings went on. Our neighbor Scott Schpero, one of Reid's best friends, was playing golf at our town's public course, just two blocks from our street. On the hole closest to our house, Scott hit a miraculous shot that cleared a ravine and a stream by bouncing across a footbridge. He turned to see a hawk standing behind him.

In the spring, one of Reid's friends posted this on the wall of his In Memoriam Facebook page:

> ok reid, supposedly people have been seeing this hawk around and they think its you and thats cool and all but i thought u would choose a much bigger animal like a bear or something. That would be sweet.

In September, Reid signaled me again on a golf course. Scott Rogerson and I stood on the tee of a par five when a hawk began circling directly above our heads. "That's Reid," I said. Scott grinned and patted me on the back. I nailed my drive 240 yards down the center of the fairway.

We did not see a hawk again until...the last week of November, as the first anniversary of Reid's accident approached. Then, on the way home from church on *December 2, 2007*, as we prepared to go to the cemetery for the one-year memorial service, a hawk flew low over our car and took up his perch on the roof of the house at the end of our street.

The coup de grâce happened three months later. In late March 2008, just before the baseball season began, the *Boston Globe* and other newspapers reported that a red-tailed hawk had swooped down over a group of middle school students who were taking a tour of Fenway Park, and grazed a thirteen-year-old girl from Connecticut named Alexa Rodriguez. For the

uninitiated, this was newsworthy not only because of the attack,
but also because Red Sox fans hate the New York Yankees, and
at that time, a Yankees' star player was Alex Rodriguez.

Attending many Opening Days, I had never seen a hawk
at Fenway. But on Opening Day 2008, April 8, just after the
Red Sox raised their 2007 World Championship banner on the
flagpole in center field, a red-tailed hawk, presumably the same
one that had swooped down on Alexa, took a lazy tour above the
stands and eventually flew less than twenty feet over my head.
He was so close I could see the markings on his feathers. I have
a picture.

"Hi, Reid," I said. I was wearing Reid's Red Sox cap, by the
way. Two days later, Jeff Goldberg of the *Courant* reported this:

BOSTON – Just days after Alexa Rodriguez, 13, of
Bristol got buzzed by a red-tailed hawk at Fenway Park,
the hawk was spotted several times swooping over
Fenway during the home opener Tuesday, as its legend
grows.

Turns out, there are actually two red-tailed hawks that
make Fenway home, one male, one female. The guys in
the control room at Fenway have named them Layla and
Sharpie. It was not confirmed which of the two attacked
Alexa last Thursday.

If these hawk sightings were really Reid or his spirit visiting
us on a schedule, then the next hawk sighting would occur in
November 2008, as we approached two years from the accident.
During the last ten days of the month, a red-tailed hawk—who
I think had taken up residence in the cemetery—swooped low
over my car as I was driving away from Reid's grave. A few

days later, Ellen and Martha watched a hawk walk across the
lawn in our backyard.

~

Since a hawk is a powerful symbol but not something one
keeps as a pet, other memorials became vital—anything through
which Reid's spirit might be preserved.

A neighbor conceived the idea of the women and girls in the
neighborhood wearing silver crosses in Reid's memory. Nothing
gaudy or ornate, just a cross an inch and a half on the vertical
and half as much on the horizontal. This gesture connected our
neighborhood.

I was not to be outdone by the crosses. I started my own
hunt through jewelry stores for a pendant, necklace, or bracelet
charm that would preserve the angel theme that I had presented
in the eulogy. My second stop was a downtown Hartford store.
I asked the lady behind the counter if she had something that
featured an angel.

It was as if she had been planted there, waiting for me to
show up. Without hesitation and without having to move right or
left or find a key to a drawer, she reached below the counter and
brought up three pendants with identical angel figures, except
that two were large and one was about three-quarters of the size
of the other two. In other words, a mommy angel, a daddy angel,
and a kid angel. Each was flat, with a simple S-curve on each side
to frame the wings, a perfectly round head, and two black lines
tracing the figurative folds in the robe. I gave one of the larger
ones to Ellen and the other to my mother, and the smaller one
to Martha. Ever since, Ellen's daily jewelry has consisted of the

silver cross hanging side-by-side with the silver angel, along with a heart pendant that Reid and Martha had given her for Christmas.

Martha and I helped ourselves to Reid's clothes. His polo shirts became a regular part of Martha's school wardrobe, and in addition to his Red Sox cap, I took a bunch of his ties, now the most colorful I wear. I also donned his Fossil wristwatch. I came to think of my morning routine as Reid helping me get ready for work.

In the spring, as a fundraiser for Camp Overlook, the summer sports camp that Reid so loved, one of Reid's friends commissioned several hundred wristbands with "Reid Samuel Hollister 12-2-06" embossed in the rubber. Here too the color choice was no choice at all: aqua, as in Reid's eyes. Ellen and I bought a bunch, and within a few weeks our family, friends, and neighborhood were one, with a blue-green rubber stripe at the end of our left or right arm.

One of those instantaneous decisions we made was to create a memorial fund for Reid that would benefit our church's new day-care center. The school opened its doors in September 2006, and it inhabited the space where Reid once gathered his legion on Sunday morning. The school had been created to serve one of Hartford's poorest neighborhoods, and its need for financial support was plain. Ellen was aware, from her energetic involvement in the school's creation, that while a combination of government funds is available to pay some tuition for the area's neediest families, there are many households who are above the income level for financial help but still unable to afford the school's cost. The school, the neighborhood, and the church needed scholarships.

If we had an expectation, it was modest. Ellen and I were unprepared for the response, precipitated by nothing more than three lines in the obituary, stating our wish that contributions be made to the church for the benefit of the center.

At the time we set up the fund, we expected to be able to provide scholarships for a few years, but by mid-2007 we had enough to establish an endowment, and so formally created the Reid Samuel Hollister Memorial Fund. In setting it up, Ellen and I authorized its board to dip into the fund's principal one time to pay for a climbing wall, an enclosure six feet high and ten feet wide. Across the front bar is engraved "Reid's Climbing Wall." When the school's youngsters are tuckered out from climbing and need to sit still for story time, five of them can nestle their little behinds into "Reid's Rockers," pint-size rocking chairs purchased for the center by our church's Women's Fellowship.

Director Irene Garneau and her staff at the center wrote to us in May:

> Your gift in the form of the Reid Samuel Hollister Memorial Fund is so much more than my words or any words can describe. It means that children from the Asylum Hill neighborhood will have high-quality early care and education. It means that they will get a leg up on the challenges they will face in a demanding world. It means for them the achievement gap will be dramatically reduced and their chances for success will be dramatically increased. It means children can jump, climb, swing, and laugh on Reid's climbing wall and monkey bars.

~

Mike Borea (as in "I'm going to Mike's house") made Reid a star. For Reid's birthday, Mike presented us with a framed certificate signifying that a star in the Hercules constellation is now recognized by the U.S. Copyright Office as being named for Reid Hollister. With the certificate, we received a booklet and an enlarged map of the section of the sky showing where Hercules is located and, in a red circle just below Hercules's extended arm, where Reid's star shines. The booklet explains that about two thousand of the brightest stars in eighty-eight constellations have names conferred by professional astronomers, using the Greek alphabet, such as Alpha Orion, but the Guide Star Catalog prepared in conjunction with the Hubble Space Telescope contains the numbers and coordinates of more than fifteen million stars. Our Star Registry map located all the constellations, and for Hercules, the major stars that mark his feet, legs, chest, head, and bow and arrow. Reid's star is locatable by reference to these markers.

I have binoculars, and when the conditions are just so I can now look in the northeastern sky, within the Hercules constellation, for the 11.6-magnitude star located at RA [Right Ascension] 18h12m33.07s D [Declination] 27°43'56.98", Reid's singular home in the cosmos.

~

And then there's the street.

I work regularly with home builders. When Reid was about eight, I took him out on a midwinter Saturday afternoon to a site in Ellington, Connecticut, for which I had helped obtain the local approvals and which I knew to be in such a mid-construction mess as to allow me to explain to Reid the stages of construction, from land clearing to house framing.

We walked around, gaping at the backhoes, bulldozers, and detention basins. Our steps led us to the part of the subdivision where a street was "roughed out"—the storm drains installed and connected, the base course of the street in place, curbing set, and the individual lots marked.

"Where are the street signs?" Reid asked.

"They put those in last," I explained.

He mulled this over. "How do they name the streets?"

"Well, usually the developers get to choose the names, but they have to check with the fire department to make sure they don't name two streets the same—that would be confusing." Then I made a big mistake.

"You know, Reid, sometimes the builders name streets after their kids."

His eyes lit up. Any distinction I might make between a developer and a developer's attorney was lost on him. "You mean, you could name a street after me?" He was suddenly so excited that I felt badly when I had to tamp it down.

"No, it's not up to me—and all of the streets here are named." He scrunched his lips and furrowed his brow, and we moved on.

And then in the summer of 2007, I discovered that one of my clients had received permits for a residential development, but several streets remained unnamed.

I called the project's landscape architects. I recounted my story. I did not have to go far before they got the idea. Within a few days, a street in the Meadowood development in Simsbury,

Connecticut, had a proposed street, "Reid Drive." The fire
department approved.

Silver crosses, angel pendants, aqua wristbands, hawks,
a memorial-fund-now-endowment, a climbing wall, rocking
chairs, a star in a constellation, a street sign. All for Reid.

~

So the memorial train chugged along—until we learned
a lesson from another father about memorials that essentially
stopped us in our tracks.

Until late 2008, Reid's room was as he had left it on
December 1, 2006. Except for the ties and a few other items
that Martha and I had borrowed, his closet was untouched. The
shirts, sneakers, sweatshirts, shoes, school memorabilia—they
were wiped a few times of dust but otherwise were intact and
unmoved. Had Reid returned to change clothes, he would have
found his underwear, socks, T-shirts, and everything else in
their familiar places. The gum, the CDs, the penknife, the iPod,
the *Sports Illustrated* swimsuit issues, the James Bond 2007
calendar, his school ID card, the baseball cards—they became,
to me, museum pieces; I was a curator as much as a father.

Then, in October I received a letter from our former
minister, the Rev. Dr. James L. Kidd. Dr. Kidd and his wife,
Joanne, lost not one but two sons to cystic fibrosis. In direct
response to a prideful explanation I had given him about how
we had preserved Reid's room as it was, as a shrine right in our
home, Dr. Kidd wrote:

> I think you have fulfilled your grief assignment.
> Now I want to suggest you complete that task with the

final act of faith and that is surrender. We found it was necessary, after we had expressed our grief in numerous ways, many not unlike your own, to self-consciously surrender them to God's care and their new adventures in His Kingdom. In fact, we had the distinct impression that they were hanging around following their funeral services and their lively spiritual presence was messing up our lives. So we addressed them each and said in words something like this, "Bruce (later Peter), we loved you while you were alive and we love you still and your death has broken our hearts. But now God has another task for you and it is not here. So we give you permission to leave home, to enter God's realm, your new home, and be about your spiritual business as a new angel. We will always love you, but now we need to get about the business of making a new life for ourselves without you. We need to face The Way Things Are. One day it is our prayer that we will meet again. By that time you will be so far beyond us in your spiritual growth we will hardly recognize you. But, as you know so well, we will always be together in the love of God in Jesus Christ. Now we need you to go. You have new worlds to conquer—and so do we." So we said to each of them.

It was amazing. We were able to move on with new freedom. We broke up their rooms and gave away most of their treasures. So I suggest it might be helpful for you to do the same and make another use of Reid's bedroom.

Dr. Kidd correctly diagnosed that we were preserving Reid's memory in a way that was or would become an obstacle to moving forward. He showed us that the ultimate act of tending the memory of a child who has died is to remember and preserve in a way that not only honors the child, but allows the living to go on.

In the next two weeks, Ellen, Martha, and I cleaned out Reid's room. We gave some clothes to our church's discount clothing shop, some to Reid's friends. We preserved a few precious items, such as his best school papers, but we also threw out things that, if we were honest, were nothing more than stuff.

That space at the northeast corner of the second floor will always be Reid's room, but it is no longer the Reid Samuel Hollister Memorial Exhibition and Museum. This part of his memory floated for a long time but then had to settle. In the immediate aftermath of Reid's passing, we had groped for every conceivable connection, no matter how remote or contrived. But this aspect of parenting Reid evolved—just as do the roles of fathers and mothers of living kids.

11

❧

The Company We Keep

"True friendship is a plant of slow growth, and must undergo and withstand the shocks of adversity before it is entitled to the appellation."

—George Washington

Within two weeks of Reid's death, the central Connecticut chapter of The Compassionate Friends sent us a package of materials explaining the organization's purpose, methods, and schedule of meetings. A friend who is a psychologist encouraged Ellen and me to attend, but cautioned us to wait until we were ready. At that time, late December, this was confusing. If this group could help us through our disbelief and shock, should we not attend as soon as possible? Months later, however, after attending three meetings, I saw that we had done the right thing by waiting until March. I came to understand that participation in a support group that provides conversation and fellowship requires regrouping, a partial restoration of one's own mental foundation.

Ellen and I were told that we would be terrified about attending that first gathering, and we were. We put the date, time, and location on our kitchen's block calendar and then did not discuss it, even as we got into our car for the five-minute drive to the meeting place. Our simmering dread erupted into full-fledged panic as we entered the building. Ellen was crying; I determined that if I started to also, we would get back in the car and ask ourselves for the next month why we had not persevered. There was the predictable dread of a room in which we would know no one, but our fears were broader. We were about to enter a room of unfathomable emotional proportions, a place where the currency of interpersonal connection would be devastation. We were about to attend a meeting whose goal was not friendship or even camaraderie but relief from wracking anguish.

TCF meetings are strictly confidential and off-the-record, and I must honor that privacy. What I can say is that it was both comforting and appalling to see so many people there. Introductions were unbearably awkward; "Nice to meet you" was out of place. The moment of silence while we held hands in a circle was comforting. Going around the circle to explain who we were and why we were there was excruciating. I was our spokesman, and I congratulated myself for choking my way through it, even as Ellen clenched my wrist like a vice. But as we revealed ourselves without having to justify ourselves, I sensed that we would benefit from this group and would return.

At that first meeting, our loss was the most recent. When we relinquished this "distinction" at the next meeting, we realized that TCF's membership grows with tragedy; who will be new at future meetings depends on deaths that are about to happen.

Without betraying confidences, I will mention two encounters from our first ventures that define why support groups like TCF exist and the specific comfort, perspective, and relief that one can find.

First, we met a couple whose seventeen-year-old son had died in a one-car accident, four months before Reid. We learned that their son had been in the hospital for a day, on life support, and they were forced to make a decision to turn it off. As they told us about their son's life, I marked several similarities to Reid. We met them nine months after their tragedy. Their sharp pain was still evident, yet they could not have been warmer in welcoming us to that first TCF meeting. I immediately identified them in my mind as role models. I tried again to banish comparative thoughts, without success, and concluded that though differences were apparent, theirs was a tragedy that was most comparable to ours, and this was comforting.

Then there was a powerfully built man in his mid-thirties, a single father, whose son had gone into the hospital for routine surgery and had died from a doctor's egregious error. We met this man three years after his loss. All he had left was litigation against the doctor, who was still practicing. It seemed to me that his anger had overwhelmed his grief, which was understandable. Every day was the pursuit of vengeance within the tortuous path of our legal system. He was trapped in the game by which the law assigns a dollar value to human life, and in fact assigns a lower value to children whose education and promise have not yet developed to the point where future earning capacity can be estimated. In my legal practice, I have never been involved in

that type of work, but I have seen the excesses and deficiencies
of the personal-injury system. Now I was seeing it through the
eyes of a plaintiff, a father stripped of his child and thrust into
a world of trying to understand pages written by lawyers but
blurred by his tears.

For Ellen and me, The Compassionate Friends was
Heaven-sent. Each month we connected with others to discuss
a devastating characteristic of our lives. As we gathered in that
circle, we metaphorically inflated our children for the group to
see, described the circumstances that destroyed the balloon, and
revealed how many tears we had shed over the deflated remains.
"Bonding" is almost too weak a word. These connections among
the parents were gossamer-thin but made of steel, if that makes
any sense. Our child became the group's child. The pain became
distributed, and so slightly more tolerable.

~

Beyond the support group, some longtime friends are now
closer because they revealed to me after Reid died, for the
first time, their own past losses. In other cases, folks I have
known for more than twenty years deepened our relationship by
proving that they could, in fact, imagine my pain.

The most jarring transformation of a long-term acquaintance
into a deeper friendship was precipitated by a letter that I
received from a man I had known through my work for more
than twenty years. He is an accomplished professional, married
and a father. Friends would not call him jaunty but not overly
serious either; he is equally adept at telling a joke and patiently
parsing a complicated problem.

Here is what he wrote: "When I was a teenager, I lost my three sisters in a fire."

I read his note several times because it was handwritten, in somewhat indecipherable script. I was sure at first that I had misread it. But that is what it said. He had never mentioned anything about this, never even hinted that his background harbored such a catastrophe.

That single sentence became like a seed that produces a complex and multicolored flower. Suddenly I appreciated his character and his life's work in so many more ways. I recognized his courage; his ability to move on; and his humility. I was also made aware of his pain, a pain that made mine seem small by comparison, and not in an unwelcome way.

I recalled seeing him at the calling hours, weeks before he sent his note. I saw him again some weeks after he wrote. There were others around, so I simply looked him in the eye, and he returned my gaze, and without any words between us, our years of professional acquaintance ripened into an emotional bond.

Other acquaintances and friends shared their losses, often in conversations or phone calls that gave me the impression that it would be too painful for them to explain in writing what had happened. Ed's son fell off the balcony of his college fraternity. Joanne's seven-year-old daughter died during a routine operation. Rob lost his eight-year-old son to illness. Another man's son had been in an accident and then in a vegetative state for *ten years*, and had spent the last several years of his life at home, attended around the clock. One of Ellen's best friends told us that her best friend's husband, the father of her godchild, had been killed while he was changing a tire, by an intoxicated eighteen-year-old driver.

I hesitate to say that I am grateful that these friends revealed their losses to me. Being entrusted with this information is a complex emotion, difficult to pin down. To be privy to the most painful details of these other lives, I first had to join the club, but my induction brought great uncertainty about how to react. Learning about another's loss led to what felt like a choice between feeling better because their tragedy had been arguably worse, or worse because they had proved that it was possible to move on, while I had yet to do so.

Lance Corporal Lawrence Philippon was a nineteen-year-old Marine when he died in Iraq in 2005. His family live in our neighborhood and are members of our church. Lawrence wanted to serve his country. The president of the United States and the governor of Connecticut took personal note of his death. The Philippons have a folded American flag and the gratitude of a nation. Did these things make his death any easier on his parents? I have heard Leesa Philippon, Larry's mother, speak on two occasions in church, once before Reid's death and once after, and both times her pain seemed unconsoled.

A question that floats among the community of bereaved parents: While each child's death is different and each parent's reaction and grief journey are idiosyncratic and unpredictable, is there a commonality beyond the basic reality of a terrible loss? Or is the only shared experience the parade of unanswerable questions that invade our minds and torture us for months and years?

My eye is now drawn magnetically to news accounts of teen driving tragedies, especially multiple fatalities in situations where everyone's first reaction is: What were they doing on that road, in that car, at that hour? Each crash is a figurative knife in my stomach as I am transferred back in time to the lobby of Hartford Hospital. I now hang on the macabre details of the news accounts: the type of car, where they were going, any evidence of speeding or substance abuse, the time of day or night, the road conditions, any insight into the life or lives now ended. My prayers for these families include not just sympathy and empathy, but even attempts at telepathy.

~

I have explained earlier that Reid's birth mother found her way to our church and the cemetery the day after the memorial service and, having made the connection with us, agreed to wait a while for the day when we might talk face to face.

Reconnecting with Laura brought me back to our first meeting with her. Several weeks after we brought Reid home from the care of a foster mother in Danbury, at a time when Laura and Mike had terminated their legal rights but Ellen and I were still legally Reid's custodians (and thus not yet his parents), we met with Laura and Mike at the adoption agency in Norwalk. The meeting had no stated purpose; Laura and Mike, not married, had made their decision, and Reid was ensconced in our home. The unspoken agenda for Ellen and me was to glean as much as we could about what lay ahead for us regarding things like health, looks, and personality. Laura and Mike, we assumed, wanted to make sure that we, these two strangers to whom they had entrusted their biological son, would keep the promises that we had made in our profile.

The days before the meeting were stressful, but within minutes of sitting down, all worries dissipated. They were indeed a head-turning couple. Laura's long, very curly brown hair framed her sparkling eyes and long, fluttering eyelashes. Through her nervousness I could see that she was bubbly and energetic. Mike was ruggedly handsome and quiet.

But the focus of the day was Kyle—now Reid—and trust and gratitude. "This is for you," Ellen said as she handed Laura a jewelry store's box that contained a heart pendant. When Laura, not sure what to do, put the box aside for later, Alice, the agency social worker, noticed the tension in Ellen's face and said, "I think they want you to open it now."

A warm conversation followed. As if she were hiring us as babysitters for a weekend, Laura reviewed our baby's first eleven weeks and gave us photos. If she had any concerns about our renaming him Reid, she did not voice them.

Ultimately, the part of that get-together that struck me then and stayed with me through the years was our parting. We said our goodbyes and good-lucks in the conventional way, but the clear, unstated message of the moment was "We will see you again, sometime in the future. None of us can know where, when, how, or under what circumstances—but again."

Through December and January, Ellen and I both struggled with reengaging with Laura. It was impossible to understand what her frame of mind might be. Seventeen years had passed. Was Reid still Kyle to her? Would she be uninterested or less interested, or would her maternal instincts be as strong as the day she gave birth? How had her own life evolved? Did she, or would she, blame us for Reid's death? Had we betrayed her trust? Would she want a detailed biography or a summary, or perhaps nothing at all? There were so many questions, and the last thing Ellen or I needed at that time was another emotional burden of unknown dimension. Reid's attempts to distance himself from our discipline by declaring, "You're not my real parents," still rang uncomfortably in our ears. And Ellen, who wanted to believe that this was all a bad dream and that Reid would return to us at any moment, did not wish to go anywhere near a situation where she would have to compete for Reid's affection.

In mid-February, I gave in to my instinct to reach out to this woman who was suffering in her own unique way. We agreed to meet at a diner for coffee, mid-morning on a Saturday.

The day before I met with Laura, I happened upon the letter that Ellen and I had written in support of Reid's private-school applications for the sixth grade:

> We adopted Reid when he was eleven weeks old. We mention this at the beginning for two reasons. First, discovering the talents and abilities and predicting the interests of an adopted child is a more daunting task than for a biological child; we are unguided by genetics (but also uninfluenced by preconceptions). Second, because we met Reid's birth parents after we had adopted him, our mission of providing the best possible education for our son is motivated in part by our promise to the courageous young couple to whom we owe a great debt. Certainly most parents are devoted to their children's education, but this is a little different.

Meeting someone seventeen years later is an odd event. Obviously, both of us had aged, but in Laura's face I saw my son, starting with her—his—dazzling eyes. As we greeted each other, it was a powerful moment.

Laura was gracious, understanding, and comforting beyond what I could have reasonably expected. She is married and has a handsome family. She showed me pictures, and I provided a few photos of Reid at various ages, filling in the gaps. I learned that we have a few mutual acquaintances, from whom she had gleaned some of Reid's life.

At the end of our conversation, I thanked her for the wreath she had left at Reid's grave at Christmas and for the trust that she had placed in us, a time ago that now seemed very short.

She harbored no rancor, no regrets. Later, she sent a card:

Tim and Ellen, May you find peace within your hearts through your grief for the loss of Reid. I know that he couldn't have been blessed with a better family and can see he was an outstanding young man. I am so sad for his passing and pray that God embraces him. I have always loved him, and will forever. Please find peace in his memory.

As the weeks turned to months, Laura and I corresponded by email twice about what if any contact we should have going forward. I explained to Laura that, despite her hopeful words, Ellen was still struggling with the concept of two mothers on the scene, and obviously our grief was still fresh and unfolding in ways we had not foreseen. To bring Laura further into our lives would be a step with an unpredictable emotional content, and we wished to proceed slowly, until we all felt that the time was right. Laura responded:

Ellen should just feel like Reid always had 2 very special moms, a birth mom who loved him so much but just couldn't do the job, so she made the ultimate sacrifice, gave him up, found an awesome woman in a huge stack of possibilities that she knew would be a wonderful mom. I am glad, in a strange sort of way that she is so grief stricken still, it just confirms all the more that I chose the perfect mom for him, a mom that can

hardly stand life without him she loved him so much! I
am in no hurry to see her, it will happen when the time
is right, and our silent hug will say it all. I will tell her
how much I love you both, that's all. What happened
with Reid was beyond anyone's control. You know as
much as I do, his life was God's from the day he was
born. Every day he had was a gift from Him. There was
nothing we could do, it was no one's fault.

My brief discussions with Laura brought up the name of
Reid's birth father. We had known his first name, of course, but
not his last. Laura had not seen Mike in several years and had
talked to him only occasionally. She mentioned his last name
and where he lived. At the time, it rang a faint bell but I could
not remember where or how.

Then, months later, I went back through the online
guestbooks—and there, in mid-December, just ten days after
the accident, was an email from Mike, a message that I had
completely overlooked at the time. We had received several
messages from friends of Reid's whom we did not know. But
now, on second reading, the words "I know that he couldn't
have been blessed with a better family" and "I have always
loved him, and will forever" suddenly transformed a message
buried amid dozens to one of the most special. I sent Mike a
reply, apologizing for our oversight and returning our gratitude
for the privilege of raising his biological child. I expected no
response, and none came.

~

I have said relatively little, intentionally, about Martha and
her grief. If you know any young ladies who consent to having

their fathers write about their teenage years in a book, please let me know.

My love for my daughter will always be framed by how she came into my life. We adopted Reid in October 1989, and two years later, we decided that Reid needed a sibling. We began the adoption process again. In mid-June of 1992, Ellen called me at work and coyly asked, "What would be the best present you could get for Father's Day?"

My response was instantaneous: "A Tom Seaver–autographed baseball." Tom, the Hall of Fame pitcher, is my boyhood hero.

With a crack in her voice, Ellen replied, "How about a daughter?"

On June 16, 1992, Martha Jenny Hollister, who had been born on May 3, arrived in our home. Reid, then a few weeks short of turning three, did not understand what all of the commotion was about until we placed this bundle into the backseat of our car. He frowned.

I will simply say this about my daughter, alternately known as Marshmallow or Little Bear: Just a few weeks after Reid's death, she asked us, somewhat urgently, for help. We arranged to get her what she needed. She has struggled, of course, but persevered. Martha has always been an excellent student, proud of her work ethic, her focus, and her analytical intelligence. To our amazement, her academic pride never flagged after Reid's death.

Reid was, if nothing else, time-consuming, and when he was alive Martha was left to her own amusement more than she should have been. Certainly not neglected, but plainly not the one who commanded the greater share of her parents' attention.

She was self-reliant, and this was self-perpetuating. But in our grief, the three of us needed to realign our relationships, both because we needed time with each other and because now we had time that we had not had before. The first steps were small and tentative, a combination of reaching out and checking in, but also giving a teenager personal space. We initiated new evening routines, such as watching *Jeopardy* and playing Scat, Quiddler, and Cribbage.

Martha is emblematic of the phenomenon that teens and younger children experience delayed grief and that the sorrow of siblings is difficult to comprehend. Martha and Reid were as close as brother and sister could be; he was her protector and confidant and thus, unlike many other sisters, she did not lose a rival, a competitor, an annoyance, or a mere relative. Yet in those first few months after the accident, when she was only fourteen, her grief was rivulets, not waves, because she had not developed and did not understand coping mechanisms. Also, she made a decision, whether conscious or not, that she needed to be strong while Ellen sobbed night after night after night. Thus, it was only after months that Martha was able to grieve, and it was not until the anniversary of Reid's death that she did in full.

In late November, we could see it building, first as despondence and then as intermittent tears and finally as unalloyed recognition of what she had lost. For me, all of this was captured and then displayed in a single moment when Martha buried her face in Ellen's coat at the anniversary memorial service. The tears flowed as they never had, and the heaviness of her heart and soul were suddenly evident. Perhaps it was when her healing began.

~

The Grief Books are replete with admonitions about the fragility of a marriage after the death of a child. In general, they outline two possibilities: Either the relationship will splinter or husband and wife will grow closer, but things will never be as they were.

I now understand three dimensions of this reality. The first is that the child's death flattens the romantic part of a relationship like Silly Putty under the wheel of a steamroller. Intimacy becomes inappropriate and self-indulgent. Second, every child's death presents the possibilities of blame between the parents and anger at a third party, either about the death or about how the parents individually and collectively raised and treated the child now dead. Third, there simply is no situation for a couple that presents a greater need for interdependence than a child's passing. Here, perhaps more than anywhere else, the facts of what happened dictate how the couple winds its way through this minefield.

In the case of Ellen and me, neither of us blamed the other for Reid's death; we made each of our Instantaneous and Irreversible Decisions together without rancor, dissension, or second-guessing; we were united in turning our attention to Martha; and we nursed our anger about Reid's expulsion. While we had disagreed at times about how and when to discipline Reid, ultimately there was no connection between our interactions and his car going into a spin. We agreed that had Reid asked for permission to go to Mike's house that night, it would have been granted. The unanimity of our decisions about the services and the memorials was seamless and complete, and looking back, there is not a detail that either of us would change.

It is, however, easy for me to envision how any small, different detail, any real or imagined basis for blame, could have derailed our concurrence. Continuing as a father is a different proposition from remaining a husband. It seems to me that whether a marriage endures through the death of a child is a game of inches, and Ellen and I were very lucky to make our way, through the storm and then the fog, together.

12

A Step Aside to Reassess

Since 1979, when I moved to Boston to go to school, four
of us have regularly attended Opening Days at Fenway Park.
Getting tickets has not been difficult, because only diehards
trying to uphold a silly tradition would voluntarily and annually
brave three or more hours outdoors in Boston in early April.
We—Harry, Marge, Dave, and I—have joked that in thirty-plus
years, we have seen temperatures in the twenties with snow
and bright sunshine in the seventies and everything in between,
sometimes on the same day.

In 2007, the tradition continued. It was chilly but calm, and
therefore bearable. I arrived at Fenway an hour before game
time, bought a steaming cup of Legal Seafood chowder, and
went to my seat. I was not only the first of our group to arrive,
but the seats around me were still mostly empty. The most
discernible sound was the familiar, intermittent crack of bats in
the batting cage.

A tide of good memories washed over me. Reid and I
had sat in those seats at least once each year since the mid-
1990s. The progression of those years unfolded in my head,
from the early ones, when I had to explain balls and strikes; to
later games, when we tried to figure out together whether the
manager was about to give the hit-and-run sign; and then to the
past two or three years, when I was the source of money for hot
dogs and popcorn but otherwise Reid asked me to leave him
alone, especially if he had a friend with him.

So I sat there, a bit chilled but not cold, until Dave arrived,
the tradition renewed itself, and the banter spanning decades
continued. In the back of my mind, though, was the connection
that Reid and I, like countless other fathers and sons in America
for a century, had made watching baseball.

The next day, on my way to work, I took my Opening
Day ticket and stuck it inside the temporary metal marker at
Reid's gravesite, behind the plastic that covered his name. Not
obscuring the name, but complementing it. I was glad that this
was one tradition with Reid that I could continue.

Then in early May, I took Martha and two friends to
Fenway. This time I had an ulterior motive and a plan. I had an
envelope in my pocket. After three innings of summoning the
courage to go through with it, I walked down the aisle between
the field-level box seats, past the vendors, to the young man who
sits on a stool next to the left-field stands and corrals foul balls.
He was kibitzing with kids and parents in the boxes, signing an
occasional autograph, even posing for a photo. As I approached,
I tried to smile, just another fan and another day at the ballpark,
but I suspect the tension in my face concerned him.

"Yes, sir?"

I pulled out the envelope. "Would you...um...be so kind as to put some dirt from the field in here?" I asked.

To my relief, he laughed. "Sure thing!" He bounded a few steps onto the field, grabbed a handful of dirt and a few blades of grass for good measure, and stuffed it in the pouch.

I tried to maintain my composure, but failed. Now the folks in the boxes were staring at me as I blinked back tears. He handed back the envelope somewhat slowly. His expression conveyed the questions, "Are you OK?" and "What's this for?"

"Gravesite," I mumbled, said thank you, looked down at my shoes, and headed back to my seat. I sealed the flap, folded it twice, and wrote "Fenway Dirt" on the back.

~

In late May, Michelle Volpe of Volpe Monuments signaled us that she had asked the staff of the Fairview Cemetery to pour the concrete foundation that would support Reid's headstone. This requires digging a hole above the middle of the casket, with the bottom of the hole being well below the frost line, which in our part of the world is forty-two inches below the surface.

Every other day for ten days I checked to see if the hole had been dug. Finally, on a sunny morning in the third week of May, there it was. Rectangular, roughly two feet by four feet, and deep, with a piece of plywood laid across to keep it dry.

Once again, I confronted something I wanted to see, but not really. I moved the plywood and peered down into the hole. I tried to orient the hole to where the casket was. I looked in.

I was trembling as the emotions of the burial day came rushing back. I confronted again the reality that Reid's body was entombed in a casket that, if not visible, was within inches of showing itself.

I could not see it, and I was thankful for that.

It was 8:30, and even though I knew that Ellen was transporting Martha to school, I called them on my cellphone and told them that the hole was there and that they should come right away with the Fenway dirt and the Atlantis sand.

Ellen and Martha arrived a few minutes later, and after a quick look around to see if anyone was watching, I pulled back the plywood again, unsealed the envelope, and poured in the magical Fenway dirt, the Red Sox dust, the hallowed Fenway ground. I threw in the envelope for good measure.

Ellen poured most of the Atlantis sand into the hole, saving the last bit to sprinkle on the new grass that was now growing unevenly above the gravesite.

At this particular moment, there was no crying—perhaps because Martha was with us, perhaps because Ellen and I were relieved to have accomplished our mission, months in the making.

Two days later, the cemetery staff filled the hole with cement. When I arrived at the grave, again around 8:30, the top of the cement was still wet. Martha was already at school, but I called Ellen and told her to come quickly.

So, on the morning of May 25, Ellen and I took a golf tee out of the trunk of my car, and we carved "Love, Mom, Dad, Martha, Gracie" into the top of the cement, all the while looking around to see if someone was watching and wondering what we were doing.

~

Not unlike parenting, part of coping with loss is embracing distractions when they become available. Parents need not only to impose time-outs, but to take them for themselves. For me, if a diversion involves physical exercise in the company of friends, so much the better. In the spring, I ventured back onto the golf course.

Golf has always been solace for me, four or five hours outdoors, measuring myself against bogey. In those years I was fortunate to have hooked up with a very-early-Saturday-morning group in eastern Connecticut, a cast of congenial characters mostly associated with the U.S. Coast Guard Academy in New London.

But in the spring and summer of 2007, as I sought a few hours of distraction on the fairways, my game stunk and became simply another source of frustration. I played wearing my aqua "Reid Samuel Hollister 12-2-06" wristband, but at some point in every round I began to think about Reid, sometimes about playing golf with him, sometimes about our challenges or what might have been. My concentration vanished, and fat shots, pulled putts, near-shanks, hooks, and slices followed. I considered quitting. Ultimately I kept playing, carried along mostly by the company of my buddies, who understood what I was going through and kept the collective mood upbeat.

~

May 25, Reid's class's graduation. We received several phone calls and notes from parents of Reid's classmates, letting us know that they recognized what a difficult day it must be.

And so it was. The lost promise of his life and our anger at his expulsion were compressed and magnified. I found myself

looking at my watch throughout the morning, estimating what
was going on at the ceremony at that moment. There was joy in
my heart for Reid's friends as they passed their milestone, but
I was also hoping that the entire assemblage had to withhold a
tear when noting an absence during the distribution of diplomas
to those whose last names begin with H.

At this school's graduations, the boys wear striped school
ties with a white shirt, while the girls wear white dresses
and carry red roses. Late in the afternoon on the Friday of
graduation, Mike Borea draped his tie over Reid's temporary
marker, and two girls laid their roses over his grave.

As I looked at the tie and the roses, I felt an urge to add my
own memorial. Reid did not have a graduation but he would
have an emblem. I opened the trunk of my car, took a handful of
tees out of my golf bag, and arranged them with into an "07" at
the head of his grave.

~

Midsummer confronted me with Reid's eighteenth birthday,
on July 22. We had worked to be sure that the headstone would
be in place by that day. The stone arrived and was installed on
July 11—that is, 7/11/7. Perfectly balanced.

It was beautifully executed. The slanted face that bore
Reid's name was polished so finely as to give the appearance of
a pane of glass overlaid on the gray granite, yet it was simply
stone rubbed smooth. The rectangle with his name was set off
by a sharp-edged groove from the rough-hewn texture of the
perimeter of the nameplate. Within the rectangle in the upper
left was the cross and in the upper right the hawk—wings
spread, peering across Reid's name, surveying the site, the

figurative wind beneath its wings evoking midair suspension and constant vigilance.

The large block letters of Reid's engraved name jumped out for their absolute precision and symmetry. Where the incision had been made into the stone, the darker, shadowed inside of the cut gave the impression that the letters had been painted on. The care in the carving was comforting to me; someone in Michigan who never knew my son had spent days meticulously rendering thirty-one letters and eleven numbers, creating a marker that will endure longer than anyone who knew him.

At a brief service to dedicate his headstone, the family gathered, just left of the pine tree. It was a return under the summer sun and different circumstances to that awful, now-familiar place where we had gathered in the cold seven months earlier.

Peter Grandy officiated. He suggested that we invoke the three gifts of the Spirit stated in I Corinthians 13—Faith, Hope, and Love—and that we match these to the three engravings on the headstone: the cross symbolizing Faith, the hawk signifying Hope, and Reid's name standing for Love. The Faith piece would open with the Lord's Prayer, in unison; a reading from Colossians 3:12–17 ("Put on love, that binds everything together in perfect harmony"); and words from Revelation 21:3–6 ("and God himself will be with them; he will wipe away every tear from their eyes, and death shall be no more, neither shall there be mourning nor crying nor pain any more . . ."). We repeated the Litany of Affirmation:

I believe God's promises are true.
I believe Heaven is real.

I believe we will meet again.
I believe God will see me through.
I believe nothing can separate me from God's love.
I believe God has work for me to do.

For Hope, Peter would ask Mary Way, whose request for a sign had led to the hawk's first visit at the church, to explain why the hawk had become our reminder of Reid being with us in spirit.

I read part of an essay that Reid had written in eighth grade about Gracie, a piece that we had found among Reid's papers. It captured Reid's voice. Standing behind his headstone, I called out his words:

> I was three when I realized how much I loved dogs. When I told my mom and my dad, they said that they loved them too, but told me that our yard was too small. We would need to buy a bigger house.

> When it was time to start my Christmas list, I had "dog" for my first present. Then on Christmas morning, I looked for a box with holes that would let a dog breathe, but there was nothing. The next year, the first thing that was on my list again was a dog. And once again, still there was no dog for me on Christmas morning. By now I was sad because I had tried so hard to convince my parents to let me have a dog, but it was not working.

> Then came the Christmas of 1998. We had a bigger house. Like every other Christmas, I went downstairs and opened up all of the presents, and guess what, there was nothing.

> It is a tradition for my family to get together at my grandma and grandpa's house because my grandma can't walk very well. At my grandparents' house I got

another very small present from my mom and dad. I opened it with a frown on my face because I had not gotten a dog and I thought it was hopeless. Then, when I saw what it was, I shouted with glee. It was a collar and a leash. I ran over to my mom and dad and said, "Details." They told me that we were getting a dog on the twenty-ninth of January. I yelled to my sister and told her the news; even though she was right next to me, I had to tell the news.

Soon it was January the twenty-ninth. When we got to Mrs. Dunn's farm, I looked at the puppies and they were in four groups. The first group was the energetic dogs. The second group was the calm and lazy dogs. The third group was the mean dogs. The fourth group was the shy and playful dogs.

Gracie was in the shy group. We saw her, and then we saw her walk. When she walked she shook her butt from side to side.

In the car on the way home, I got to hold Gracie most of the way. This was partly because my sister was too young and we were scared she would drop Gracie. When we were turning the corner onto my street a dog outside barked really loudly. Gracie was scared. I had heard that dogs pee when they are scared, so I gave her to my sister.

At the moment that we gathered at the grave, just left of the pine tree, to begin the service, the sun went behind a cloud and the 5:00 p.m. shadows that all of us surrounding Reid were casting on his headstone and the flower-strewn grass disappeared, and then stayed away for the duration of our time together. Shadows remained in our hearts, but I was grateful for the reminder that they do in fact dissolve.

~

In August I went to my doctor for a physical. I had not seen him since the fall of 2006, and he was unaware of Reid's death. He said: "Don't think of Reid's death as dragging you down, but expanding your emotional range. A beautiful sunset or similar experience is now more appreciated because the distance from your sorrow to this wonderful moment is greater." In those few sentences, Dr. Carley provided a perspective that I have mulled over regularly since.

~

In October, I finally mustered the courage, if that's the right word, to look at the records from the Hartford Hospital emergency room. They had been sitting on my desk since April. The reality was that most of it was incomprehensible to me. I had no idea what an "acute parenchymal hemorrhage" was or the significance of "both femoral heads" being "well seated within their respective acetabula."

I resolved to ask Rich and Joanne Kuntz, our doctor-neighbors, for help. A few weeks later, at a neighborhood party, Joanne and I drifted into a corner of the kitchen. She recounted the night of December 1 from her perspective.

Joanne, Rich, Jessica's mother Sue, and several other neighbors had been socializing when Jessica, fresh out of the car at the accident scene, called her mother on her cellphone. Sue rushed out to Plainville. Eventually, word came to those still at the party that two kids were being taken to Hartford Hospital but a third was in cardiac arrest and was headed to New Britain

General, which was closer to the accident scene. At that point the parents did not know who was who.

Joanne took me through those hours, in small bits.

"As we drove, I began to see that this was going to be bad. En route to Hartford Hospital I learned from the emergency dispatch that, yes, there was an accident on 84, there were three people being transported, two to Hartford and one to New Britain General. The one going to New Britain was a traumatic cardiac arrest. I felt as if I was going to be sick. Patients who have no pulse and no blood pressure rarely survive."

As Joanne talked, I started to realize the excruciating conflicts that she had endured that night.

"When we got to Emergency, they had little information, another bad sign because it often means the crew is busy taking care of the patient. The first ambulance arrived. Did I dare wish it was Rachel, Reid, or Jessica? My mind was racing. I hoped that someone I had never met was the one being transported to New Britain. Rachel arrived first, injured but awake, crying and very much alive."

Joanne recounted her cellphone call to the emergency room in New Britain. "They had a male patient, but he had no identification." Joanne told the doctor to "look at his eyes, and if they are the most amazing eyes you've ever seen, that's Reid Hollister." The doctor looked, returned to the phone, and told Joanne, "I'm sorry to tell you this but this is your friend's son."

She then explained the next conflict that arose, between her roles as close friend and medical professional with access to information. "Ellen arrived just before the next ambulance. It carried Jessica. Ellen collapsed briefly and frantically asked me, 'Where is he?' I went inside and called New Britain. I knew I couldn't tell Ellen what was going on. I've heard of people getting news that a family member has died, only to find out later that the victim was misidentified."

As we talked, I began to admire the courage that Joanne had brought to the unfolding tragedy, even as I also started to appreciate that it had taken months for her to be able to recount for me, face-to-face, her conversations and fears.

She explained that since she knew the New Britain doctor personally, he had provided the details of Reid's conditions. "He told me that Reid had a blood pressure and strong pulse, some burns and clearly intra-abdominal bleeding. They didn't think that Reid would survive a trip to the burn unit in Bridgeport, which is standard for a burn victim, but I got the sense that the burns were the least of Reid's problems."

Then came word of a medical decision that revealed to Joanne the severity of Reid's injuries. "When New Britain said that Reid was being moved to Hartford, I almost collapsed. I didn't want Reid to die in the back of an ambulance."

Joanne was there, with Ellen, when Reid finally arrived at Hartford Hospital about 20 minutes later. The emergency team was ready for him. He needed CPR three times in the trauma room.

As I listened, gratefully, to this full rendition of the medical side of the accident night, I reached a point where I couldn't speak, and so Joanne continued and finished: "Every improvement was turning out to be a false hope. The chest tubes continued to drain blood and what was happening became clearer. I remembered thanking God that I was privileged to work with such compassionate people." Joanne explained that while everyone was busy in the trauma room, "I quietly leaned down and I spoke to Reid, praying to God to spare him this. I remember stepping out of the room and seeing Richard anxiously waiting. I wept and said, 'Honey, I think Reid is dying.'"

They decided to take Reid to the operating room to get control of the bleeding that was occurring in his abdomen. The surgeon then went and spoke to Ellen. "When he came back," Joanne told me, "he said he didn't have the heart to tell Ellen that he didn't think Reid would make it. I found myself unable to take away what little hope she had."

Finally, Joanne revealed that for six months after that unholy night, she took herself off the list of physicians available to work in the Hartford Hospital ER. She just couldn't deal with it.

Fortified by Joanne's explanation, I went back to the medical records on my own. Again, there were medical terms that I did not understand. For example, the "History" section stated that Reid had "suffered hemopneumothorax, grade 4 splenic laceration, lower lumbar fractures, cardiac arrest [that part I got], coagulopathy, metabolic acidosis, retroperitoneal hematoma. During the resuscitation, the patient was quite labile and unstable. . . ." I had the gist of it: blood in his chest cavities, damage to his spleen, broken bones, blood clots, loss of oxygen to the brain.

My reading, however, only served to reframe, rather than resolve, questions that had been churning in my parental mind for months: When did he lose consciousness? After that happened, did he feel any pain? Is being unconscious the same as the cessation of brain function? When the doctors restarted his heart, did that restore any functions other than the pumping of blood? In other words, when was he unconscious, when did his brain cease, and when did his vital organs shut down? Why was 3:10 a.m. recorded as the time of his death?

None of this armchair doctoring would bring Reid back,
so why did I even open the envelope again? It was clear: I was
carrying out the role of caretaker, obligated to ask questions lest
something important to his memory be overlooked or incorrectly
remembered. To forge an ongoing relationship with Reid, I
needed to understand as fully as possible what had happened on
that awful day. The dust had settled, and I had opportunities to
see more clearly. Among what became clearer was that Reid's
injuries were so substantial as to be beyond medical help. He
was so badly hurt that he did not suffer.

In early November, I learned that the state police had issued
a report several months earlier about the accident. They had not
sent me a copy, but Jessica's parents had obtained one when
dealing with an insurance company. For a few months, they had
assumed that we had a copy.

The report merely confirmed what I already knew: Reid,
Jessica, and Rachel had gone for a ride and gotten lost in
Plainville while trying to reverse direction on I-84, back toward
West Hartford. They had finally turned around at Exit 32,
which the report noted is the only place between Plainville and
Waterbury where one can get off the highway and back on in the
eastbound direction. Rachel said the car was going "pretty fast"
and passing other cars, but Jessica said the speed seemed normal
and she was not scared or alarmed. Rachel then recalled the car
spinning, but neither girl recalled anything after that.

The trooper concluded that the causes of the accident
were likely excessive speed due in part to Reid trying to get
Jessica home by her curfew; operator inexperience; operator
unfamiliarity with that roadway; and the sharp curve at Exit 34.

The report also noted that "the operator was unable to give a
statement."

~

It would be nice to be able to say that I have succeeded eventually in putting what happened to Reid at his school behind me. That day has not yet arrived.

Going through Reid's messages on Facebook, we found one he had written the day before Thanksgiving, five days before his disciplinary hearing, to a 2006 graduate. It seemed to us that in that context, Reid never expected that anyone would ever see the message except this other student. That is, in sending that message on that day, Reid had no reason to lie. His message said that what he had been accused of had "never happened."

Then in February 2007, the underclassman to whom Reid had passed the marijuana posted a message on Reid's memorial site on Facebook. It was addressed to Reid and said, "I just want you to know that I never ratted you out."

A few months later, we got a further report about what had happened during the expulsion process. We sent a long letter to the chair of school's trustees. We did not ask the board to do anything about Reid's case but said that the board should be concerned about the school's disgraceful disciplinary system. We received a patronizing note, informing us that the trustees have nothing to do with discipline of students. We later learned that this was not true.

Later in the spring, a member of our church, father of a student at the school, asked me about a rumor that the school had expelled Reid because of "drug paraphernalia found in his locker." I exploded. Ellen and I sent a letter to all of Reid's classmates and their parents, enclosing a copy of Reid's

statement to the committee. Several parents called us to say
thank you for putting a stop to the rumor mill.

~

During that second half of 2007, the second six months
of my new and different fatherhood, the mind games that had
begun in the late winter and early spring continued. I never quite
knew when one of them would leap into my consciousness, or
whether the game would be brand new or a refinement of an
earlier version. The one thing I could count on was intrusion,
distraction, and frustration.

Above all, death became part of my routine. My to-do list
devolved into something like "CVS, Stop & Shop, cleaners,
cemetery, bank." I knew that this was not only inevitable
but psychologically necessary; if I was bound to visit Reid's
gravesite regularly, I needed to get beyond the stage where each
visit was a debilitating challenge, and eventually I got there.

But then I got angry with myself for relegating my visits to
that sacred site to a *routine*. One of Reid's classmates sent us a
touching email that captured part of what I was feeling:

> To the Hollisters: I've heard that the best thing for
> pain like this, is time, but it's been almost six months
> now since Reid's passing and although the clock has
> continued ticking and the days have turned into months,
> the pain hasn't gotten any smaller. If anything, the pain
> doesn't go away it's more like your body just becomes
> stronger and becomes accustomed to the pain.

Theoretically, I was free to come and go as I pleased, but
grief was a perpetual drag on my movements. The sound of
Reid's voice, his tall and skinny frame, the aqua eyes, his smell,

even his surliness—each was dissipating in small pieces because time was diminishing the clarity of the details. I could not detain him; he was departing one puzzle piece at a time.

I also noticed that life's funniest and most lighthearted moments were not as funny or light, and the lowest moments were spent at a new and unprecedented depth. I was capable of laughter, equivalent to the high point of a musical scale, but my lowest moments became dirges played on the far left of the keyboard.

I began to think about events using December 2, 2006, as if it were the divider between B.C. and A.D. When the Red Sox won the World Series in 2004, Reid was alive, but when they won in 2007 he wasn't. President Bush's re-election? Before. The world's new attention to global warming? Before. Ellen's surgery? Before. Obama's rise to national prominence? After. And so on.

Martha, like millions of other kids, is a Harry Potter fanatic, so in July 2007 we went to see the latest movie, which implanted in my brain another lasting image. At Hogwarts School, the characters in paintings move. I began to look at photos of Reid and Martha together—especially the Thanksgiving 2006 picture taken in our kitchen, with tall Reid in a white polo with his arm draped over Martha's shoulder—as ones in which one side, Martha, was aging while the other, Reid, remained frozen in time.

~

I became intensely curious about other parents who had lost a child, especially those who had lost a teen in an automobile crash, and particularly those whose loss was several or more years ago. I looked to them for clues as to what lay ahead for me, and what I saw was more chilling than comforting. Those whose loss had occurred relatively close in time to Reid's death still seemed to be recovering from shock. Those who were five years out seemed to be predominantly sad, showing some ability to look on the bright side but still clearly engulfed by their tragedy. One mother, her daughter's death seven years past, confided to me that she had "turned a corner" in that she could "recall memories without pain." Another couple, whose seventeen-year-old died in 1990, seemed to be mostly enjoying their busy, purposeful lives, with their son's memory now sustainable. All of which revealed, and continued to remind me, that I had a long way to go.

~

I expected the days leading up to the one-year anniversary of Reid's December 2 accident to be anguished, the actual day to be one of despair and regret, and the day after, December 3, to be one of relief. How wrong I was.

During the two weeks prior, Ellen and I, together and individually, had replayed what had happened on those days one year ago: Ellen's being called to the school and informed that Reid was a drug dealer. The weekend days when we interrogated Reid, got to the truth, and assembled that long list of discipline to which Reid would voluntarily submit, the list that we were certain the school could not reasonably refuse. Our baffling meetings with school officials, and the changing accusation. Reid's preparation meeting with his faculty advocate, by which time we all had the dreaded sense that the die had been cast and Reid had no chance to overcome faceless accusers and rumors. The night of the expulsion hearing, that surreal phone call with the decision. The Tuesday-night kitchen confrontation, the visits to Dr. Jarvis, the contract, the discussions among Ellen, Reid, and me about who was allowed to go where and when. Ellen's fishing the crumpled yearbook page out of the trash.

In a way, there was so much to remember that the effort overwhelmed us. I suppose that Ellen and I had made clear to each other that between us, there would be no blame, no regrets about that night. Given our joint feeling that our son, though he had grievously misbehaved, had been punished beyond justification and most needed our support and trust, we concluded that we would have conducted ourselves the same again, given the same circumstances and information.

Yet those days were now governed by the tyranny of hindsight. Neither of us can recall with precision the last time and place that we saw him in person or what our final words were. We thought at the time that the conversations were routine and would continue. How could we have been so blind? As parents, why had we not cherished each day?

As we faced those anniversary days, we employed a strategy that, by November, we knew would work well on days when waves of grief threatened to wash over us: Keep busy. While I occupied myself with work and writing, Ellen fell in with a group of women from The Compassionate Friends, the support group for bereaved parents. Each year the Wadsworth Atheneum, Hartford's venerable art museum, conducts a "Festival of Trees," in which groups and individuals compete by decorating and displaying a holiday tree with unique and colorful ornaments. Ellen and her group bought a white artificial tree, and over the course of a month, they fashioned more than one hundred deep-blue origami butterflies and attached each

one with a white ribbon, on which was printed the name of
a child who had died. Among the butterflies and ribbons, the
ladies hung flat ornaments bearing the words "Precious" and
"Beloved" and "Good" and "Forever." Somehow, Reid's ribbon
ended up in a prominent place on the tree, front and upper left.

The trees, after their week of display, go on sale. Ellen and
I bought The Compassionate Friends tree, brought it home in
pieces, and reassembled it in our den, where it served as our
2007 Christmas tree.

~

Our headstone dedication ceremony in July had been
small—the first anniversary, however, seemed to generate its
own momentum.

Midday on December 2, 2007, a hundred strong gathered
at Fairview. Steve Mitchell sang "Try to Remember" from *The
Fantasticks*, the song that says, "Deep in December, our hearts
should remember."

Martha's tears flowed in a way that we had not seen before.
As she buried her head in Ellen's chest, we could see and feel a
heaviness—the weight of recognition, I guess—in her sobs. In a
reversal of the 2006 memorial service, Ellen comforted Martha.

For years, Ellen and I have had a special bond with our
neighbor and friend Leslie Hadra, a mother of three whose
husband, Reed, had died several years earlier in a hospital due
to a misdiagnosis. Leslie suggested to us a memorial gesture:
helium balloons, each bearing a handwritten message, released
into the sky together at the end of the service. A breeze would
have scattered the balloons, but at that windless moment, all
fifty or so proceeded straight up in a column. For almost a full

minute they hung together, and so from the ground formed an ever-changing pattern, a midair kaleidoscope. The pink dots turned gray and then black and then disappeared from view, still without dispersing.

The next day, Monday, as I drove to work, I began to cry, so much so that I pulled onto the shoulder of the highway. The world would now truly be expecting me to move on. It was unlikely that we would ever again assemble a hundred people at Reid's grave. From now on, there would be small gatherings only on July 22 and December 2. The community that had surrounded us the day before would slip away forever.

I was overcome by the feeling that this was the first day of the rest of my life. The horizon of my new reality was no longer the next memorial event or the next addition to Reid's train of memorials, but the rest of my own time on earth, to be lived under a cloud. My sorrow was concrete that was setting.

Nearly every time in 2007 when I visited Reid's grave, two or three times per week, something had changed. The stone pedestal and semicircle of mulch that Ellen had installed in front of the stone regularly sported flowers, plants, notes, stones, dolls, balloons, ornaments, photos, quarters, pennies, and crosses.

Then, in mid-December we discovered the downside of our gravesite choice. New England's recent winters had been unusually warm—December 2006, for example, was more like a September. But in December 2007 we had an ice storm, and when I went to the cemetery for one of my regular visits, I thought my eyes were deceiving me. The letters and numbers on the slanted face of Reid's headstone had vanished. The stone was encased in ice, and the ice had filled in the engraved letters and numbers.

Two weeks later, two major snowstorms arrived, three days apart, depositing more than fifteen inches. When I went to the cemetery, the top of the headstone was not visible, and the grave was accessible only by navigating twenty feet through knee-high snow. This was all very depressing. Now not only could I not tend Reid's grave, I couldn't even reach it without a shovel and boots.

Reid's physical presence was gone, and details of his life were slipping away, too. I felt akin to the night watchman of a museum who is bound and gagged and watches helplessly as thieves make off with precious, irreplaceable pieces of the collection. At the end of 2007, I was relegated to cherishing, securing, and polishing what remained, by fighting back, in the name of my son, against the force of months and years dissipating the memories of his life and character.

Those months were a time to repair misunderstandings and allow the fog to dissipate further. I confronted the physiology of his crash, measured the geometry of his resting place, dealt with rumors that threatened his memory, learned the benefits of distractions, and discovered little surprises. The second half of that year after was, above all, necessary. It became the prelude to cobbling together the connection by which Reid and I would carry each other forward.

13

❧

And Lead Us Not
Into Penn Station

I am blessed to be, if not a "born again" Christian in the evangelical sense, one whose religious faith is the result of a life-changing experience that occurred when I was nineteen. Throughout my attention to Reid's memory, this faith served me constantly, even when I did not recognize it at the time.

I do not take my faith for granted. A fellow I know through work lost his son at age thirty-two to cancer. Aware from past conversations and our December 2006 letter how our family was relying on faith, he conveyed his appreciation of our beliefs, saying, "At least you have your religion. For us, life just sucks."

I have pondered this comment many times. My life as I knew it and envisioned it disappeared, and faith did not insulate me from dreading much of daily life. My friend's comment was a backhand suggestion that facing grief without faith is more difficult. He was not painting my faith or anyone else's as a crutch, a convenience, or magical thinking. Still, like his, my life sucked, and continued for a long time to suck, and my faith did not change this reality. Faith was not necessarily an antidepressant.

So which is it? Was my life a shambles, or did my faith ameliorate my pain?

Neither. Both. Faith helps in one critical realm, but it does not cure or transform the part of life that has the capacity to suck.

When I was growing up in New York City, in our family, religion was optional. My father was born and raised on the Upper West Side of Manhattan in a family that was nominally Jewish; he was bar mitzvahed and his family observed the most basic rituals of Judaism, but his household was neither spiritual nor practicing. In 1947, after serving for two years on a minesweeper in the Pacific, finishing college at New York University, and studying economics at Leyden University in the Netherlands, he began to look for work on Wall Street. He quickly realized that being a Jew limited his employment opportunities. As a result, at the age of twenty-four, my dad changed his name to Hollister. He got a job at a venerable brokerage firm and went on to a successful career as a certified financial analyst of the nation's utility companies.

In the early 1960s, as my sister, Liz, and I came of age, my father decided that religious instruction should be part of our formative years. He joined a Presbyterian congregation and became an active member, even rising to various leadership positions. He introduced my sister and me to Sunday school and church, and as we got older and began to resist, he insisted on our attendance.

My mother's parents both immigrated from Finland, and her household was nominally Lutheran but, as in my father's home, neither devout nor practicing. Throughout my childhood, my mom did not attend church with my dad, my sister, and me, in part because she was a night owl, legendary among her family and friends for staying up late and sleeping late. Mom's not attending church and Dad's Protestant conversion, in a subtle way, reinforced that faith is a choice and not a measure of goodness.

Eventually, this perception that religion played no major part in an adult's worthiness sowed a seed of conflict between my father and me about attending Sunday school and church. When I became a teenager, I began to protest it. I became creative in avoiding Sunday morning, making up sore throats, headaches, colds, unfinished homework, and other dodges, excuses, and weaves.

This was painful to my father, especially when he had assumed leadership posts in the church. He could not persuade his own children and wife to join him on Sunday morning? It did not help his cause or my interest that in the 1960s and 1970s, Protestant churches in New York City were in decline.

Somewhere in my teen years, the early 1970s, either I prevailed or my father quit trying, because when I graduated from high school, faith, spirituality, and participation in a church were not options that I intended to exercise in the foreseeable future.

This state of affairs lasted for only two years, until the spring of 1976, when I had a life-altering experience.

In high school, I had two very nice girlfriends, but I was always a bit awkward with the opposite sex. Then in early 1976, while attending college in Connecticut, I met Virginia. She was beautiful, smart, and engaging. I was a sophomore; she was a freshman. I struck up as many conversations as I could. I walked far out of my way across campus to ensure that our paths would cross.

To my monumental disappointment, Virginia was not only engaging to talk to but *engaged*, at least informally, to a student at Yale. I was amazed that a college student would be so irrevocably committed to one person, but as best I could tell this attachment was real, and there was no room in Virginia's life for me in the way that I hoped.

This attachment, pure and chaste from afar, continued for several months until Virginia disappeared from campus, not just for the weekend but for a few days, then a week, then ten days. As soon as she returned, I knew that something was terribly wrong. In fact there was. Her fiancé had been killed in a traffic accident. Virginia had been away to attend his funeral.

When she returned to campus, Virginia was, of course, grief-stricken—at that time I had no idea what that meant—but also in need of a friend and companion who could help integrate her into the campus's social life. Selflessly, I volunteered. Friendship morphed into romance. It was spring. I now had the attention of this lovely lady. I should have been pinching myself. Instead, I was miserable, because I simply could not understand how this relationship, something I had wanted so much, had resulted from such tragic circumstances. While this may sound trifling, I assure you that my anguish was real. I was

nineteen and in love, but recoiling from it. It made no sense. I
was despondent when I should have been ecstatic.

I reached out to the Rev. Bill Tolley, senior pastor of our
Presbyterian church in New York. Maybe my Dad had exposed
me to religion just enough to help me realize that faith is an
option when we are out of options. I called Rev. Tolley to tell
him the situation, and then I drove from Connecticut to meet
him face to face.

We met at his office in early May. I remember that as
I walked toward the rectory, the day was not beautiful, the
temperature was not pleasant, the sky was not blue. The best I
could say was that it was not raining.

I explained my quandary in detail. He was well prepared to
respond. He described to me the writings of a British theologian
named Leslie Weatherhead who, in Rev. Tolley's view, had best
stated the theological approach appropriate to my misery: (at
the risk of gross oversimplification) that God is the source of
all good things that happen in the world, but cannot stop the
bad and the evil. God is beneficence but not omnipotence, in
the sense of controlling everything that occurs and warding off
human pain and suffering. This was the core idea, at any rate,
and it was a powerful one.

My life-changing experience occurred in the several minutes
after I left Rev. Tolley's office. I walked down the front steps
of the church and looked up and around, at the sky, the trees,
the flowers in the front yards of the houses across the street.
What I saw, and what has stayed with me through the more than
thirty years since, was the colors. The sky was suddenly the
deepest blue imaginable. The sun was bright yellow and filtering

through the trees in well-defined beams. Those leaves were a green of indescribable vibrancy. The flowers were purple and red and orange and yellow and blue. Everywhere, colors.

My heart was unburdened. I felt the transformative and restorative power of belief in the beneficence of God. Virginia's fiancé's passing was suffering that God does not eliminate from life. We are left with decisions about whether to enjoy the blessings that God has provided to us.

Now, the cynic might say, how convenient. What unburdened my heart was a rationalization that allowed me to resume my love life. I had that discussion with myself in the days and weeks that followed but in time, and certainly now, I know that not to be true. That moment when the colors exploded propelled me on a faith journey that continues today. I became motivated to explore belief in God and to deepen, articulate, and internalize the emotion of that moment in 1976. My newfound faith outlasted my relationship with Virginia, which went on for only another year or so. Since then, I have always been an active, seeking member of some church.

There was one more consequence of what I now refer to as my "born again" experience. It helped me to understand a powerful memory from my childhood that I had never quite known how to handle.

I was about nine, old enough that my parents would let me walk by myself the four city blocks to Third Avenue, a busy street of stores, restaurants, and gas stations, including stores that sold baseball cards, gum, candy, ice cream, and comic books. On a spring day, I decided to spend my one-dollar allowance on baseball cards, hoping specifically that one of my packs would include the newest New York Mets cards. As I left our apartment building, my friends Matt and Richie were headed out to play touch football, and they needed me to join. But the gravitational pull of those Mets cards was substantial, so I told them I would race up to Nat's store and be back in ten minutes.

I crossed Third Avenue, bought the cards, tore open the four packs, was disappointed to find Yankees but no Mets, raced out the front of the store, and began to sprint back across the street.

As I stepped off the sidewalk, a man firmly grabbed the back of my shirt. As I turned to look at him, I felt the passenger-side mirror of a car go *inches* past my face. The man was in his sixties, wearing a gray suit, a gray fedora, and black shoes. He was carrying a black umbrella. He had a kind, round, avuncular face. I looked down Third Avenue at that car, speeding away, that would have killed me had I taken one more step. I turned again to thank the man for pulling me back.

But there was no one there, nor anyone close on my side of the street.

~

I moved to Hartford in 1982 and soon after, at the invitation of a co-worker, joined Asylum Hill Congregational Church. There, the senior minister, the Rev. Dr. James Kidd, helped me understand what faith requires and provides.

Jim Kidd was one of America's great preachers. He was not a pulpit-pounding, fire-and-brimstone fearmonger, but one who conveyed spiritual messages in plain language sprinkled with down-home humor. He regularly left his parishioners with bits of wisdom that they could chew on for weeks. After listening to his sermons from 1982 to 1998, I took away four points. First, we cannot change what he called "The Way Things Are"—life's facts, including the painful ones. Second, faith is a decision we make, consciously and purposefully. Third, "all things work together for good for those who love the Lord." Finally, if you have faith the size of a mustard seed, you can move mountains.

I even learned enough about the New Testament to develop what I regard as my personal creed, the passage that has most frequently provided me with a sense of direction when I have been unsure of myself. One translation of Romans 12:2 is: "Do not be conformed to the present world, but be transformed by the renewal of your own mind." In other words, relying on faith, make your own decisions instead of doing what others may expect of you. These words have served me well.

Jim Kidd was a man to be listened to because his own faith had been severely tested. As mentioned earlier, Jim and his wife, Joanne, lost two sons, in their teenage years, to cystic fibrosis. When Jim was my pastor, this fact compelled me and many others to stand in awe of the depth of his faith. Anyone who could lose not one but two sons and emerge with his faith intact is a man who can teach others. Certainly the faith he taught me became my anchor, starting on December 2, 2006.

Thus, when I was young, faith was optional; in 1976, I had a born-again experience, one that set me on a journey. On December 2, 2006, I began taking a test. I am still taking it.

But I feel as though I studied enough before the test and have now applied enough learning to achieve a passing grade. My faith has been intact for more than thirty years. I have felt receptive to ministers' and others' teaching me and supporting me, never more than the free fall at the hospital when Rev. Miller cradled me in his arms, and the moment at Reid's burial when Rev. Verasco held my hand, stopped the leakage, and replenished my spirit while we interred hope and dreams.

Through my grief, then, the colors of my life have remained vibrant. I have been flattened by pain but as I have lain on my back, the sky has remained blue, the grass green, and the flowers as vibrant as they were on that afternoon in 1976. Even Reid's story features colors: the pink polos, his aqua eyes, the red-tailed hawk. The shock, pain, and sadness have not rendered the world gray.

I appreciate that each believer's route is different. I can only say that I am grateful that I confronted Reid's death fortified by a faith that had been built up over decades and strengthened by events and challenges that caused me to take stock. I guess I can say that when the flood came, I was already on high ground, and my faith and my ministers held me firmly in place against forces that could have swept me away.

14

❧

Small Mercies

"Morning by morning, new mercies I see."

—William Runyan, "Great Is Thy Faithfulness"

Attending to my obligations as a father after Reid's crash, preserving his memory, discovering from innumerable sources who he was at the time of his passing, and rearranging my relationships with just about everyone in my life were all necessary to creating a new tether to my son. Yet I still needed to *want* him as a permanent presence. Our bond needed tensile strength. Over time I realized that to solidify our ongoing relationship, I needed to count my blessings, to balance the loss with what was undamaged, preserved, and even gained.

I forced myself to write a list of the positives, of circumstances, causes, and events that either happened in a particularly good way or thankfully did not happen at all.

Borrowing from the Rt. Hon. The Earl Spencer's eulogy for his sister Princess Diana, I called them "small mercies":

That Reid had two passengers with him when he crashed. He cared about those girls, and as a result I have no doubt that he did not intend to wreck his car. But given what had happened in the four days prior, if he had been by himself, I would have wondered forever whether he pushed the envelope out of frustration or anger.

Laura and Mike entrusted Ellen and me with their biological child, providing us with years of joy.

Reid and Martha were as close as any brother and sister I have ever known.

Reid was blessed with memorable eyes, a handsome face, a lanky frame, and a sense of humor. What a combination.

Along the way, several extraordinary teachers pulled the best out of Reid.

Two child psychologists accurately evaluated Reid's learning capabilities and disability and gave us invaluable guidance.

Reid's greatest quality as a person was his empathy for others.

Reid's greatest gift was his ability to relate to young children.

Before he died, Reid fell in love with a wonderful girl, Lauren.

Reid and I replicated the father-son bonding of generations of Americans in the stands at Fenway Park and Shea Stadium.

Reid went to Disneyland and Disney World, as every little kid should.

Reid had a beautiful tenor voice.

When we most needed it, Dr. Jarvis settled Reid down and mediated family tensions.

A senior's belief in an untested freshman resulted in Reid's being plucked from the crowd and inserted into one of the singular experiences of his life, Spartan 7.

Though he claimed to protest it at the time, Reid's outdoor experience with the Appalachian Mountain Club transformed him, by showing him possibilities for personal growth of which he was not aware.

Our August 2006 college trip allowed me to understand who my son was at age seventeen, and the promise and challenges that lay ahead.

When I was so exasperated with Reid that I was ready to throttle him, Scott Rogerson advised me to hug him and tell him I loved him, which I did.

Reid's final consequential action on earth, his personal statement to the Citizenship Committee, was probably the best piece of writing he did in his life, and it was a statement of repentance.

On the night of November 30, Ellen fished that yearbook page out of the trash.

Reid and Martha spent the early evening hours of December 1 together.

At the crash scene, Reid did not suffer long.

One of the first at the scene at Exit 34 was someone we knew, who was able to confirm quickly to us that Reid lost consciousness almost immediately.

I did not get stranded in Chicago in that snowstorm.

I was able to drive from Washington, D.C., to Hartford along Interstate 95, one of the busiest traffic corridors in the U.S., with no traffic.

On the night of December 1, Ellen was comforted until I got there.

Ellen saw Reid as they wheeled him into Hartford Hospital.

Our senior minister, Gary Miller, met me at the door of Hartford Hospital.

I have no doubt that those first at the crash scene, and then the ambulance people, and then the medical staffs at New Britain and Hartford did everything they could reasonably have done to save Reid.

Reid's crash did not kill anyone else.

With the help of Rev. Miller and Rev. Grandy, I was able to spend a few final moments with Reid.

Ellen and I were able to make those numerous, pressurized decisions together, unanimously, and without dissent, rancor, or regret.

We found a casket that matched his personality and life.

With family help, we crafted in five hours a fitting obituary.

With help from a gifted ad hoc committee, I was able to draft the eulogy.

Randy Molloy and his funeral-home staff were sensitive and professional throughout.

We found a gravesite that is peaceful, accessible, and shaded.

After the calling hours, Reid's best friends had a final open-casket moment with him.

At the memorial service, Spartan 7 sang beautifully.

My reluctant-speaker sister, Liz, delivered a sound bite, "You will get up," that has resonated ever since with every person who attended the service.

Rev. Miller carried Mike Borea when his emotional bond with Reid prevented him from continuing.

Wick Sloane turned my eulogy into a stem-winder.

Karen Tomasko took a big pile of photos and turned them into a work of art.

Martha's drawing of Reid, the one that went into his casket, was at once a touching tribute from a sister and a revelation of her artistic talent.

At the calling hours, so many demonstrated their dedication by persevering on a freezing night.

Other than the cold, from December 2 to 6, the New England weather cooperated.

At the burial, the Rev. Sarah Verasco, merely by holding my hand, made a difference in my life.

Steve Mitchell modified the words of "Bring Him Home" so that the words matched the situation, allowing us to experience the incomparable power of that song.

More than seven hundred kids coalesced in Reid's memory on Facebook in a matter of days.

On that dreadful "What Happened?" Facebook site, Martha stepped in to protect her brother and effectively shut it down.

The Compassionate Friends proved to be a timely source of recognition that Ellen and I were not alone.

Michelle Volpe guided us through the delicate task of choosing and designing Reid's headstone.

My Coast Guard golf buddies distracted me when I needed it and kept smiling when they knew why my concentration had evaporated.

We were able to add a whimsical touch to Reid's grave with Atlantis sand and the Fenway dirt.

No one saw us depositing either one.

Several parents reached out to us on graduation day when we had nothing to do.

Many people wrote to us in a way that demonstrated, months after Reid's crash, that they were *still* thinking about us.

Through the ministry of the Rev. Dr. James L. Kidd at Asylum Hill, I faced Reid's death with my faith intact, with an ability to articulate what I believe.

Reid's memorial fund drew contributions at a pace and level of generosity that left us stunned.

So many people helped Martha in ways that Ellen and I could not.

A client graciously agreed to name a street in a new development after Reid.

Dozens of people, unknown to us, left flowers and envelopes at Reid's grave, reminding us that he is remembered further and wider than we know.

Ellen and I have no second-guesses or blame about our conduct as parents.

Throughout this ordeal, our ministers were with us every step of the way.

Dr. Kidd gave us timely advice to dismantle the museum that was Reid's room.

I had enough time with Reid to get to know him, not as an adult, but enough to see the promise of his life.

Reid kept me laughing when I wasn't crying or swearing under my breath; there were no dull moments.

For all of the challenges and angst, I was the father of a unique and amazing young man.

If and when I get to that point where I can recall the good times with Reid unburdened by the pain of losing him, I will be blessed because those happy times, though fewer than I would have liked, were rich and varied.

Reid is an identifiable star in the firmament, if one has binoculars, a clear sky, and a map.

In contrast to parents of teenagers everywhere, I know where my son is, 24/7.

15

Dear Buddybear,

Dear Buddybear,

    I have faced the unthinkable and relentless demands of being your father still. I have learned more about your character, while regretting that I did not appreciate it earlier and better. The debate about how I raised you, how I weighed exposure against protection, how I balanced teaching against self-discovery, has quieted in my mind. I have new and closer friends, reaffirmed faith, and much more knowledge about grief, obituaries, eulogies, condolences, memorials, the Internet, Facebook, and driving. I have counted my blessings and shared our story that others may benefit.

    So let me return to the question I have most struggled with: How are we to carry on? What are you in my life from now on?

    I know some things that you are not. You are not that useless lump of lead, furrowed in the comforter on the bed in your room, who needs to get his sorry butt up and out or be late for school.

You are not an extra pair of hands to help me stack wood, rake leaves, move chairs into the dining room for Thanksgiving dinner or Christmas or birthdays, haul the picnic table from the back porch to the garage, or clear the snow from the driveway.

Except for attending to the physical condition of your gravesite, your physical safety and well-being are no longer my responsibility. No more curfews or inspections.

When and how people remember you are, however, most definitely my responsibility. I am the principal steward of the legacies of your seventeen-plus years.

In trying to figure us from now on, I thought of some of the songs I can still hear your voice singing in the house or in the car, like this one from Starlight Express:

> *Starlight Express, Starlight Express,*
> *Are you real, yes or no?*
> *Starlight Express, answer me yes.*
> *I don't want you to go.*

You are here and you are gone at the same time. You are my Starlight Express.

Transforming you into something agreeably attached and portable is difficult because it hurts to remember you. Alleviating the pain requires recalling you less frequently, less longingly, which I don't want to do. So, in a way, I choose to keep punishing myself in order to preserve you in my consciousness.

Yes, I know. Abstractions were not your favorite. Sorry again. Let me try to return to concrete simplicity.

As I carry you around, as we remain figuratively connected, it will help if your presence will make me smile. We need to fit like Abbott and Costello, Lewis and Martin, Belushi and Aykroyd, or Penn and Teller.

Needing a concept to connect us, I reflected and meditated and pondered and ruminated and racked my brain, until it came to me—what you are, in my life, from now on:

You are my traveling companion.

You will be the guy always next to me as I go places.

You will be the voice off my shoulder that helps me decide which path to take and which way to turn.

We will read life's map together.

We will be inseparable.

You will be my American Express card: I will never leave home without you.

So, I conclude, we did not bury you. You changed from a person to a presence. You may no longer be here in the flesh, but your spirit is now an integral part of the magnet in my compass. I'm not dragging you along, but walking with you, checking in on occasion but always content to feel you near. A Son app on my DadPhone. I can work with this concept. Off we go.

One last thing before we head off to wherever. Since you are still my charge, you will need to observe a bit of decorum. The Hollister family has standards. I am determined to carry out my role as half a duo, as tender of your memory, with purpose, dignity, eloquence, and grace. I will be proud of you. I will not, therefore, stand for one thing you did as a teenager that irked me to no end, and that is—you guessed it—wearing your pants or shorts so low as to leave your underwear visible. No gangster-style. So, before we step outside:

Pull your pants up, please.

. . . .

Higher.

Love, Dad

Reader's Guide

1. *His Father Still* uses "tether" as a metaphor for the connection between parents and their children. Does this image capture how your parents raised you during your teenage years, or how you raised your own teens?

2. Chapters 3 through 6 describe Tim's flashbacks, as he was writing Reid's obituary and eulogy, to the decisions that he and his wife made about which school Reid should attend, and later whether to keep him in that school. What do you think about their decisions?

3. The story recounts Tim and Ellen's discipline of Reid through his teenage years, including times when their approaches differed. How important is it that parents be "on the same page"?

4. Did Tim make the right choice by omitting Reid's educational turmoil and expulsion from the obituary, but then including a reference to it in the eulogy? What else could have been or should have been said, or stated differently?

5. In the months after Reid's passing, Tim and his family received many letters and email messages, sending condolences but also commenting on Reid's life and character. Which messages did you find most eloquent? Touching? Appropriate? Inappropriate? Instructive for your own use?

6. What did you learn about sending condolences from the book's discussion of the messages that Tim and his family received?

7. Will Chapter 8, "Our Electronic Funeral," change the way you will approach sending online condolence messages, or participate in condolences sent through social media such as Facebook?

8. At the end of Chapter 10, the Rev. Dr. Kidd counsels Tim and Ellen to end their preservation of every item in Reid's room just as he had left it on the day of his crash, and to give away most of Reid's possessions. What did you think about this advice, especially its timing? Is there any benefit in preserving what a loved one has left behind, and how does one know it is time to move on?

9. What is your assessment of how Tim handled his role as a father after Reid's passing? What could he have done differently?

10. Reflecting on your own loss of loved ones, what did you do (and perhaps are still doing) to establish an acceptable and sustainable relationship after their passing? Is establishing or reestablishing a "relationship" even the right way to think about a loved one who has passed away?

11. How would you characterize Tim and Reid's relationship at the end of the book? Fragile? Strong? Sustainable? Did the last chapter leave you with the impression that their relationship will – or must – continue to evolve? Do our relationships with loved ones who have passed away continue to change, just like our friendships and interactions with those still living?

Questions and Answers with author
Tim Hollister, May 2015

The title *His Father Still: A Parenting Memoir* gives us some idea of what the book is about – but what do you think it's about?

It's the story of parenting a rebellious yet fearful teenager; a father continuing his obligations after losing a child; and building a sustainable relationship after a loved one's passing.

I resist calling this book a "grief journey" or advice about how to recover from a tragedy. It's about parenting.

This said, the book is about a long list of things that don't necessarily or logically fit together, but shaped my experience as a father, both before and after Reid's passing. So, in no particular order:

- balancing protection against freedom when raising a teen;
- choosing a school;
- managing teen misbehavior and rebellion;
- delivering effective discipline, including the challenge of having both parents being in sync;
- reacting to a school's discipline, especially when it has gone wrong;
- supervising a new teen driver;
- writing an obituary for a teen;
- writing a eulogy for a teen;
- composing a condolence message for anyone;
- conveying condolences through email and social media;
- planning a funeral;
- establishing memorials for a person who has passed away;

- giving away possessions;
- identifying opportunities for friendship in the aftermath of a loved one's passing;
- counting blessings after a tragedy;
- rebuilding a relationship after a loved one is gone; and
- appreciating the power of faith communities to care for those who have lost.

The Introduction explains your dissatisfaction with what you call "the Grief Books" – grief memoirs and instructional books on dealing with tragedy. Why did you find these books unhelpful? Was your experience so different that how-to books were less relevant?

When it came to writing the story told in this book, my mantra was that I am not a professional counselor, I'm a dad. My need wasn't understanding grief and recovery from tragedy as a clinical or psychological process. I needed to answer two questions: Had I been a good father? And who had Reid been as a person when he passed away, and how had I shaped his character? I most needed a retrospective on my parenting, which was surely based in part on the fact that he died at age seventeen. In other words, when I started writing, I was doing so not to unburden myself from grief–I did that in other ways–but to consider my role as Reid's father and what he had taken from my almost-complete efforts to raise a self-sufficient, responsible adult. Thus, as I wrote and wrote, a perspective emerged that seemed different from and more satisfying than the Grief Books. It was not that the Grief Books were unhelpful, but that they did not respond to the particular questions that were gnawing at me. When I had addressed my own need by reconsidering my parenting, I discovered that I had told a story that might be useful not only to parents trying to move beyond loss, but also to those with happy, healthy kids.

How would you summarize your emotional stages and progressions as a parent during the story the book tells?

For me, because the three years preceding Reid's crash were his rebellion years, my teen parenting experience was predominated by anguish, uncertainty, and fear of bad choices that would either hurt Reid or come back to haunt him later. I struggled to keep him from rebelling further, and to stay in school. These preoccupations blinded me to his character, his friendships with so many, and his potential. Hope and satisfaction were mostly beneath the surface of our relationship. The best times were those in which he offered glimpses of maturity, but those were fleeting and intermittent.

Then, in the immediate aftermath of his crash, I endured more than a year of emotional devastation—no other way to say it. At that point I began to write, to reflect on the cards and emails and letters we had received, to think about the conversations I had had and was still having with so many friends, and to consider how faith might pull me up and forward. Eventually, I began to recognize "the chasm deep in our souls" as Anna Quindlen has called it so eloquently, a hole in the center of who we are that never completely mends, but can be put in its place so it isn't a shadow that overwhelms every day. This phase gave way to what some call "memories without anguish," sadness softened by recognition of small mercies. My most recent stage has been greater appreciation of friends, faith, and family, and how I am so blessed to have each one in great measure.

What advice do you have for parents of teens?

Don't let the daily challenges of raising a teen blind you to character, integrity, goodness, or promise. The rebellion will pass. Focus on instilling values and lessons, even if it seems as though they are not taking hold or being heard. Recognize that separation—letting out the tether—is painful and scary, but ultimately necessary. Remember that, for better or worse, you will always be a mother or father, no matter where or how your child goes through life. Put another way, one of my common experiences is to listen to parents of teens complain long and loud about misbehavior, rebellion, lack of caring, etc.–and all the while, thinking that I long to be in their shoes.

How have the experiences you describe in the book changed you as a person?

I am more appreciative of my friends, if only out of gratitude for the innumerable acts of kindness and caring that I have experienced, especially from people with busy lives and their own worries and concerns. So many took extraordinary time to take care of me when I needed to offload my responsibilities and to be on the receiving end of care and grace. That gratitude extends to those who helped my wife and daughter.

I am less tolerant of wasting time. And I am glad to say that one of the dividends of this whole experience is that I am a better writer. Working with professional writers, agents, and editors on this book has helped me to express myself better than I ever could before.

What is the one memory from the events described in the book that you most cherish?

Writing the Small Mercies chapter was transformative. A friend recommended the process to me, and I forced myself to do it, but the amazing thing was that once I started compiling a list of blessings, I challenged myself to keep going, to keep thinking of things for which I was genuinely grateful throughout the months and years of tragedy and tears. When I felt I had listed as many as I could possibly imagine, the result was positively uplifting. I never dreamed that there had been so many good things that had happened along the way. I highly recommend "counting your blessings," as cliché as that is, to anyone experiencing a tough time.

What do you miss most about Reid?

Nearly every day at some point I think about where he would be today, given who he was and the promise of his life when he died. When I was in college, I had a history professor who gave "counterfactual" tests, essay questions in which we were asked to predict how the arc of history would have been different based on one key fact being changed. So I think about how Reid's life would have developed, using the evidence I have, to predict an outcome: where would his interests, abilities, challenges, character, advantages, and even disabilities have taken him? I recognize that it's speculation, and ultimately a sad exercise, but it's a part of how I keep his memory alive in my mind and heart.

Acknowledgements

Some books take a village. This one certainly did.

My wife Ellen and my daughter Martha have given me the precious gift of permission to write this story of our family life, so that others may benefit. I know this book is an intrusion on their privacy, and I appreciate their recognition of the good cause.

Inexpressible thanks go to my immediate and extended families, Deutsch, Jansen, Pierce, Boga, Safino, Horvat, Hollister, Jackson, and Swearingin, who have loved us through hell and high water.

Thanks also to the Quish, Schpero, Way, and Bier families, and to so many others in West Hartford who, in the months after Reid's passing and since, have cared for us and stuck with us.

My agent Joy Tutela has guided me since 2009 through the tribulations of the publishing industry in general and countless revisions of proposals and the manuscript in particular. I may never understand her devotion to this book, but I certainly appreciate it. Her colleagues at the David Black Literary Agency, especially Antonella Iannarino and Luke Thomas, have always been responsive, encouraging, and insightful.

Curt Clarisey of Clarisey Consulting in Simsbury, Connecticut, by creating and maintaining my blog, has been a vital part of my publishing platform. Thank you Curt, and Betsy too.

Wick Sloane was a sage advisor through the events recounted in this book, and as noted, I made a wise choice in asking him to deliver the eulogy that I had written.

The National Organizations for Youth Safety, known as NOYS, has embraced *His Father Still* from its earliest drafts as consistent with its focus on guiding families through the challenges of adolescence. First Sandy Spavone and Nicole Graziosi, and now Anita Boles have been valued partners in bringing this book to publication.

My thanks to those whose letters, emails, and social media posts appear in this book. While it is not possible to name all of them, my special thanks to Mark Pierce, Sara Pierce, John Boyer, Diane Bier, the late Rev. Jim Kidd, Rev. Gary Miller, Mike Borea, Tom Quish, Steve Quish, Tom Gersky, Liz Swearingin, Kathleen Graham, Ann Taylor, Cassie Trammel, Sarah DeFilippis, Sandra Chase, Dan Doyle, Ron and Cindy White, Sam Fuller, Karen Perry, Carol Morano, Diana Garfield, Jessie Rodriguez, Karin Stahl, Lynne Lawrence, Jim Wakim, John Mason, Lynda Fitzgerald, Karen Mortensen, Beth Critton, Judith Melchreit, and Irene Garneau.

The ministers, staff, and members of the Asylum Hill Congregational Church in Hartford, Connecticut are as much the heroes of this book as anyone. They have been a critical part of our family's support network, and in doing so have demonstrated time and again the healing power of a committed, caring community of faith. Thanks especially to the Rev. Gary Miller, the Rev. Peter Grandy, Steve Mitchell, Kathleen Graham, and Mary Way.

Thank you to Attorney Leon Rosenblatt for his assistance with legal matters after Reid's passing. My gratitude also to several of my Shipman & Goodwin colleagues who helped with the publication of this book: Cathy Intravia, Ryan Leichsenring, Patty Chouinard, Tasha Marrero, and Lou Schatz.

My assistant for twenty-two years, Erin Fitzgerald, has helped with innumerable administrative tasks and, along with Jeanne Swayner, Carolyn Lawrence, Deanna Alvarez, and Jessie Rodriguez, revised the manuscript again and again.

My law firm, in the fall of 2007, granted me a mini-sabbatical by which, for three months, I stayed at home on weekday mornings and wrote of the first draft of this book. Thank you as well as all of my Practice Group colleagues, particularly Joe Williams and Matt Ranelli, for being patient with me during times when I was struggling personally.

Our firm's wonderfully talented graphic designer, Maria Ramsay, designed the cover of the book.

Elizabeth Stein, Luke Dempsey, Michael Critelli, and Mary-Ann Tirone Smith not only edited the manuscript, but gave it new direction and organizing themes, and better oriented it to its potential audiences. They cut what needed to be cut and provided insights that were simply beyond my view.

Thank you to Myles McDonnell for his eagle-eyed copy edit, which revealed that my belief that I had mastered grammar and punctuation was a delusion.

I am grateful to many friends who commented on drafts of the manuscript. Hoping to not have overlooked anyone, thanks to Rick Green, Duby McDowell, Warren Olsen, the late David Lentini, Leslie Wertam, Fay Dupuis, Steve Chinn, Mark Hayes, Bob Haggeman, Jodi Wilinsky Hill, Fred Schpero, the Rev. Sarah Verasco, Marianne Dubuque, the Rev. Sara Salomons, Sona Pancholy, Sam Fuller, Karin Stahl, Peter Eisenhardt, Nicolle Burnham, Tom and Sally Tresselt, Mally Cox-Chapman, Kathy Mintz, Shelby Rogerson, Gene Gaddis, Brent Marchant, Steve Boga, and Anne Dranginis.

I must thank my "traffic safety friends," those I have been so blessed to work with on safe teen driving, and who helped make *Not So Fast* a success: Cathy Gillen, Brandy Nannini, Bill Seymour, Pam Fischer, Piña Violano, Joe Cristalli, Sharon Silke Carty, Bruce Hamilton, the late Dave Preusser, Neal Chaudhury, Karen Sprattler, Kathy Bernstein Harris, Dr. Brendan Campbell, Garry Lapidus, and Kevin Borrup.

Special thanks to my friend, mentor, and hero Sherry Chapman, and everyone at Mourning Parents Act, for their inspiration.

Thanks to Jill Konopka and her colleagues at WFSB-TV, the CBS affiliate in Connecticut, for their continued interest in Reid's story as a cautionary tale for parents and teens.

To Reid's Class of 2007 classmates and their families, thank you for your continuing words and reminders that remind us that Reid remains in your hearts and memories.

Finally, thanks to my best friends: Harry Castleman, Marge Dolan, Dave Tately, Jenny Erickson, Suzanne Jorgensen, Donna Thiel, Kristy Bulleit, Marion Hobbs, Tom Rollins, Scott Rogerson, Rob Ayer, Mike Howell, Karen Tomasko and Bob Goodman, and Mark Pazniokas and Laura Post.

I am blessed to inhabit such a wonderful village.

About the Author

Tim Hollister's seventeen-year-old son, Reid, died in a one-car crash on an interstate highway in central Connecticut in December 2006. A year later, and after several other fatal crashes in the state, Connecticut's Governor M. Jodi Rell appointed Tim as a bereaved parent to a task force charged with reexamining the state's teen driver laws. That task force led Connecticut in 2008 to transform its law from one of the most lenient in the nation to one of the strictest.

After serving on the task force, Tim began speaking and writing about safer teen driving. In 2009, he launched his national blog for parents of teen drivers, "From Reid's Dad," www.fromreidsdad.org. The blog has been featured on the *CBS Evening News with Scott Pelley* and Kyra Phillips's *Raising America* on HLN, and has been covered by the *Huffington Post*, television and radio stations, newspapers, newsletters, websites, and other blogs. It is now relied upon by parents, government agencies, driving schools, law enforcement, and traffic safety advocates across the country. In 2010, U.S. Department of Transportation and the National Highway Transportation Safety

Administration honored Tim's advocacy with their Public Service Award, the nation's highest civilian award for traffic safety.

In 2013, Tim published *Not So Fast: Parenting Your Teen Through the Dangers of Driving*. *Publisher's Weekly* called the book "A practical, concise, and potentially life-saving book that should be required reading for every parent before their teen gets behind the wheel." In 2014, the Governors Highway Safety Association, which represents the Highway Safety Offices of all 50 states, recognized *Not So Fast* with a national public service award. *Not So Fast* has also been featured on KMOX Radio and on the "Home and Family" show on the Hallmark Channel.

Now, in *His Father Still*, Tim Hollister tells the story of his life with his son during Reid's teenage years, and in the aftermath of Reid's fatal crash.

Tim is a partner in a law firm, practicing land use and environmental law. For the past several years he has been listed among the *Best Lawyers in America*. He lives in Connecticut with his wife and daughter.